NOSTRADAMUS
The Complete Prophecies of the Seer

by Constantin Vaughn

Erebus Society

Erebus Society

First published in Great Britain in 2017
by Erebus Society

First Edition

Editor: Constantin Vaughn

ISBN: 978-0-9933284-5-9

TABLE OF CONTENTS

PREFACE

Greetings and happiness to César Nostradamus my son.

Your late arrival, César Nostredame, my son, has made me spend much time in constant nightly reflection so that I could communicate with you by letter and leave you this reminder, after my death, for the benefit of all men, of which the divine spirit has vouchsafed me to know by means of astronomy.

And since it was the Almighty's will that you were not born here in this region and I do not want to talk of years to come but of the months during which you will struggle to grasp and understand the work I shall be compelled to leave you after my death: assuming that it will not be possible for me to leave you such writing as may be destroyed through the injustice of the age (1555). The key to the hidden prediction which you will inherit will be locked inside my heart.

Also bear in mind that the events here described have not yet come to pass, and that all is ruled and governed by the power of Almighty God, inspiring us not by bacchic frenzy nor by enchantments but by astronomical assurances: predictions have been made through the inspiration of divine will alone and the spirit of prophecy in particular.

On numerous occasions and over a long period of time I have predicted specific events far in advance, attributing all to the workings of divine power and inspiration, together with other fortunate or unfortunate happenings, foreseen in their full unexpectedness, which have already come to pass in various regions of the earth. Yet I have wished to remain silent and abandon my work because of the injustice not only of the present time but also for most of the future. I will not commit to writing.

Since governments, sects and countries will undergo such sweeping changes, diametrically opposed to what now obtains, that were I to relate events to come, those in power now - monarchs, leaders of sects and religions would find these so different from their own imaginings that they would be led to condemn what later centuries will learn how to see and understand. Bear in mind also Our Saviour's words: Do not give anything holy to the
dogs, nor throw pearls in front of the pigs lest they trample them with their feet and turn on you and tear you apart. For this reason I withdrew my pen from the paper, because I wished to amplify my statement touching the Vulgar Advent, by means of ambiguous and enigmatic comments about future causes, even those closest to us and those I have perceived, so that some human change which may come to pass shall not unduly scandalize delicate sensibilities. The whole work is thus written in a nebulous rather than plainly prophetic form. So much so that,

You have hidden these things from the wise and the circumspect, that is from the mighty and the rulers, and you have purified those things for the small and the poor, and through Almighty God's will, revealed unto those prophets with the power to perceive what is distant and thereby to foretell things to come. For nothing can be accomplished without this faculty, whose power and goodness work so strongly in those to whom it is given that, while they contemplate within themselves, these powers are subject to other influences arising from the force of good. This warmth and strength of prophecy invests us with its influence as the sun's rays affect both animate and inanimate entities.

We human beings cannot through our natural consciousness and intelligence know anything of God the Creator's hidden secrets, For it is not for us to know the times or the instants, etc.
So much so that persons of future times may be seen in present ones, because God Almighty has wished to reveal them by means of images, together with various secrets of the future vouchsafed to orthodox astrology, as was the case in the past, so that a measure of power and divination passed through them, the flame of the spirit inspiring them to pronounce upon inspiration both human and divine. God may bring into being divine works, which are absolute; there is another level, that of angelic works; and a third way, that of the evildoers.

But my son, I address you here a little too obscurely. As regards the occult prophecies one is vouchsafed through the subtle spirit of fire, which the understanding sometimes stirs through contemplation of the distant stars as if in vigil, likewise by means of pronouncements, one finds oneself surprised at producing writings without fear of being stricken for such impudent loquacity. The reason is that all this proceeds from the divine power of Almighty God from whom all bounty proceeds.

Preface

And so once again, my son, if I have eschewed the word prophet, I do not wish to attribute to myself such lofty title at the present time, for whoever is called a prophet now was once called a seer; since a prophet, my son, is properly speaking one who sees distant things through a natural knowledge of all creatures. And it can happen that the prophet bringing about the perfect light of prophecy may make manifest things both human and divine, because this cannot be done otherwise, given that the effects of predicting the future extend far off into time. God's mysteries are incomprehensible and the power to influence events is bound up with the great expanse of natural knowledge, having its nearest most immediate origin in free will and describing future events which cannot be understood simply through being revealed. Neither can they be grasped through men's interpretations nor through another mode of cognizance or occult power under the firmament, neither in the present nor in the total eternity to come. But bringing about such an indivisible eternity through Herculean efforts, things are revealed by the planetary movements.

I am not saying, my son - mark me well, here - that knowledge of such things cannot be implanted in your deficient mind, or that events in the distant future may not be within the understanding of any reasoning being. Nevertheless, if these things current or distant are brought to the awareness of this reasoning and intelligent being they will be neither too obscure nor too clearly revealed.

Perfect knowledge of such things cannot be acquired without divine inspiration, given that all prophetic inspiration derives its initial origin from God Almighty, then from chance and nature. Since all these portents are produced impartially, prophecy comes to pass partly as predicted. For understanding created by the intellect cannot be acquired by means of the occult, only by the aid of the zodiac, bringing forth that small flame by whose light part of the future may be discerned.

Also, my son, I beseech you not to exercise your mind upon such reveries and vanities as drain the body and incur the soul's perdition, and which trouble our feeble frames. Above all avoid the vanity of that most execrable magic formerly reproved by the Holy Scriptures - only excepting the use of official astrology.

For by the latter, with the help of inspiration and divine revelation, and continual calculations, I have set down my prophecies in writing. Fearing lest this occult philosophy be condemned, I did not therefore wish to make known its dire import; also fearful that several books which had lain hidden for long centuries might be discovered, and of what might become of them, after reading them I presented them to Vulcan. [i.e. burned them]. And while he devoured them, the flame licking the air gave out such an unexpected light, clearer than that of an ordinary flame and resembling fire from some flashing cataclysm, and suddenly illumined the house as if it were caught in a furnace. Which is why I reduced them to ashes then, so that none might be tempted to use occult labours in searching for the perfect transmutation, whether lunar or solar, of incorruptible metals.

But as to that discernment which can be achieved by the aid of planetary scrutiny, I should like to tell you this. Eschewing any fantastic imaginings, you may through good judgement have insight into the future if you keep to the specific names of places that accord with planetary configurations, and with inspiration places and aspects yield up hidden properties, namely that power in whose presence the three times [past, present, and future]are understood as Eternity whose unfolding contains them all: for all things are naked and open.

That is why, my son, you can easily, despite your young brain, understand that events can be foretold naturally by the heavenly bodies and by the spirit of prophecy: I do not wish to ascribe to myself the title and role of prophet, but emphasize inspiration revealed to a mortal man whose perception is no further from heaven than the feet are from the earth. I cannot fail, err or be deceived, although I may be as great a sinner as anyone else upon this earth and subject to all human afflictions.

But after being surprised sometimes by day while in a trance, and having long fallen into the habit of agreeable nocturnal studies, I have composed books of prophecies, each containing one hundred astronomical quatrains, which I want to condense somewhat obscurely. The work comprises prophecies from today to the year 3797.

This may perturb some, when they see such a long time-span, and this will occur and be understood in all the fullness of the Republic; these things will be universally understood upon earth, my son. If you live the normal lifetime of man you will know upon your own soil, under your native sky, how future events are to turn out.

For only Eternal God knows the eternity of His light which proceeds from Him, and I speak frankly to those to whom His immeasurable, immense and incomprehensible greatness has been disposed to grant revelations through long, melancholy inspiration, that with the aid of this hidden element manifested by God, there are two principal factors which make up the prophet's intelligence.

The first is when the supernatural light fills and illuminates the person who predicts by astral science, while the second allows him to prophesy through inspired revelation, which is only a part of the divine eternity, whereby the prophet comes to assess what his divinatory power has given him through the grace of God and by a natural gift, namely, that what is foretold is true and ethereal in origin.

And such a light and small flame is of great efficacy and scope, and nothing less than the clarity of nature itself. The light of human nature makes the philosophers so sure of themselves that with the principles of the first cause they reach the loftiest doctrines and the deepest abysses. But my son, lest I venture too far for your future perception, be aware that men of letters shall make grand and usually boastful claims about the way I interpreted the world, before the worldwide conflagration which is to bring so many catastrophes and such revolutions that scarcely any lands will not be covered by water, and this will last until all has perished save history and geography themselves. This is why, before and after these revolutions in various countries, the rains will be so diminished and such abundance of fire and fiery missiles shall fall from the heavens that nothing shall escape the holocaust. And this will occur before the last conflagration.

For before war ends the (20th) century and in its final stages it will hold the century under its sway. Some countries will be in the grip of revolution for several years, and others ruined for a still longer period. And now that we are in a republican era, with Almighty God's aid, and before completing its full cycle, the monarchy will return, then the Golden Age. For according to the celestial signs, the Golden Age shall return, and after all calculations, with the world near to an all-encompassing revolution

- from the time of writing 177 years 3 months 11 days, plague, long famine and wars, and still more floods from now until the stated time. Before and after these, humanity shall several times be so severely diminished that scarcely anyone shall be found who wishes to take over the fields, which shall become free where they had previously been tied.

This will be after the visible judgement of heaven, before we reach the millennium which shall complete all. In the firmament of the eighth sphere, a dimension whereon Almighty God will complete the revolution, and where the constellations will resume their motion which will render the earth stable and firm, but only if He will remain unchanged for ever until His will be done.

This is in spite of all the ambiguous opinions surpassing all natural reason, expressed by Mahomet; which is why God the Creator, through the ministry of his fiery agents with their flames, will come to propose to our perceptions as well as our eyes the reasons for future predictions.

Signs of events to come must be manifested to whomever prophesies. For prophecy which stems from exterior illumination is part of that light and seeks to ally with it and bring it into being so that the part which seems to possess the faculty of understanding is not subject to a sickness of the mind.

Reason is only too evident. Everything is predicted by divine afflatus and thanks to an angelic spirit inspiring the one prophesying, consecrating his predictions through divine unction. It also divests him of all fantasies by means of various nocturnal apparitions, while with daily certainty he prophesies through the science of astronomy, with the aid of sacred prophecy, his only consideration being his courage in freedom.

So come, my son, strive to understand what I have found out through my calculations which accord with revealed inspiration, because now the sword of death approaches us, with pestilence and war more horrible than there has ever been - because of three men's work - and famine. And this sword shall smite the earth and return to it often, for the stars confirm this upheaval and it is also written: I shall punish their injustices with iron rods, and shall strike them with blows.
For God's mercy will be poured forth only for a certain time, my son, until the majority of my prophecies are fulfilled and this fulfillment is complete. Then several times in the course of the doleful tempests the Lord shall say: Therefore I shall crush and destroy and show no mercy; and many other circumstances shall result from floods and continual rain of which I have written more fully in my other prophecies, composed at some length, not in a chronological sequence, in prose, limiting the places and times and exact dates so that future generations will see, while experiencing these inevitable events, how I have listed others in clearer language, so that despite their obscurities these things shall be understood: When the time comes for the removal of ignorance, the matter will be clearer still.

So in conclusion, my son, take this gift from your father M. Nostradamus, who hopes you will understand each prophecy in every quatrain herein. May Immortal God grant you a long life of good and prosperous happiness.

Salon, 1 March 1555

EPISTLE TO KING HENRY II

TO THE MOST INVINCIBLE MOST POWERFUL AND MOST CHRISTIAN HENRY, KING OF FRANCE THE SECOND: MICHEL NOSTRADAMUS, HIS VERY HUMBLE AND VERY OBEDIENT SERVANT AND SUBJECT, WISHES VICTORY AND HAPPINESS

Ever since my long-beclouded face first presented itself before the immeasurable deity of your Majesty, O Most Christian and Most Victorious King, I have remained perpetually dazzled by that sovereign sight. I have never ceased to honour and venerate properly that date when I presented myself before a Majesty so singular and so humane. I have searched for some occasion on which to manifest high heart and stout courage, and thereby obtain even greater recognition of Your Most Serene Majesty. But I saw how obviously impossible it was for me to declare myself.

While I was seized with this singular desire to be transported suddenly from my long beclouded obscurity to the illuminating presence of the first monarch of the universe, I was also long in doubt as to whom I would dedicate these last three Centuries of my prophecies, making up the thousand. After having meditated for a long time on an act of such rash audacity, I have ventured to address Your Majesty. I have not been daunted like those mentioned by that most grave author Plutarch, in his Life of Lycurgus, who were so astounded at the expense of the offerings and gifts brought as sacrifices to the temples of the immortal gods of that age, that they did not dare to present anything at all. Seeing your royal splendour to be accompanied by such an incomparable humanity, I have paid my address to it and not as those Kings of Persia whom one could neither stand before nor approach.

It is to a most prudent and most wise Prince that I have dedicated my nocturnal and prophetic calculations, which are composed rather out of a natural instinct, accompanied by a poetic furor, than according to the strict rules of poetry. Most of them have been integrated with astronomical calculations corresponding to the years, months and weeks of the regions, countries and most of the towns and cities of all Europe, including Africa and part of Asia, where most of all these coming events are to transpire. They are composed in a natural manner. Indeed, someone, who would do well to blow his nose, may reply that the rhythm is as easy as the sense is difficult.

That, O Most Humane king, is because most of the prophetic quatrains are so ticklish that there is no making way through them, nor is there any interpreting of them.

Nevertheless, I wanted to leave a record in writing of the years, towns, cities and regions in which most of the events will come to pass, even those of the year 1585 and of the year 1606, reckoning from the present time, which is March 14, 1557, and going far beyond to the events which will take place at the beginning of the seventh millenary, when, so far as my profound astronomical calculations and other knowledge have been able to make out, the adversaries of Jesus Christ and his Church will begin to multiply greatly.

I have calculated and composed all during choice hours of well-disposed days, and as accurately as I could, all when Minerva was free and not unfavourable. I have made computations for events over almost as long a period to come as that which has already passed, and by these they will know in all regions what is to happen in the course of time, just as it is written, with nothing superfluous added, although some may say, There can be no truth entirely determined concerning the future.

It is quite true, Sire, that my natural instinct has been inherited from my forebears, who did not believe in predicting, and that this is natural instinct has been adjusted and integrated with long calculations. At the same time, I freed my soul, mind and heart of all care, solicitude and vexation. All of these prerequisites for presaging I achieved in part by means of the brazen tripod.

There are some who would attribute to me that which is not mine at all. The eternal God alone, who is the thorough searcher of humane hearts, pious, just and merciful, is the true judge, and it is to him I pray to defend me from the calumny of evil men. These evil ones, in their slanderous way, would likewise want to inquire how all your most ancient progenitors, the Kings of France, have cured the scrofula, how those of other nations have cured the bite of snakes, how those of yet other nations have had a certain instinct for the art of divination and still others which would be too long to recite here.

Notwithstanding those who cannot contain the malignity of the evil spirit, as time elapses after my death, my writings will have more weight than during my lifetime. Should I, however, have made any errors in my calculation of dates, or prove unable to please everybody, I beg that your more than Imperial Majesty will forgive me. I protest before God and his Saints that I do not propose to insert any writings in this present Epistle that will be contrary to the true Catholic faith, whilst consulting the astronomical calculations to the best of my ability.

Such is the extent of time past, subject to correction by the most learned judgement, that the first man, Adam, came 1,242 years before Noah. About 1,080 years after Noah and the universal flood came Abraham, who, according to some, was a first-rate astrologer and invented the Chaldean alphabet. About 515 or 516 years later came Moses, and from his time to that of David about 570 years elapsed. From the time of David to that of out Savior and Redeemer, Jesus Christ, born of the unique Virgin, 1,350 year elapsed, according to some chronographs. Some may object that this calculation cannot be true, because it differs from that of Eusebius. From the time-of the human redemption to the detestable heresy of the Saracens about 621 years elapsed. From this one can easily add up the amount of time gone by.

Although my calculations may not hold good for all nations, they have, however, been determined by the celestial movements, combined with the emotion, handed down to me by my forebears, which comes over me at certain hours. But the danger of the times, O Most Serene King, requires that such secrets should not be bared except in enigmatic sentences having, however, only one sense and meaning, and nothing ambiguous or amphibological inserted.
Rather they are under a cloudy obscurity, with a natural infusion not unloke the creation of the
world, according to the calculation and Punic Chronicle of Joel: I will pour out my spirit upon all flesh and your sons and daughters will prophesy. But such Prophecy proceeded from the mouth of the Holy Ghost who was the sovereign and eternal power, together with the heavens, and caused some of them to predict great and marvellous events.

As for myself, I would never claim such a title, never, please God. I readily admit that all proceeds from God and render to Him thanks, honour and immortal praise. I have mixed therewith no divination coming from fate. All from God and nature, and for the most part integrated with celestial movements. It is much like seeing in a burning mirror, with clouded vision, the great events, sad, prodigious and calamitous events that in due time will fall upon the principal worshippers. First, upon the temples of God; secondly, upon those who, sustained by the earth, approach such a decadence. Also a thousand other calamitous events which will be known to happen in due time.

For God will take notice of the long barrenness of the great dame, who thereupon will conceive two principal children. But she will be in danger, and the female to whom she will have given birth will also, because of the temerity of the age, be in danger of death in her eighteenth year, and will be unable to live beyond her thirty-sixth year. She will leave three males, and one female, and of these two will not have had the same father.

There will be great differences between the three brothers, and then there will be such great cooperation and agreement between them that the three and four parts of Europe will tremble. The youngest of them will sustain and augment the Christian monarchy, and under him sects will be elevated, and suddenly cast down, Arabs will be driven back, kingdoms united and new laws promulgated.

The oldest one will rule the land whose escutcheon is that of the furious crowned lions with their paws resting upon intrepid arms.

The one second in age, accompanied by the Latins, will penetrate far, until a second furious and trembling path has been beaten to the Great St. Bernard Pass. From there he will descend to mount the Pyrenees, which will not, however, be transferred to the French crown. And this third one will cause a great inundation of human blood, and for a long time Lent will not include March.

The daughter will be given for the preservation of the Christian Church. Her lord will fall into the pagan sect of the new infidels. Of her two children, one will be faithful to the Catholic Church, the other an infidel.

The unfaithful son, who, to his great confusion and later repentance, will want to ruin her, will have three widely scattered regions, namely, the Roman, Germany and Spain, which will set up diverse sects by armed force. The 50th to the 52th degree of latitude will be left behind.
And all will render the homage of ancient religions to the region of Europe north of the 48th parallel. The latter will have trembled first in vain timidity but afterwards the regions to its west, south and east will tremble. But the nature of their power will be such that what has been brought about by concord and union will prove insuperable by warlike conquests.

In nature they will be equal, but very different in faith.

After this the barren Dame, of greater power than the second, will be received by two of the nations. First, by them made obstinate by the one time masters of the universe. Second, by the latter themselves.

The third people will extend their forces towards the circuit of the East of Europe where, in the Pannonias, they will be overwhelmed and slaughtered. By sea they will extend their Myrmidons and Germans to Adriatic Sicily. But they will succumb wholly and the Barbarian sect will be greatly afflicted and driven out by all the Latins.

Then the great Empire of the Antichrist will begin where once was Attila's empire and the new Xerxes will descend with great and countless numbers, so that the coming of the Holy Ghost, proceeding from the 48th degree, will make a transmigration, chasing out the abomination of the Christian Church, and whose reign will be for a time and to the end of time.

This will be preceded by a solar eclipse more dark and gloomy than any since the creation of the world, except that after the death and passion of Jesus Christ. And it will be in the month of October than the great translation will be made and it will be such that one will think the gravity of the earth has lost its natural movement and that it is to be plunged into the abyss of perpetual darkness.

In the spring there will be omens, and thereafter extreme changes, reversals of realms and mighty earthquakes. These will be accompanied by the procreation of the new Babylon, miserable daughter enlarged by the abomination of the first holocaust. It will last for only seventy-three years and seven months.

Then there will issue from the stock which had remained barren for so long, proceeding from the 50th degree, one who will renew the whole Christian Church. A great place will be established, with union and concord between some of the children of opposite ideas, who have been separated by diverse realms. And such will be the peace that the instigator and promoter of military factions, born of the diversity of religions, will remain chained to the deepest pit. And the kingdom of the Furious One, who counterfeits the sage, will be united.

The countries, towns, cities, realms and provinces which will have abandoned their old customs to gain liberty, but which will in fact have enthralled themselves even more, will secretly have wearied of their liberty. Faith lost in their perfect religion, they will begin to strike to the left, only to return to the right. Holiness, for a long time overcome, will be replaced in accordance with the earliest writings.
Thereafter the great dog, the biggest of curs, will go forth and destroy all, the same old crimes being perpetrated again. Temples will be set up again as in ancient times, and the priest will be restored to his original position and he will begin his whoring and luxury, and will commit a thousand crimes.

At the eve of another desolation, when she is atop her most high and sublime dignity, some potentates and warlords will confront her, and take away her two swords, and leave her only the insignia, whose curvature attracts them. The people will make him go to the right and will not wish to submit themselves to those of the opposite extreme with the hand in acute position, who touch the ground, and want to drive spurs into them.

And hereupon it is that there is born of a branch long sterile one who will deliver the people of the world from this benevolent slavery to which they had voluntary submitted. He will put himself under the protection of Mars, stripping Jupiter of all his honours and dignities, and establish himself in the free city in another scant Mesopotamia. The chief and governor will be cast out from the middle and hung up, ignorant of the conspiracy of one of the
conspirators with the second Thrasibulus, who for a long time will have directed all this.

Then the impurities and abominations, with a great shame, will be brought out and manifested in the shadows of the veiled light, and will cease towards the end of the change in reign. The chiefs of the Church will be backward in the love of God, and several of them will apostatize from the true faith. Of the three sects, that which is in the middle, because of its own partisans, will be thrown a bit into decadence. The first one will be exterminated throughout all Europe and most of Africa by the third one, making use of the poor in spirit who, led by madmen to libidinous luxury, will adulterate.

The supporting common people will rise up and chase out the adherents of the legislators. From the way realms will have been weakened by the Easterners, it will seem that God the Creator has loosed Satan from the prisons of hell to give birth to the great Dog and Doham, who will make such an abominable breach in the Churches that neither the reds nor the whites without eyes or hands will know what to make of it, and their power will be taken from them.

Then will commence a persecution of the Churches the like of which was never seen. Meanwhile, such a plague will arise that more than two thirds of the world will be removed. One will be unable to ascertain the true owners of fields and houses, and weeds growing in the streets of cities will rise higher than the knees. For the clergy there will be but utter desolation. The warlords will usurp what is returned from the City of the Sun, from Malta and the Isles of Hyères. The great chain of the port which wakes its name from the marine ox will be opened.

And a new incursion will be made by the maritime shores, wishing to deliver the Sierra Moreпa from the first Mahometan recapture. Their assaults will not all be in vain, and the place which was once the abode of Abraham will be assaulted by persons who hold the Jovialists in veneration. And this city of "Achem" will be surrounded and assailed on all sides by a most powerful force of warriors. Their maritime forces will be weakened by the Westerners, and great desolation will fall upon this realm. Its greatest cities will be depopulated and those who enter • will fall under the vengeance of the wrath of God.

The sepulchre, for long an object of such great veneration, will remain in the open, exposed to the sight of the heavens, the Sun and the Moon. The holy place will be converted into a stable for a herd large and small, and used for profane purposes. Oh, what a calamitous affliction will pregnant women bear at this time.

For hereupon the principal Eastern chief will be vanquished by the Northerners and Westerners, and most of his people, stirred up, will be put to death, overwhelmed or scattered. His children, offspring of many women, will be imprisoned. Then will be accomplished the prophecy of the Royal Prophet, Let him hear the groaning of the captives, that he might deliver the children of those doomed to die.

What great oppression will then fall upon the Princes and Governors of Kingdoms, especially those which will be maritime and Eastern, whose tongues will be intermingled with all others: the tongue of the Latins, and of the Arabs, via the Phoenicians. And all these Eastern Kings will be chased, overthrown and exterminated, but not altogether, by means of the forces of the Kings of the North, and because of the drawing near of our age through the three secretly united in the search for death, treacherously laying traps for one another. This renewed Triumvirate will last for seven years, and the renown of this sect will extend around the world. The sacrifice of the hole and immaculate Wafer will be sustained.

Then the Lords of "Aquilon", two in number, will be victorious over the Easterners, and so great a noise and bellicose tumult will they make amongst them that all the East will tremble in terror of these brothers, yet not brothers, of "Aquilon".

By this discourse, Sire, I present these predictions almost with confusion, especially as to when they will take place. Furthermore, the chronology of time which follows conforms very little, if at all, with that which has already been set forth. Yet it was determined by astronomy and other sources, including Holy Scriptures, and thus could not err. If I had wanted to date each quatrain, I could have done so. But this would not have been agreeable to all, least of all to those interpreting them, and was not to be done until Your Majesty granted me full power to do so, lest calumniators be furnished with an opportunity to injure me.

Anyhow, I count the years from the creation of the world to the birth of Noah as 1,506, and from the birth of Noah to the completion of the Ark, at the time of the universal deluge, as 600 I hold that the Sacred Scriptures use solar years. And at the end of these 600 years, Noah entered the Ark to be saved from the deluge. This deluge was universal, and lasted one year and two months. And 295 years elapsed from the end of the flood to the birth of Abraham, and 100 from then till the birth of Isaac. And 60 years later Jacob was born. 130 years elapsed between the time he entered Egypt and the time he came out. Between the entry of Jacob into Egypt and the exodus, 430 years passed. From the exodus to the building of the Temple by Solomon in the fourth year of his reign, 480 years. According ot the calculations of the Sacred Writings, it was 490 years from the building of the Temple to the time of Jesus Christ. Thus, this calculation of mine, collected from the holy writ, comes to about 4,173 years and 8 months, more or less. Because there is such a diversity of sects, I will not go beyond Jesus Christ.

I have calculated the present prophecies according to the order of the chain which contains its revolution, all by astronomical doctrine modified by my natural instinct. After a while, I found the time when Saturn turns to enter on April 7 till August 25, Jupiter on June 14 till October 7, Mars from April 17 to June 22, Venus from April 9 to May 22, Mercury from February 3 to February 24. After that, from June 1 to June 24, and from September 25 to October 16, Saturn in Capricorn, Jupiter in Aquarius, Mars in Scorpio, Venus in Pisces, Mercury for a month in Capricorn, Aquarius and Pisces, the Moon in Aquarius, the Dragon's head in Libra: its tail in opposition following a conjunction of Jupiter and Mercury with a quadrature of Mars and Mercury, and the Dragon's head coinciding with a conjunction of the Sun and Jupiter. And the year without an eclipse peaceful.

But not everywhere. It will mark the commencement of what will long endure. For beginning with this year the Christian Church will be persecuted more fiercely than it ever was in Africa, and this will last up to the year 1792, which they will believe to mark a renewal of time.

After this the Roman people will begin to re-establish themselves, chasing away some obscure shadows and recovering a bit of their ancient glory. But this will not be without great division and continual changes. Thereafter Venice will raise its wings very high in great force and power, not far short of the might of ancient Rome.

At that time the great sails of Byzantium, allied with the Ligurians and through the support and power of "Aquilon", will impede them so greatly that the two Cretans will be unable to maintain their faith. The arks built by the Warriors of ancient times will accompany them to the waves of Neptune. In the Adriatic great discord will arise, and that which will have been united will be separated. To a house will be reduced that which was, and is, a great city, including "Pampotamia" and "Mesopotamia" of Europe at 45, and others of 41, 42 and 37 degrees.

It will be at this time and in these countries that the infernal power will set the power of its adversaries against the Church of Jesus Christ. This will constitute of the second Antichrist, who will persecute that Church and its true Vicar, by means of the power of three temporal kings who in their ignorance will be seduced by tongues which, in the hands of the madmen, will cut more than any sword.

The said reign of the Antichrist will last only to the death of him who was born at the beginning of the age and of the other one of Lyon, associated with the elected one of the House of Modena and of Ferrara, maintained by the Adriatic Ligurians and the proximity of great Sicily. Then the Great St. Bernard will be passed.

The Gallic Ogmios will be accompanied by so great a number that the Empire of his great law will extend very far. For some time thereafter the blood of the Innocent will be shed profusely by the recently elevated guilty ones. Then, because of great floods, the memory of things contained in these instruments will suffer incalculable loss, even letters. This will happen to the "Aquiloners" by the will of God.
Once again Satan will be bound, universal peace will be established among men, and the Church of Jesus Christ will be delivered from all tribulations, although the Philistines would like to mix in the honey of malice and their pestilent seduction. This will be near the seventh millenary, when the sanctuary of Jesus Christ will no longer be trodden down by the infidels who come from "Aquilon". The world will be approaching a great conflagration, although, according to my calculations in my prophecies, the course of time runs much further.

In the Epistle that some years ago I dedicated to my son, César Nostradamus, I declared some points openly enough, without presage. But here, Sire, are included several great and marvelous events which those to come after will see.

During this astrological supputation, harmonized with the Holy Scriptures, the persecution of the Ecclesiastical folk will have its origin in the power of the Kings of "Aquilon", united with the Easterners. This persecution will last for eleven years, or somewhat less, for then the chief King of "Aquilon" will fall.

Thereupon the same thing will occur in the South, where for the space of three years the Church people will be persecuted even more fiercely through the Apostatic seduction of one who will hold all the absolute power in the Church militant. The hole people of God, the observer of his law, will be persecuted fiercely and such will be their affliction that the blood of the true Ecclesiastics will flow everywhere.

One of the horrible temporal Kings will be told by his adherents, as the ultimate in praise, that he has shed more of human blood of Innocent Ecclesiastics than anyone else could have spilled of wine. This King will commit incredible crimes against the Church. Human blood will flow in the public streets and temples, like water after an impetuous rain, colouring the nearby rivers red with blood. The ocean itself will be reddened by another naval battle, such that one king will say to another, Naval battles have caused the sea to blush.

Then, in this same year, and in those following, there will ensue the most horrible pestilence, made more stupendous by the famine which will have preceded it. Such great tribulations will never have occurred since the first foundation of the Christian Church. It will cover all Latin regions, and will leave traces in some countries of the Spanish.

Thereupon the third King of "Aquilon", hearing the lament of the people of his principal title, will raise a very mighty army and, defying the tradition of his predecessors, will put almost everything back in its proper place, and the great Vicar of the hood will be put back in his former state. But desolated, and then abandoned by all, he will turn to find the Holy of Holies destroyed by paganism, and the old and new Testaments thrown out and burned.
After that Antichrist will be the infernal prince again, for the last time. All the Kingdoms of Christianity will tremble, even those of the infidels, for the space of twenty-five years. Wars and battles will be more grievous and towns, cities, castles and all other edifices will be burned, desolated and destroyed, with great effusion of vestal blood, violations of married woman and widows, and sucking children dashed and broken against the walls of towns. By means of Satan, Prince Infernal, so may evils will be commited that nearly all the world will find itself undone and desolated. Before these events, some rare birds will cry in the air: Hui, Hui and some time later will vanish.

After this has endured for a long time, there will be almost renewed another reign of Saturn, and golden age. Hearing the affliction of his people, God the Creator will command that Satan be cast into the depths of the bottomless pit, and bound there. Then a universal peace will commence between God and man, and Satan will remain bound for around a thousand years, and then all unbound.

All these figures represent the just integration of Holy Scriptures with visible celestial bodies, namely, Saturn, Jupiter, Mars and others conjoined, as can be seen at more length in some of the quatrains. I would have calculated more profoundly and integrated them even further, Most Serene King, but for the fact that some given to censure would raise difficulties. Therefore I withdraw my pen and seek nocturnal repose.

Many events, most powerful of all Kings, of the most astounding sort are to transpire soon, but I neither could nor would fit them all into this epistle; but in order to comprehend certain horrible facts, a few must be set forth. So great is your grandeur and humanity before men, and your piety before the gods, that you alone seem worthy of the great title of the Most Christian King, and to whom the highest authority in all religion should be deferred.

But I shall only beseech you, Most Clement King, by this singular and prudent humanity of yours, to understand rather the desire of my heart, and the sovereign wish I have to obey Your Most Serene Majesty, ever since my eyes approached your solar splendour, than the grandeur of my labour can attain to or acquire.

Salon, 27th of June, 1558.

Almanacs: 1555-1563

Almanac of 1555

The soul touched from a distance by the divine spirit presages,
Trouble, famine, plague, war to hasten:
Water, droughts, land and sea stained with blood,
Peace, truce, prelates to be born, princes to die.
The Tyrrhenian Sea, the Ocean for the defense,
The great Neptune and his trident soldiers:
Provence secure because of the hand of the great Tende,
More Mars Narbonne the heroic de Villars.
The big bronze one which regulates the time of day,
Upon the death of the Tyrant it will be dismissed:
Tears, laments and cries, waters, ice bread does not give,
V.S.C. peace, the army will pass away. Near Geneva terror will be great,
 Through the counsel, that cannot fail: The new King has his league prepare,
The young one dies, famine, fear will cause failure.
O cruel Mars, how you should be feared,
More is the scythe with the silver conjoined:
Fleet, forces, water, wind of shadow to fear,
Sea and land in a truce. The friends has joined L.V.
For not having a guard you will be more offended,
The weak fort, Pinquiet uneasy and pacific:
They cry "famine," the people are oppressed,
The sea reddens, the Long one proud and iniquitous.
The five, six, fifteen, late and soon they remain,
The heirâs bloodline ended: the cities revolted:
The herald of peace twenty and three return,
The open?hearted five locked up, news invented.
At a distance, near the Aquarius, Saturn turns back,
That year great Mars will give a fire opposition,
Towards the North to the south the great proud female,
Florida in contemplation will hold the port.
Eight, fifteen, and five what disloyalty
The evil spy will come to be permitted:
Fire in the sky, lightning, fear, Papal terror,
The west trembles, pressing too hard the Salty wine.
Six, twelve, thirteen, twenty will speak to the Lady,

The older one by a woman will be corrupted:
Dijon, Guienne hail, lightning makes the first cut into it,
The insatiable one of blood and wine satisfied.
The sky to weep for him, made to do that!
The sea is being prepared, Hannibal to plan his ruse:
Denis [drops anchor], fleet delays, does not remain silent,
Has not known the secret, and by which you are amused!
Venus Neptune will pursue the enterprise,
Pensive one imprisoned, adversaries troubled:
Fleet in the Adriatic, cities towards the Thames,
The fourth clamor, by night, the reposing ones wounded.
The great one of the sky the cape will give,
Relief, Adriatic makes an offer to the port:
He who will be able will save himself from dangers,
By night the Great One wounded pursues.
The port protests too fraudulently and false,
The maw opened, condition of peace:
Rhone in crystal, water, snow, ice stained,
The death, death, wind, through rain the burden broken.

Almanac of 1558

The young King makes a funeral wedding soon,
Holy one stirred up, feasts, of the said, Mars dormant:
Night tears they cry, they conduct the lady outside,
The arrest and peace broken on all sides.
Vain rumor within the Hierarchy,
Genoa to rebel: courses, offenses, tumults:
For the greater King will be the monarchy,
Election, conflict, covert burials.
Through discord in the absence to fail,
One suddenly will put him back on top:
Towards the North will be noises so loud,
Lesions, points to travel, above.
On the Tyrrhenian Sea, of different sail,
On the Ocean there will be diverse assaults:
Plague, poison, blood in the house of canvas,

Prefects, Legates stirred up to march high seas.
There where the faith was it will be broken,
The enemies will feed upon the enemies:
Fire rains [from the] Sky, it will burn, interrupted,
Enterprise by night. Chief will make quarrels.
War, thunder, forces fields, depopulated,
Terror and noise, assault on the frontier:
Great Great One fallen, pardon for the exiles,
Germans, Spaniards, by the sea the Barbarian banner.
The noise will be vain, the faltering ones bundled up,
The Shaven Ones captured: the all?powerful One elected:
The two Reds and four true crusaders to fail,
Rain troublesome to the powerful Monarch.
Rain, wind, forces, Barbarossa Hister, the Tyrrhenian Sea,
Vessels to pass Orkneys and beyond Gibraltar,
grain and soldiers provided:
Retreats too well executed by Florence, Siena crossed,
The two will be dead, friendships joined.
Venus the beautiful will enter Florence.
The secret exiles will leave the place behind:
Many widows, they deplore the death of the Great One,
To remove from the realm, the Great Great one does not threaten.
Games, feasts, nuptials, dead Prelate of renown.
Noise, peace of truce while the enemy threatens:
Sea, land and sky noise, deed of the great Brennus,
Cries gold, silver, the enemy they ruin.

Almanac of 1560

Dayâs journey, diet, interim, no council,
The year peace is being prepared, plague, schismatic famine:
Put outside inside, sky to change, domicile,
End of holiday, hierarchical revolt.
Diet to break up, the ancient sacred one to recover,
Under the two, fire through pardon to result:
Consecration without arms: the tall Red will want to have,
Peace of neglect, the Elected One, the Widower, to live.
To be made to appear elected with novelty,

Place of day?labor to go beyond the boundaries:
The feigned goodness to change to cruelty,
From the suspected place quickly will they all go out.
With the place chosen, the Shaved Ones will not be contented,
Led from Lake Geneva, unproven,
They will cause the old times to be renewed:
They will expose the frighten off the plot so well hatched.
Savoy peace will be broken,
The last hand will cause a strong levy:
The great conspirator will not be corrupted,
And the new alliance approved.
A long comet to wrong the Governor, Hunger,
burning fever, fire and reek of blood:
To all estates Jovial Ones in great honor, Sedition by the Shaven ones, ignited.
Plague, famine, fire and ardor incessant,
Lightning, great hail, temple struck from the sky:
The Edict, arrest, and grievous law broken,
The chief inventor his people and himself snatched up.
Deprived will be the Shaven Ones of their arms,
It will augment their quarrel much:
Father Liber deceived lightning Albanians,
Sects will be gnawed to the marrow.
The modest request will be received,
They will be driven out and then restored on top:
The Great Great woman will be found content,
Blind ones, deaf ones will be put uppermost.
He will not be placed, the New Ones expelled,
Black king and the Great One will hold hard:
To have recourse to arms. Exiles expelled further,
To sing of victory, not free, consolation.
The mourning left behind, supreme alliances,
Great Shaven One dead, refusal given at the entrance:
Upon return kindness to be in oblivion,
The death of the just one perpetrated at a banquet.

Almanac of 1562

Season of winter, good spring, sound, bad summer,
Pernicious autumn, dry, wheat rare:
Of wine enough, bad eyes, deeds, molested,
War, mutiny, seditious waste.
The hidden desire for the good will succeed,
Religion, peace, love and concord:
The nuptial song will not be completely in accord,
The high ones, who are low, and high, put to the rope.
For the Shaven Ones the Chief will not reach the end,
Edicts changed, the secret ones set at large:
Great One found dead, less of faith, low standing,
Dissimulated, shuddering, wounded in the boarâs lair.
Moved by Lion, near Lion he will undermine,
Taken, captive, pacified by a woman:
He will not hold as well as they will waver,
Placed unpassed, to oust the soul from rage.
From Lion he will come to arouse to move,
Vain discovery against infinite people:
Known by none the evil for the duty,
In the kitchen found dead and finished.
Nothing in accord, worse and more severe trouble,
As it was, land and sea to quieten:
All arrested, it will not be worth a double,
The iniquitous one will speak, Counsel of annihilation.
Portentous deed, horrible and incredible,
Typhoon will make the wicked ones move:
Those who then afterwards supported by the cable,
And the greater part exiled on the fields.
Right put on the throne come into France from the sky,
The whole world pacified by Virtue:
Much blood to scatter, sooner change to come,
By the birds, and by fire, and not by vers.
The colored ones, the Sacred malcontents,
Then suddenly through the happy Androgynes:
Of the great part to see, the time not come,
Several amongst them will make their soups weak.
They will be returned to their full power,
Conjoined at one point of the accord, not in accord:
All defied, more promised to the Shaven Ones,
Several amongst them outflanked in a band.

For the legate of terrestrial and dawn,
The great Cape will accommodate himself to all:
Tacit LORRAINE, to be listening,
He whose advice they will not want to agree with.
The enemy wind will impede the troop,
For the greatest one advance put in difficulty:
Wine with poison will be put in the cup,
To pass the great gun without horse?power.
Through crystal the enterprise is broken,
Games and feats, in LYONS to repose more:
No longer will he take his repast with the Great Ones,
Sudden catarrh, blessed water, to bathe him.

Almanac of 1564

The sextile year rains, wheat to abound, hatreds, Joy to men,
Princes, King divorced:
Herd to perish, human mutations,
People oppressed and poison under the surface.
Times very diverse, discord discovered,
Council of war, change taken in, changed:
The Great Woman must not be, conspirators through water lost,
Great hostility, for the great one all steady.
The bit of the enemy's tongue approaches,
The Debonair one to peace will want to reduce:
The obstinate ones will want to lose the kinswoman,
Surprised, Captives, and suspects fury to injure.
Fathers and mothers dead of infinite sorrows,
Women in mourning, the pestilent she?monster:
The Great One to be no more, all the world to end,
Under peace, repose and every single one in opposition.
Princes and Christendom stirred up in debates,
Foreign nobles, Christ's See molested:
Become very evil, much good, mortal sight.
Death in the East, plague, famine, evil treaty.
Land to tremble, killed, wasteful, monster,
Captives without number, to do, undone, done:
To go over the sea misfortune will occur,
Proud against the proud evil done in disguise.

Almanacs

The unjust one lowered, they will molest him fiercely,
Hail, to flood, treasure, and engraved marble:
Chief of Persuasion people will kill to death,
And attached will be the blade to the tree.
Of what not evil? inexcusable result,
The fire not double, the Legate outside confused:
Against the worse wounded the fight will not be made,
The end of June the thread cut by firing.
Fine bonds enfeebled by accords,
Mars and Prelates united will not stop:
The great ones confused by gifts of mutilated bodies,
Dignified ones, undignified ones will seize the well endowed.
From good to the evil times will change,
The peace in the South, the expectation of the Greatest Ones:
The Great Ones grieving Louis too much more will stumble,
Well?known Shaven Ones have neither power not understanding.
This is the month for evils so many as to be doubled,
Deaths, plague to drain all, famine, to quarrel:
Those of the reverse of exile will come to note,
Great Ones, secrets, deaths, not to censure.
Through death, death to bite, counsel, robbery, pestiferous,
They will not dare to attack the Marines:
Deucalion a final trouble to make,
Few young people: half?dead to give a start.
Dead through spite he will cause the others to shine,
And in an exalted place some great evils to occur:
Sad concepts will come to harm each one,
Temporal dignified, the Mass to succeed.
Almanac of 1566
For the greatest ones death, loss of honor and violence,
Professors of the faith, their estate and their sect:
For the two great Churches diverse noise, decadence,
Evil neighbors quarreling serfs of the Church without a head.
Waste, great loss, and not without violence,
All those of the faith, more for religion,
The Greatest Ones will lose their lives, their honor and fortunes
Both the two Churches, the sin in their faction.
For the two very Great Ones pernicious loss to arise,
The Greatest Ones will cause loss, goods, of honor, and of life,
As much great noises will run, the urn very odious,
Great maladies to be, meeting?house, mass in envy.
The servants of the Churches will betray their Lords,

Of other Lords also by the undivided of the fields:
Neighbors of meeting?house and mass will quarrel amongst them,
Rumors, noises to augment, to death are several lying.
Of all blessings abundance, the earth will produce for us,
No din of war in France, sedition put outside:
Man?slayers, robbers one will find on the highway,
Little faith, burning fever, people in commotion.
Between people discord, brutal enmity,
War, death of great Princes, several parts:
Universal plague, stronger in the West,
Times good and full, but very dry and exhausted.
The grains not to be plentiful, in all other fruits, plenty,
The Summer, spring humid, winter long, snow, ice:
The East in arms, France reinforces herself,
Death of beasts much honey, the place to be besieged.
Through pestilence and fire fruits of trees will perish,
Signs of oil to abound. Father Denis not scarce:
Some great ones to die, but few foreigners will sally forth in attack,
Offense, Barbarian marines, and dangers at the frontiers.
Rains very excessive, and of blessings abundance,
The cattle price to be just, women outside of danger:
Hail, rain, thunder: people depressed in France,
Through death they will work, death to reprove people.
Arms, plagues to cease, death of the seditious ones,
Great Father Liber will not much abound:
Evil ones will be seized by more malicious ones,
France more than ever victorious will triumph.
Up to this month the great drought will endure,
For Italy and Provence all fruits to half:
The Great One less of enemies prisoner of their band,
For the scroungers, Pirates, and the enemy to die.
The enemy so much to be feared to retire into Thrace,
Leaving cries, howls, and pillage desolated:
To leave noise on sea and land, religion murdered,
Jovial Ones put on the road, every sect to become angry.

CENTURY I

I.

Estant assis de nuict secret estude, Seul reposé sur la selle d'ærain: Flambe exigue sortant de solitude, Fait prosperer qui n'est à croire vain.

Sitting alone at night in secret study; it is placed on the brass tripod.
A slight flame comes out of the emptiness and makes successful that which should not be beleived in vain.

II.

La vierge en main mise au milieu de Branches De l'onde il moulle & le l'imbe & le pied:
Vn peur & voix fremissent par les manches: Splendeur diuine. Le diuin pres s'assied.

The wand in the hand is placed in the middle of the tripod's legs. With water he sprinkles both the hem of his garment and his foot.
A voice, fear: he trembles in his robes. Divine splendour; the god sits nearby.

III.

Quand la lictiere du tourbillon versee, Et seront faces de leurs manteaux couuers, La republique par gens nouveaux vexee, Lors blancs & rouges iureront à l'enuers.

When the litters are overturned by the whirlwind and faces are covered by cloaks, the new republic will be troubled by its people.
At this time the reds and the whites will rule wrongly.

IV.

Par l'vnivers sera faict vn monarque, Qu'en paix & vie ne sera longuement: Lors
se perdra la piscature barque, Sera regie en plus grand detriment.

In the world there will be made a king who will have little peace and a short life.
At this time the ship of the Papacy will be lost, governed to its greatest detriment.

V.

Chassez seront pour faire long combat, Par les pays seront plus fort greuez:
Bourg & cité auront plus grand debat.
Carcas. Narbonne auront coeur esprouuez.

They will be driven away for a long drawn out fight. The countryside will be most
grievously troubled.
Town and country will have greater struggle.
Carcassonne and Narbonne will have their hearts tried.

VII.

Tard arriué l'execution faicte,
Le vent contraire lettres au chemin prinses: Les coniurez XIIIJ. d'vne secte,
Par le Rousseau senez les entreprinses.

Arrived too late, the act has been done.
The wind was against them, letters intercepted on their way.
The conspirators were fourteen of a party.
By Rousseau shall these enterprises be undertaken.

VIII.

Combien de fois prinse cité solitaire Seras changeant ses loix barbares & vaines:
Ton mal s'aproche. Plus seras tributaires Le grand Hardie recouurira tes veines.

How often will you be captured, O city of the sun ?

Century I

Changing laws that are barbaric and vain.
Bad times approach you. No longer will you be enslaved.
Great Hadrie will revive your veins.

IX.

De l'Orient viendra le coeur Punique Fascher Hadrie, & les hoires Romulides, ,
Acompagne de la classe Libique, emples Melites & proches Isles vuides.

From the Orient will come the African heart to trouble Hadrie and the heirs of Romulus.
Accompanied by the Libyan fleet
the temples of Malta and nearby islands shall be deserted.

X.

Serpens transmis en la cage de fer, Ou les enfans septains du Roy sont pris:
Les vieux & peres sortirons bas de l'enfer, Ains mourir voir de fruict mort & cris.

A coffin is put into the vault of iron, where seven children of the king are held.
The ancestors and forebears will come forth from the depths of hell, lamenting
to see thus dead the fruit of their line.

XI.

Le mouuement de sens, coeur pieds & mains, Seront d'accord. Naples, Lyon, Sicile.
Glaiues, feux, eaux, puis aux nobles Romains, Plongez, tuez, morts par cerueau debile

The motion of senses, heart, feet and hands
will be in agreement between Naples, Lyon and Sicily. Swords fire, floods, then
the noble Romans drowned, killed or dead because of a weak brain.

XII.

Dans peu dira fauce brute fragile De bas en haut esleué promptement: Puis en
istant desloyale & labile,
Qui de Veronne aura gouuernement.

There will soon be talk of a treacherous man, who rules a short time, quickly
raised from low to high estate.
He will suddenly turn disloyal and volatile.
This man will govern Verona.

XIII.

Les exilez par ire, haine intestine, Feront au Roy grand coniuration: Secret
mettront ennemis par la mine, Et ses vieux siens contre eux sedition.

Through anger and internal hatreds, the exiles will hatch a great plot against the
king.
Secretly they will place enemies as a threat,
and his own old (adherents) will find sedition against them.

XIV.

De gent esclaue chansons, chants & requestes, Captifs par Princes & Seigneurs
aux prisons: A l'aduenir par idiots sans testes,
Seront receus par diuines oraisons.

From the enslaved populace, songs, chants and demands, while Princes and
Lords are held captive in prisons.
These will in the future by headless idiots be received as divine prayers

XV.

Mars nous menasse par sa force bellique, Septante fois fera le sang espandre:
Auge & ruyne de l'Ecclesiastique
Et plus ceux qui d'eux rien voudront entendre.

Mars threatens us with the force of war and will cause blood to be spilt seventy
times.
The clergy will be both exalted and reviled moreover, by those who wish to learn
nothing of them.

XVI.

Faux à l'estang ioinct vers le Sagittaire, En son haut AVGE de l'exaltation, Peste,
famine, mort de main militaire, Le siecle approche de renouation.

A scythe joined with a pond in Sagittarius at its highest ascendant.
Plague, famine, death from military hands; the century approaches its renewal.

XVII.

Par quarante ans l'Iris n'apparoistra, Par quarante ans tous les iours sera veu:
La terre aride en siccité croistra,
Et grands deloges quand sera apperceu.

For forty years the rainbow will not be seen. For forty years it will be seen every
day. The dry earth will grow more parched,
and there will be great floods when it is seen.

XVIII.

Par la discorde Negligence Gauloise, Sera passage à Mahommet ouuert:
De sang trempé la terre & mer Senoise, Le port Phocen de voiles & nerfs couuert.

Because of French discord and negligence
an opening shall be given to the Mohammedans. The land and sea of Siena will
be soaked in blood,
and the port of Marseilles covered with ships and sails.

XIX.

Lors que serpens viendront circuer l'arc, Le sang Troyen vexé par les Espaignes:
Par eux grand nombre en sera faicte tarc,
Chef fruict, caché aux marcs dans les saignes.

When the snakes surround the altar,
and the Trojan blood is troublerd by the Spanish. Because of them, a great number will be lessened. The leader flees, hidden in the swampy marshes.

XX.

Tours, Oriens, Blois, Angers, Reims & Nantes, Cités vexees par subit changement.
Par langues estranges seront tenduës tentes, Fleuues, dards Renes terre & mer tremblement.

The cities of Tours, Orleans, Blois, Angers, Reims and Nantes are troubled by sudden change.
Tents will be pitched by (people) of foreign tongues; rivers, darts at Rennes, shaking of land and sea.

XXI.

Profonde argille blanche nourrit rocher, Qui d'vn abysme istra lacticineuse,
En vain troublez ne l'oseront toucher, Ignorant estre au fond terre argilleuse.

The rock holds in its depths white clay which will come out milk-white from a cleft
Needlessly troubled people will not dare touch it, unaware that the foundation of the earth is of clay.

XXII.

Ce que viura & n'ayant aucun sens, Viendront leser à mort son artifice: Autun, Chalon, Langres, & les deux Sens, La gresle & glace fera grand malefice.

Century I

A thing existing without any senses
will cause its own end to happen through artifice.
At Autun, Chalan, Langres and the two Sens there will be great damage from
hail and ice.

XXIII.

Au mois troisiesme se leuant le Soleil, Sanglier, Leopart, au champ mars pour
côbatre Leopart lassé au ciel estend son oeil,
Vn Aigle autour du Soleil voyt s'esbatre.

In the third month, at sunrise,
the Boar and the Leopard meet on the battlefield.
The fatigued Leopard looks up to heaven and sees an eagle playing around the
sun.

XXIV.

A cité neuue pensif pour condamner, L'oisel de proye au ciel se vient offrir: Apres
victoire à captif pardonner,
Cremone & Mâtoue grâds maux aura souffert.

At the New City he is thoughtfil to condemn; the bird of prey offers himself to
the gods.
After victory he pardons his captives.
At Cremona and Mantua great hardships will be suffered.

XXV.

Perdu trouué caché de si long siecle, Sera pasteur demy Dieu honnore:
Ains que la Lune acheue son grand siecle, Par autres vents sera deshonnoré.

The lost thing is discovered, hidden for many centuries. Pasteur will be celebrated almost as a god-like figure.
This is when the moon completes her great cycle, but by other rumours he shall
be dishonoured.

XXVI.

Le grand du foudre tumbe d'heure diurne, Mal, & predict par porteur postulaire:
Suiuant presage tumbe de l'heure nocturne, Conflict Reims, Londres, Ettrusque
pestifere.

The great man will be struck down in the day by a thunderbolt.
An evil deed, foretold by the beare of a petition.
According to the prediction another falls at night time. Conflict at Reims, London, and pestilence in Tuscany.

XXVII.

Dessouz le chaine Guien du ciel frappé, Non loing de là est caché le thresor: Qui
par longs siecles auoit esté grappé, Trouué mourra, l'oeil creué de ressort.

Beneath the oak tree of Gienne, struck by lightning, the treasure is hidden not
far from there.
That which for many centuries had been gathered, when found, a man will die,
his eye pierced by a spring.

XXVIII.

La tour de Boucq craindra fuste Barbare, Vn temps, long temps apres barque
hesperique: Bestail, gês, meubles, tous deux ferôt grâd tare,
Taurus, & Libra, quelle mortelle picque?

Tobruk will fear the barbarian fleet for a time, then much later the Western fleet.
Cattle, people, possessions, all will be quite lost.
What a deadly combat in Taurus and Libra.

XXIX.

Quand le poisson terrestre & aquatique Par forte vague au grauier sera mis,
Sa forme estrange suaue & horrifique, Par mes aux meurs bien tost les ennemis.

Century I

When the fish that travels over both land and sea is cast up on to the shore by a great wave,
its shape foreign, smooth and frightful.
From the sea the enemies soon reach the walls.

XXX.

La nef estrange par le tourment marin, Abordera pres de port incogneu: Nonobstant signes de rameau palmerin, Apres mort pille bon aduis tard venu.

Because of the storm at sea the foreign ship will approach an unknown port.
Notwithstanding the signs of the palm branches, afterwards there is death and pillage. Good advice comes too late.

XXXI.

Tant d'ans en Gaule les guerres dureront, Outre la course du Castulon monarque:
Victoire incerte trois grands couronneront, Aigle, Coq, Lune, Lyon, Soleil en marque.

The wars in France will last for so many years beyond the reign of the Castulon kings.
An uncertain victory will crown three great ones,
the Eagle, the Cock, the Moon, the Lion, the Sun in its house.

XXXII.

Le grand Empire sera tost translaté
En lieu petit, qui bien tost viendra croistre, Lieu bien infime d'exigue comté,
Où au milieu viendra poser son sceptre.

The great Empire will soon be exchanged
for a small place, which soon will begin to grow.
A small place of tiny area
in the middle of which he will come to lay down his sceptre.

XXXIII.

Pres d'vn grand pont de plaine spatieuse, Le grand Lyon par forces Cesarees,
Fera abbatre hors cité rigoreuse,
Par effroy portes luy seront reserrees.

Near a great bridge near a spacious plain the great lion with the Imperial forces
will cause a falling outside the austere city.
Through fear the gates will be unlocked for him.

XXXIV.

L'oyseau de proye volant à la senestre, Auant conflict faict aux Fran&cced;ois
pareure:
L'vn bon prendra, l'vn ambique sinistre, La partie foible tiendra par son augure.

The bird of prey flying to the left,
before battle is joined with the French, he makes preparations.
Some will regard him as good, others bad or uncertain.
The weaker party will regard him as a good omen.

XXXV.

Le lyon ieune le vieux surmontera, En champ bellique par singulier duelle:
Dans cage d'or les yeux luy creuera, Deux classes vne, puis mourir, mort cruelle.

The young lion will overcome the older one, in a field of combat in single fight:
He will pierce his eyes in their golden cage; two wounds in one, then he dies a
cruel death.

XXXVI.

Tard le monarque se viendra repentir, De n'auoir mis à mort son aduersaire: Mais
viendra bien à plus haut consentir, Que tout son sang par mort fera deffaire.

Too late the king will repent

10

that he did not put his adversary to death.
But he will soon come to agree to far greater things which will cause all his line
to die.

XXXVII.

Vn peu deuant que le Soleil s'absconde, Conflict donné, grand peuple dubiteux:
Profligez, port marin ne faict response, Pont & sepulchre en deux estranges lieux

Shortly before sun set, battle is engaged.
A great nation is uncertain.
Overcome, the sea port makes no answer, the bridge and the grave both in for-
eign places.

XXXVIII.

Le Sol & l'Aigle au victeur paroistront, Response vaine au vaincu l'on asseure:
Par cor ne crys harnois n'arresteront, Vindicte paix par mors si acheue à l'heure.

The Sun and the Eagle will appear to the victor.
An empty answer assured to the defeated.
Neither bugle nor shouts will stop the soldiers.
Liberty and peace, if achieved in time through death.

XXXIX.

De nuict dans lict le supresme estranglé, Pour trop auoir seiourné blond esleu.
Par trois l'Empire subrogé exanclé,
A mort mettra carte, & pacquet ne leu.

At night the last one will be strangled in his bed because he became too involved
with the blond heir elect.
The Empire is enslaved and three men substituted. He is put to death with neither letter nor packet read.

XL.

La trompe fausse dissimulant folie, Fera Bisance vn changement de loix, Histra
d'Egypte, qui veut que l on deffie Edict changeant monnoyes & aloys.

The false trumpet concealing maddness will cause Byzantium to change its laws.
From Egypt there will go forth a man who wants the edict withdrawn, changing
money and standards.

XLI.

Siege en cité est de nuict assallie, Peu eschappé, non loin de mer conflict: Femme
de ioye, retours fils defaillie, Poison & lettres cachees dans le plic.

The city is beseiged and assaulted by night; few have escaped; a battle not far
from the sea. A woman faints with joy at the return of her son,
poison in the folds of the hidden letters.

XLII.

Le dix Calendes d'Auril de faict Gotique, Resuscité encor par gens malins:
Le feu estainct, assemblee diabolique, Cherchant les os du d'Amant & Pselin.

The tenth day of the April Calends, calculated in Gothic fashion is revived again
by wicked people.
The fire is put out and the diabolic gathering seek the bones of the demon of
Psellus.

XLIII.

Auant qu'aduienne le changement d'Empire, Il aduiendra vn cas bien merueilleux:
Le camp mué, le pillier de porphire, Mis, transmué sus le rocher noilleux.

Before the Empire changes
a very wonderful event will take place. The field moved, the pillar of porphyry

put in place, changed on the gnarled rock.

XLIV.

En bref seront de retour sacrifices, Contreuenans seront mis à martyre:
Plus ne seront moines, abbes, ne nouices, Le miel sera beaucoup plus cher que
cire.

In a short time sacrifices will be resumed, those opposed will be put (to death) ˙
like martyrs. The will no longer be monks, abbots or novices.
Honey shall be far more expensive than wax.

XLV.

Secteur de sectes grand peine au delateur, Beste en theatre dressé le ieu scenique,
Du faict antique ennobly l'inuenteur,
Par sectes monde confus & schismatiques.

A founder of sects, much trouble for the accuser: A beast in the theatre prepares
the scene and plot.
The author ennobled by acts of older times; the world is confused by schismatic
sects.

XLVI.

Tout apres d'Aux de Lestore & Mirande Grand feu du ciel en trois nuicts tombera:
Cause aduiendra bien stupende & mirande, Bien peu apres la terre tremblera.

Very near Auch, Lectoure and Mirande
a great fire will fall from the sky for three nights.
The cause will appear both stupefying and marvellous; shortly afterwards there
will be an earthquake.

XLVII.

Du lac Leman les sermons fascheront, Des iours seront reduits par des sep-
maines,
Puis moys, puis an, puis tous failliront, Les Magistras danneront leur loix vaines.

The speeches of Lake Leman will become angered, the days will drag out into
weeks,
then months, then years, then all will fail.
The authorities will condemn their useless powers.

XLVIII.

Vingt ans du regne de la Lune passez, Sept mil ans autre tiendra sa monarchie:
Quand le Soleil prendra ses iours lassez: Lors accomplir & mine ma prophetie.

When twenty years of the Moon's reign have passed another will take up his
reign for seven thousend years.
When the exhausted Sun takes up his cycle then my prophecy and threats will
be accomplished.

XLIX.

Baucoup auant telles menees, Ceux d'Orient par la vertu lunaire:
L'an mil sept cens feront grands emmenees, Subiungant presques le coing Aquilonaire.

Long before these happenings
the people of the East, influenced by the Moon,
in the year 1700 will cause many to be carried away, and will almost subdue the
Northern area.

L.

De l'aquatique triplicité naistra, D'vn qui fera le Ieudy pour sa feste:
Son bruit, loz, regne, sa puissance croistra, Par terre & mer aux Oriens tempeste.

From the three water signs will be born a man who will celbrate Thursday as his holiday. His renown, praise, rule and power will grow on land and sea, bringing . trouble to the East.

LI.

Chef d'Aries, Iupiter, & Saturne, Dieu eternel quelles mutations?
Puis par long siecle son maling temps retourne Gaule & Italie, quelles esmotions?

The head of Aries, Jupiter and Saturn.
Eternal God, what changes !
Then the bad times will return again after a long century; what turmoil in France and Italy.

LII.

Les deux malins de Scorpion conioinct, Le grand Seigneur meurdry dedans sa salle: Peste à l'Eglise par le nouueau Roy ioinct,
L'Europe basse & Septentrionale.

Two evil influences in conjunction in Scopio.
The great lord is murdered in his room.
A newly appointed king persecutes the Church, the lower (parts of) Europe and in the North.

LIII.

Las! qu'on verra grand peuple tourmenté, Et la loy saincte en totale ruine,
Par autres loix toute la Chrestienté, Quand d'or d'argent trouue nouuelle mine.

Alas, how we will see a great nation sorely troubled and the holy law in utter ruin.
Christianity (governed) throughout by other laws, when a new source of gold and silver is discovered.

LIV.

Deux reuolts faicts du maling falcigere, De regne & siecles faict permutation: Le mobil signe à son endroit si ingere, Aux deux esgaux & d'inclination.

Two revolutions will be caused by the evil scythe bearer making a change of reign and centuries.
The mobile sign thus moves into its house: Equal in favour to both sides.

LV.

Soubs l'opposite climat Babilonique, Grande sera de sang effusion, Que terre & mer, air, ciel sera inique, Sectes, faim, regnes pestes, confusion.

I the land with a climate opposite to Babylon there will be great shedding of blood.
Heaven will seem unjust both on land and sea and in the air.
Sects, famine, kingdoms, plagues, confusion.

LVI.

Vous verrez tost & tard faire grand change, Horreurs extremes & vindications: Que si la Lune conduite par son ange, Le ciel s'approche des inclinations.

Sooner and later you will see great changes made, dreadful horrors and vengeances.
For as the moon is thus led by its angel the heaves draw near to the Balance.

LVII.

Par grand discord la terre tremblera, Accord rompu dressant la teste au ciel, Bouche sanglante dans le sang nagera, Au sol la face ointe de laict & miel.

The trumpet shakes with great discord.
An agreement broken: lifting the face to heaven: the bloody mouth will swim with blood;

the face anointed with milk and honey lies on the ground.

LVIII.

Tranché le ventre naistra auec deux testes, Et quatre bras: quelques ans entiers viura Iour qui Alquiloye celebrera ses festes, Fossen, Turin, chef Ferrare suiura.

Through a slit in the belly a creature will be born with two heads and four arms:
it will survive for some few years.
The day that Alquiloie celebrates his festivals Fossana, Turin and the ruler of
Ferrara will follow.

LIX.

Les exilez deportez dans les isles,
Au changement d'vn plus cruel monarque Seront meurtris, & mis deux des scin-
tiles, Qui de parler ne seront estez parques.

The exiles deported to the islands
at the advent of an even more cruel king will be murdered. Two will be burnt ·
who were not sparing in their speech.

LX.

Vn Empereur naistra pres d'Italie, Qui à l'Empire sera vendu bien cher: Diront
auec quels gens il se ralie,
Qu'on trouuera moins prince que boucher.

An Emperor will be born near Italy, who will cost the Empire very dearly. They
will say, when they see his allies, that he is less a prince than a butcher.

LXI.

La republique miserable infelice Sera vastee du nouueau magistrat: Leur grand amas de l'exil malefice Fera Sueue rauir leur grand contract.

The wretched, unfortunate republic will again be ruined by a new authority. The great amount of ill will accumulated in exile will make the Swiss break their important agreement.

LXII.

La grande perte, las! que feront les lettres, Auant le ciel de Latona parfaict: Feu grand deluge plus par ignares sceptres, Que de long siecle ne se verra refaict.

Alas! what a great loss there will be to learning before the cycle of the Moon is completed.
Fire, great floods, by more ignorant rulers; how long the centuries until it is seen to be restored.

LXIII.

Les fleurs passees diminue le monde, Long temps la paix terres inhabitees: Seur marchera par ciel, terre, mer & onde, Puis de nouueau les guerres suscitees.

Pestilences extinguished, the world becomes smaller, for a long time the lands will be inhabited peacefully.
People will travel safely through the sky (over) land and seas: then wars will start up again.

LXIV.

De nuict Soleil penseront auois veu.
Quand le pourceau demy homme on verra: Bruit chant, bataille au ciel batre apperceu, Et bestes brutes à parler lon orra.

At night they will whink they have seen the sun, when the see the half pig man:

18

Noise, screams, battles seen fought in the skies.
The brute beasts will be heard to speak.

LXV.

Enfant sans mains iamais veu si grand foudre, L'enfant Royal au ieu d'oesteuf
blessé:
Au puy brises fulgures allant mouldre, Trois souz les chaines par le milieu trous-
sés.

A child without hands, never so great a thunderbolt seen, the royal child wounded at a game of tennis.
At the well lightning strikes, joining together three trussed up in the middle
under the oaks.

LXVI.

Celuy qui lors portera les nouuelles Apres vn peu il viendra respirer,
Viuiers, Tournon, Montferrant & Pradelles, Gresle & tempestes le fera souspirer.

He who then carries the news, after a short while will (stop) to breath:
Viviers, Tournon, Montferrand and Praddelles; hail and storms will make them
grieve.

LXVII.

La grand famine que ie sens approcher, Souuent tourner, puis estre vniuerselle,
Si grande & longue qu'on viendra arracher Du bois racine, & l'enfant de mam-
melle.

The great famine which I sense approaching
will often turn (in various areas) then become world wide.
It will be so vast and long lasting that (they) will grab roots from the trees and
children from the breast.

LXVIII.

O quel horrible & malheureux teurment, Trois innocens qu'on viendra à liurer
Poison suspecte, mal gardé tardiment. Mis en horreur par bourreaux enyurez.

O to what a dreadful and wretched torment are three innocent people going to
be delivered.
Poison sugested, badly guarded, betrayal.
Delivered up to horror by drunken executioners.

LXIX.

La grand montagne ronde de sept stades, Apres paix, guerre, faim, inodation,
Roulera loin abismant grands contrades, Mesmes antiques, & grands fondation.

The great mountain, seven stadia round, after peace, war, famine, flooding.
It will spread far, drowning great countries, even antiquities and their might
foundations.

LXX.

Pluye, faim, guerre en Perse non cessee, La foy trop grand trahira le monarque:
Par la finie en Gaule commencee, Secret augure pour à vn estre parque.

Rain, famine and war will not cease in Persia; too great a faith will betray the
monarch.
Those (actions) started in France will end there, a secret sign for on to be sparing.

LXXI.

La tour marine troys foys prise & reprise, Par Espagnols, Barbares, Ligurains:
Marseille & Aix, Arles par ceux de Pise, Vast, feu, fer pillé Auignon des Thurins.

The marine tower will be captured and retaken three times by Spaniards, barbarians and Ligurians.
Marseilles and Aix, Ales by men of Pisa, devastation, fire, sword, pillage at Avi-

gnon by the Turinese.

LXXII.

Du tout Marseille des habitans changee, Course & poursuite iusqu'au pres de Lyon, Narbon, Tholouse par Bourdeaux outragee, Tuez captifs presque d'vn milion.

The inhabitants of Marseilles completely changed, fleeing and pursued as far as Lyons.
Narbonne, Toulouse angered by Bordeaux; the killed and captive are almost one million.

LXXIII.

France à cinq pars par neglect assaillie, Tunys, Argal esmeuz par Persiens: Leon, Seuille, Barcellonne faillie, N'aura la classe par les Venitiens.

France shall be accused of neglect by her five partners.
Tunis, Algiers stirred up by the Persians. Leon, Seville and Barcelona having failed,
they will not have the fleet because of the Venetians.

LXXIV.

Apres seiourné vagueront en Epire, Le grand secours viendra vers Anthioche. Le noir poil crespe rendra fort à l'Empire,
Barbe d'ærain se rostira en broche.

After a rest they will travel to Epirus, great help coming from around Antioch.
The curly haired king will strive greatly for the Empire, the brazen beard will be roasted on a spit.

LXXV.

Le tyran Sienne occupera Sauonne, Le fort gaigné tiendra classe marine:
Les deux armees par la marque d'Anconne, Par effrayeur le chef s'en examine.

The tyrant of Siena will occupy Savona, having won the fort he will restrain the
marine fleet.
Two armies under the standard of Ancona: the leader will examine them in fear.

LXXVI.

D'vn nom farouche tel proferé sera, Que les trois seurs auront fato le nom:
Puis grand peuple par langue & faict dira Plus que nul autre aura bruit & renom.

The man will be called by a barbaric name that three sisters will receive from
destiny.
He will speak then to a great people in words and deeds, more than any other
man will have fame and renown.

LXXVII.

Entre deux mers dreslera promontoire, Que puis mourra par le mors du cheual:
Le sien Neptune pliera voile noire,
Par Calpre & classe aupres de Rocheual.

A promontory stands between two seas:
A man who will die later by the bit of a horse; Neptune unfurls a black sail for
his man;
the fleet near Gibraltar and Rocheval.

LXXVIII.

D'vn chef vieillard naistra sens hebeté, Degenerant par s&cced;avoir & par
armes: Le chef de France par sa soeur redouté, Champs diuisez, concedez aux
gendarmes.

To an old leader will be born an idiot heir, weak both in knowledge and in war.
The leader of France is feared by his sister, battlefields divided, conceded to the soldiers.

LXXIX.

Bazaz, Lestore, Condon, Ausch, Agine, Esmeurs par loix, querelle & monopole:
Car Bourd. Tholouse, Bay mettra en ruine: Renouueller voulant leur tauropole.

Bazas, Lectoure, Condom, Auch and Agen are troubled by laws, disputes and ,
monopolies.
Carcassone, Bordeaux, Toulouse and Bayonne will be ruined when they wish to
renew the massacre.

LXXX.

De la sixiesme claire splendeur celeste, Viendra tonner si fort en la Bourgongne,
Puis n'aystra monstre de tres hideuse beste:
Mars, Auril, May, Iuin, grâd charpin & rongne.

From the sixth bright celestial light
it will come to thunder very strongly in Burgundy. Then a monster will be born
of a very hideuos beast:
In March, April, May and June great wounding and worrying.

LXXXI.

D'humain troupeau neuf seront mis à part, De iugement & conseil separez: Leur
sort sera diuisé en depart,
Kappa, Thita, Lambda mors bannis esgarez.

Nine will be set apart from the human flock, separated from judgment and ad-
vise.
Their fate is to be divided as they depart.
K. Th. L. dead, banished and scattered.

LXXXII.

Quand les colonnes de bois grande tremblee, D'Auster conduite, couuerte de rubriche: Tant vuidera dehors grande assemblee, Trembler Vienne & le pays d'Austriche.

When the great wooden columns tremble in the south wind, covered with blood.
Such a great assembly then pours forth
that Vienna and the land of Austria will tremble.

LXXXIII.

La gent estrange diuisera butins, Saturne en Mars son regard furieux: Horrible estrange aux Toscans & Latins, Grecs qui seront à frapper curieux.

The alien nation will divide the spoils.
Saturn in dreadful aspect in Mars.
Dreadful and foreign to the Tuscans and Latins, Greeks who will wish to strike.

LXXXIV.

Lune obscurcie aux profondes tenebres, Son frere passe de couleur ferrugine: Le grand caché long temps sous les tenebres, Tiedera fer dans la playe sanguine.

The moon is obscured in deep gloom, his brother becomes bright red in colour.
The great one hidden for a long time in the shadows will hold the blade in the bloody wound.

LXXXV.

Par la response de dame Roy troublé, Ambassadeurs mespriseront leur vie: Le grand ses freres contrefera doublé, Par deux mourront ire, haine & enuie.

The king is troubled by the queen's reply. Ambassadors will fear for their lives.
The greater of his brothers will doubly disguise his action, two of them will die through anger, hatred and envy.

LXXXVI.

La grande Royne quand se verra vaincue, Fera excés de masculin courage,
Sur cheual, fleuue passera toute nue, Suite par fer: à foy fera outrage.

When the great queen sees herself conquered, she will show an excess of masculine courage.
Naked, on horseback, she will pass over the river pursued by the sword: she will have outraged her faith

LXXXVII.

Ennosigee feu du centre de terre, Fera trembler autour de cité neuue
Deux grâds rochers long têps feront la guerre, Puis Arethuse rougira nouueau fleuue.

Earthshaking fire from the centre of the earth will cause tremors around the New City.
Two great rocks will war for a long time, then Arethusa will redden a new river.

LXXXVIII.

Le diuin mal surprendra le grand Prince, Vn peu deuant aura femme espousee,
Son appuy & credit à vn coup viendra mince, Conseil mourra pour la teste rasee.

The divine wrath overtakes the great Prince, a short while before he will marry.
Both supporters and credit will suddenly diminish. Counsel, he will die because of the shaven heads.

LXXXIX.

Touts ceux de Iler ne seront dans la Moselle, Mettant à mort tous ceux de Loire
& Seine: Le cours marin viendra pres d'haute velle, Quand Espagnols ouurira toute veine.

Those of Lerida will be in the Moselle, kill all those from the Loire and Seine.
The seaside track will come near the high valley, when the Spanish open every route.

XC.

Bourdeaux, Poitiers au son de la campagne, A grande classe ira iusqu'à l'Angon,
Contre Gaulois sera leur tramontane,
Quand monstre hideux naistra pres de Orgô.

Bordeaux and Poitiers at the sound of the bell will go with a great fleet as fas as Langon.
A great rage will surge up against the French, when an hideous monster is born near Orgon.

XCI.

Les Dieux feront aux humains apparence, Ce qu'ils seront autheurs de grand conflict: Auant ciel veu serain espee & lance,
Que vers main gauche se plus grand afflict.

The gods will make it appear to mankind that they are the authors of a great war.
Before the sky was seen to bee free of weapons and rockets: the greatest damage will be inflicted on the left.

XCII.

Souz vn la paix par tout sera clamee, Mais non long temps pille, & rebellion, Par refus ville, terre & mer entamee, Morts & captifs le tiers d'vn million.

Under one man peace will be proclaimed everywhere, but not long after will be looting and rebellion.
Because of a refusal, town, land and see will be broached.
About a third of a million dead or captured.

XCIII.

Terre Italique pres monts tremblera, Lyon & Coq non trop confederez, En lieu de peur l'vn l'autre s'aidera, Seul Catulon & Celtes moderez.

The Italian lands near the mountains will tremble.
The Cock and the Lion not strongly united. In place of fear they will help each other. Freedom alone moderates the French.

XCIV.

Au port Selin le tyran mis à mort, La liberté non pourtant recouuree:
Le nouueau Mars par vindicte & remort, Dame par force de frayeur honoree.

The tyrant Selim will be put to death at the harbour but Liberty will not be re-gained, however.
A new war arises from vengeance and remorse.
A lady is honoured through force of terror.

XCV.

Deuant moustier trouué enfant besson, D'heroic sang de moine & vetustique:
Son bruit par secte langue & puissance son, Qu'on dira fort esleué le vopisque.

In front of a monastery will be found a twin infant from the illustrious and an-cient line of a monk.
His fame, renown and power through sects and speech
is such that they will say the living twin is deservedly chosen.

XCVI.

Celuy qu'aura la charge de destruire Temples, & sectes, changez par fantasie: Plus au rochers qu'aux viuans viendra nuire, Par langue ornee d'oreilles rassasie.

A man will be charged with the destruction of temples and sectes, altered by fantasy.
He will harm the rocks rather than the living, ears filled with ornate speeches.

XCVII.

Ce que fer, flamme n'a s&cced;eu paracheuer, La douce langue au conseil viendra
faire:
Par repos, songe, le Roy fera resuer, Plus l'ennemy en feu, sang militaire.

That which neither weapon nor flame could accomplish will be achieved by a
sweet speaking tongue in council.
Sleeping, in a dream, the king will see the enemy not in war or of military blood.

XCVIII.

Le chef qu'aura conduit peuple infiny Loing de son ciel, de moeurs & langue
estrange,
Cinq mil en Crete & Thessalie finy, Le chef fuyant sauué en marine grange.

The leader who will conduct great numbers of people far from their skies, to
foreign customs and language.
Five thousand will die in Crete and Thessaly, the leader fleeing in a sea going
supply ship.

XCIX.

Le grand monarque que fera compagnie Auec deux Roys vnis par amitié:
O quel souspir fera la grand mesgnie, Enfants Narbon à l'entour quel pitié.

The great king will join
with two kings, united in friendship. How the great household will sigh: around
Narbon what pity for the children.

C.

Long temps au ciel sera veu gris oyseau, Aupres de Dole & de Toscane terre:
Tenant au bec vn verdoyant rameau, Mourra tost grand & finera la guerre.

For a long time a grey bird will be seen in the sky near Dôle and the lands of

Century I

Tuscany.
He holds a flowering branch in his beak, but he dies too soon and the war ends.

CENTURY II

I.

VERS Aquitaine par insuls Britanniques De par eux-mesmes grandes incursions Pluyes, gelees feront terroirs iniques, Port Selyn fortes fera inuasions.

Towards Aquitaine by the British isles By these themselves great incursions. Rains, frosts will make the soil uneven, "Port Selyn" will make mighty invasions

II.

La teste bleue fera la teste blanche Autant de mal, que France a faict leur bien: Mort à l'anthene, grand pendu sus la branche, Quand prins des siens le Roy dira combien.

The blue head will inflict upon the white head As much evil as France has done them good:
Dead at the sail-yard the great one hung on the branch. When seized by his own the King will say how much.

III.

Pour la chaleur solitaire sus la mer, De Negrepont les poissons demy cuits: Les habitans viendront entamer, Quand Rhod & Gennes leur faudra le biscuit.

Because of the solar heat on the sea Of Euboea the fishes half cooked:
The inhabitants will come to cut them, When the biscuit will fail Rhodes and Genoa.

IV.

Depuis Monach iusqu'aupres de Sicille, Toute la plage demourra desolee:
Il n'y aura fauxbourgs, cité, ne ville, Que par Barbares pillee soit & vollee.

From Monaco to near Sicily
The entire coast will remain desolated: There will remain there no suburb, city
or town
Not pillaged and robbed by the Barbarians.

V.

Qu'en dans poisson, fer & lettre enfermee, Hors sortira, qui puis fera la guerre,
Aura par mer sa classe bien ramee, Apparoissant pres de Latine terre.

That which is enclosed in iron and letter in a fish, Out will go one who will then
make war,
He will have his fleet well rowed by sea, Appearing near Latin land.

VI.

Aupres des portes & dedans deux citez Seront deux fleaux, & onc n'apperceut
vn tel, Faim, dedans peste, de fer hors gens boutez, Crier secours au grand Dieu
immortel.

Near the gates and within two cities
There will be two scourges the like of which was never seen, Famine within
plague, people put out by steel, Crying to the great immortal God for relief.

VII.

Entre plusieurs aux isles deportez, L'vn estre nay à deux dents en la gorge Mourront de faim les arbres esbrotez,
Pour eux neuf Roy, nouuel edict leur forge.

Amongst several transported to the isles, One to be born with two teeth in his
mouth They will die of famine the trees stripped, For them a new King issues a

new edict.

VIII.

Temples sacrez prime fa&cced;on Romaine, Reietteront les gofres fondements,
Prenant leurs loix premieres & humaines, Chassant non tout des saincts les cultements.

Temples consecrated in the original Roman manner, They will reject the excess foundations,
Taking their first and humane laws, Chasing, though not entirely, the cult of saints.

IX.

Neuf ans le regne le maigre en paix tiendra, Puis il cherra en soif si sanguinaire,
Pour luy peuple sans foy & loy mourra Tué vn beaucoup plus debonnaire.

Nine years the lean one will hold the realm in peace, Then he will fall into a very bloody thirst:
Because of him a great people will die without faith and law Killed by one far more good-natured.

X.

Auant long temps le tout sera rangé, Nous esperons vn siecle bien senestre,
L'estat des masques & des seuls bien changé. Peu trouueront qu'à son rang veuille estre.

Before long all will be set in order, We will expect a very sinister century,
The state of the masked and solitary ones much changed, Few will be found who want to be in their place.

XI.

Le prochain fils de l'aisnier paruiendra Tant esleué iusqu'au regne des fors: Son aspre gloire vn chacun craindra, Mais ses enfans du regne gettez hors.

The nearest son of the elder will attain
Very great height as far as the realm of the privileged: Everyone will fear his fierce glory,
But his children will be thrown out of the realm.

XII.

Yeux clos ouuerts d'antique fantasie, L'habit des seuls seront mis à neant: Le grand monarque chastiera leur frenaisie, Ravir des temples le thresor par deuant.

Eyes closed, opened by antique fantasy,
The garb of the monks they will be put to naught: The great monarch will chastise their frenzy, Ravishing the treasure in front of the temples.

XIII.

Le corps sans ame plus n'estre en sacrifice, Iour de la mort mis en natiuité: L'esprit diuin fera l'ame felice, Voiant le verbe en son eternité.

The body without soul no longer to be sacrificed: Day of death put for birthday:
The divine spirit will make the soul happy, Seeing the word in its eternity.

XIV.

A Tours, Gien, gardé seront yeux penetrans, Descouuriront de loing la grand sereine: Elle & sa suitte au port seront entrans, Combat, poussez, puissance souueraine.

At Tours, Gien, guarded, eyes will be searching, Discovering from afar her serene Highness:

She and her suite will enter the port, Combat, thrust, sovereign power.

XV.

Vn peu deuant monarque trucidé? Castor Pollux en nef, astre crinite: Lerain public par terre & mer vuidé, Pise, Ast, Ferrare, Turin terre interdicte.

Shortly before the monarch is assassinated, Castor and Pollux in the ship, bearded star: The public treasure emptied by land and sea, Pisa, Asti, Ferrara, Turin land under interdict.

XVI.

Naples, Palerme, Sicile, Syracuses, Nouueaux tyrans, fulgures feux celestes: Force de Londres, Gand, Bruxelles & Suses, Grand hecatombe, triomphe faire festes.

Naples, Palermo, Sicily, Syracuse, New tyrants, celestial lightning fires: Force from London, Ghent, Brussels and Susa, Great slaughter, triumph leads to festivities.

XVII.

Le champ du temple de la vierge vestale, Non esloigné d'Ethne & monts Pyrenees: Le grand conduit est caché dans la male, North gettez fleuues & vignes mastinees.

The field of the temple of the vestal virgin, Not far from Elne and the Pyrenees mountains: The great tube is hidden in the trunk.
To the north rivers overflown and vines battered.

XVIII.

Nouelle & pluye subite, impetueuse, Empeschera subit deux exercites.
Pierre ciel, feux faire la mer pierreuse, La mert de sept terre & marin subites.

New, impetuous and sudden rain Will suddenly halt two armies. Celestial stone, fires make the sea stony, The death of seven by land and sea sudden.

XIX.

Nouueaux venus lieu basty sans defence, Occuper la place par lors inhabitable: Prez, maisons, champs, villes, prêdre à plaisance, Faim peste, guerre, arpen long labourage.

Newcomers, place built without defense, Place occupied then uninhabitable: Meadows, houses, fields, towns to take at pleasure, Famine, plague, war, extensive land arable.

XX.

Freres & soeurs en diuers lieux captifs, Se trouueront passer pres du monarque: Les comtempler ses rameaux ententifs. Desplaisant voir menton frôt, nez, les marques.

Brothers and sisters captive in diverse places Will find themselves passing near the monarch: Contemplating them his branches attentive, Displeasing to see the marks on chin, forehead and nose.

XXI.

L'ambassadeur enuoyé par biremes, A my chemin d'incogneuz repoussez: De sel renfort viendront quatre triremes, Cordes & chaines en Negre pont troussez.

The ambassador sent by biremes, Halfway repelled by unknown ones: Reinforced with salt four triremes will come, In Euboea bound with ropes and chains.

XXII.

Le camp Ascop d'Europe partira, S'adioignant proche de l'Isle submergee: D'Ar-
aon classe phalange pliera,
Nombril du monde plus grand voix subrogee:

The imprudent army of Europe will depart, Collecting itself near the submerged
isle: The weak fleet will bend the phalanx,
At the navel of the world a greater voice substituted.

XXIII.

Palais, oyseaux, par oyseau dechassé, Bien tost apres le prince paruenu: Combien
qu'hors fleuue ennemy repoussé, Dehors saisir trait d'oyseau soustenu.

Palace birds, chased out by a bird, Very soon after the prince has arrived:
Although the enemy is repelled beyond the river, Outside seized the trick upheld
by the bird.

XXIV.

Bestes farouches de faim fleuues tranner; Plus part du champ encontre Hister
sera, En cage de fer le grand fera treisner, Quand rien enfant de Germain obse-
ruera.

Beasts ferocious from hunger will swim across rivers: The greater part of the
region will be against the Hister, + The great one will cause it to be dragged in an
iron cage, When the German child will observe nothing.

XXV.

La garde estrange trahira forteresse, Espoir & vmbre de plus hault mariage:
Garde de&cced;eu, fort prinse dans la presse, Loyre, Saone, Rosne, Gar, à mort
oultrage.

The foreign guard will betray the fortress, Hope and shadow of a higher mar-

riage: Guard deceived, fort seized in the press,
Loire, Saone, Rhone, Garonne, mortal outrage.

XXVI.

Pour sa faueur que la cité fera,
Au grand qui tost perdra camp de bataille, Puis le rang Pau Thesin versera,
De sang, feux morts yeux de coup de taille.

Because of the favor that the city will show
To the great one who will soon lose the field of battle, Fleeing the Po position,
the Ticino will overflow
With blood, fires, deaths, drowned by the long-edged blow.

XXVII.

Le diuin verbe sera du ciel frappé, Qui ne pourra proceder plus auant: Du rese-
ruant le secret estoupé,
Qu'on marchera par dessus & deuant.

The divine word will be struck from the sky, One who cannot proceed any further:
The secret closed up with the revelation, + Such that they will march over and
ahead.

XXVIII.

Le penultiesme du surnom du Prophete, Prendra Diane pour son iour & repos:
Loing vaguera par frenetique teste,
En deliurant vn grand peuple d'impos.

The penultimate of the surname of the Prophet Will take Diana for his day and
rest:
He will wander far because of a frantic head, And delivering a great people from
subjection.

XXIX.

L'Oriental sorrira de son siege, Passer les monts Apennons voir la Gaule:
Transpercera le ciel, les eaux & neige, Et vn chacun frappera de sa gaule.

The Easterner will leave his seat,
To pass the Apennine mountains to see Gaul: He will transpire the sky, the waters and the snow,
And everyone will be struck with his rod.

XXX.

Vn qui les dieux d'Annibal infernaux, Fera renaistre, effrayeur des humains.
Oncq' plus d'horreur ne plus pire iournaux, Qu'auint viendra par Babel aux Romains.

One who the infernal gods of Hannibal Will cause to be reborn, terror of mankind Never more horror nor worse of days
In the past than will come to the Romans through Babel.

XXXI.

En Campanie le Cassilin fera tant, Qu'on ne verra d'aux les champs couuers:
Deuant apres la pluye de long temps, Hors mis les arbres rien l'on verra de vert.

In Campania the Capuan [river] will do so much That one will see only fields
covered by waters: Before and after the long rain
One will see nothing green except the trees.

XXXII.

Laict, sang grenoilles escoudre en Dalmatie.
Conflict donné preste pres de Balennes: Cry sera grand par toute Esclauonie,
Lors naistra monstre pres & dedans Rauenne.

Milk, frog's blood prepared in Dalmatia.

Conflict given, plague near Treglia:
A great cry will sound through all Slavonia, Then a monster will be born near and within Ravenna.

XXXIII.

Par le torrent qui descent de Veronne, Par lors qu'au Pau guindera son entree.
Vn grand naufrage, & non moins en Garonne, Quand ceux de Gênes marcherôt leur contree

Through the torrent which descends from Verona Its entry will then be guided to the Po,
A great wreck, and no less in the Garonne, When those of Genoa march against their country.

XXXIV.

L'ire insensee du combat furieux, Fera à table par freres le fer luire: Les desparrit blessé, & curieux,
Le fier duelle viendra en France nuire.

The senseless ire of the furious combat
Will cause steel to be flashed at the table by brothers: To part them death, wound, and curiously,
The proud duel will come to harm France.

XXXV.

Dans deux logis de nuict la feu prendra, Plusieurs dedans estoffez & rostis.
Pres de deux fleuues pour seul il aduiendra: Sol, l'Arq, & Caper tous seront amortis.

The fire by night will take hold in two lodgings, Several within suffocated and roasted.
It will happen near two rivers as one:
Sun, Sagittarius and Capricorn all will be reduced.

Century II

XXXVI.

Du grand Prophete les lettres seront prinses, Entre les mains du tyran deuiendront: Frauder son Roy seront ses entreprinses, Mais ses rapines bien tost le
troubleront.

The letters of the great Prophet will be seized, They will come to fall into the
hands of the tyrant: His enterprise will be to deceive his King,
But his extortions will very soon trouble him.

XXXVII.

De ce grand nombre que l'on enuoyera, Pour secourir dans le fort assiegez, Peste
& famine tous les deuorera,
Hors mis septante qui seront profligez.

Of that great number that one will send To relieve those besieged in the fort,
Plague and famine will devour them all, Except seventy who will be destroyed.

XXXVIII.

Des condamnez sera fait vn grand nombre, Quand les monarques seront con-
ciliez: Mais l'vn d'eux viendra si malencombre, Que guerre ensemble: ne seront
raliez.

A great number will be condemned When the monarchs will be reconciled:
But for one of them such a bad impediment will arise That they will be joined
together but loosely.

XXXIX.

Vn deuant le conflict Italique, Germains, Gaulois, Espaignols pour le fort:
Cherra l'escolle maison de republique, Où, hors mis peu, seront suffoqué morts.

One year before the Italian conflict, Germans, Gauls, Spaniards for the fort: The
republican schoolhouse will fall,

There, except for a few, they will be choked dead.

XL.

Vn peu apres non point longue interualle, Par mer & terre sera faict grand tumulte: Beaucoup plus grande sera pugne nauale, Feux, animaux, qui plus feront
d'insulte.

Shortly afterwards, without a very long interval, By sea and land a great uproar
will be raised: Naval battle will be very much greater,
Fires, animals, those who will cause greater insult.

XLI.

La grand' estoille par sept iours bruslera, Nuee fera deux soleils apparoir:
Le gros mastin toute nuit hurlera, Quand grand pontife changera de terroir.

The great star will burn for seven days, The cloud will cause two suns to appear:
The big mastiff will howl all night
When the great pontiff will change country.

XLII.

Coq, chiens & chats de sang seront repeus, Et de la playe du tyran trouué mort,
Au lict d'vn autre iambes & bras rompus, Qui n'avoit peu mourir de cruelle mort.

Cock, dogs and cats will be satiated with blood And from the wound of the tyrant found dead, At the bed of another legs and arms broken, He who was not
afraid to die a cruel death.

Century II

XLIII.

Durant l'estoille cheuelue apparente,
Les trois grands princes seront faits ennemis: Frappez du ciel paix terre tremu-
lente,
Pau, Timbre vndâns, serpent sur le bort mis.

During the appearance of the bearded star. The three great princes will be made
enemies: Struck from the sky, peace earth quaking,
Po, Tiber overflowing, serpent placed upon the shore.

XLIV.

L'Aigle poussee en tout de pauillons, Par autres oyseaux d'entour sera chassee:
Quand bruit des cymbres tube & sonnaillons Rendont le sens de la dame insensee.

The Eagle driven back around the tents Will be chased from there by other birds:
When the noise of cymbals, trumpets and bells Will restore the senses of the
senseless lady.

XLV.

Trop du ciel pleure l'Androgin procree, Pres du ciel sang humain respandu: Par
mort trop tard grand peuple recree, Tard & tost vient le secours attendu.

Too much the heavens weep for the Hermaphrodite begotten, Near the heavens
human blood shed:
Because of death too late a great people re-created, Late and soon the awaited
relief comes.

XLVI.

Apres grâd troche humain plus grâd s'appreste Le grand moteur les siecles renouuelle: Pluye sang, laict, famine, fer & peste,
Au ciel veu feu, courant longue estincelle.

After great trouble for humanity, a greater one is prepared The Great Mover renews the ages:
Rain, blood, milk, famine, steel and plague, Is the heavens fire seen, a long spark running.

XLVII.

L'ennemy grand vieil dueil meurt de poison, Les souuerains par infinis subiuguez: Pierres plouvoir, cachez soubs la toison,
Par mort articles en vain sont alleguez.

The great old enemy mourning dies of poison, The sovereigns subjugated in infinite numbers: Stones raining, hidden under the fleece, Through death articles are cited in vain.

XLVIII.

La grand copie qui passera les monts.
Saturne en l'Arq tournant du poisson Mars: Venins cachez soubs testes de saumons, Leurs chief pendu à fil de polemars.

The great force which will pass the mountains. Saturn in Sagittarius Mars turning from the fish: Poison hidden under the heads of salmon,
Their war-chief hung with cord.

XLIX.

Les conseilliers du premier monopole. Les conquerants seduits pour la Melite, Rode, Bisance pour leurs exposant pole. Terre faudra les poursuiuans de fuite.

The advisers of the first monopoly, The conquerers seduced for Malta: Rhodes, Byzantium for them exposing their pole: Land will fail the pursuers in flight.

L.

Quâd ceux d'Hainault, de Gâd & de Bruxelles, Verront à Langres le siege deuant
mis:
Derrier leurs flancs seront guerres cruelles La playe antique fera pis qu'ennemis.

When those of Hainaut, of Ghent and of Brussels Will see the siege laid before·
Langres:
Behind their flanks there will be cruel wars, The ancient wound will do worse
than enemies.

LI.

Le sang du iuste à Londres fera faute, Bruslez par foudres de vingt trois les six:
La dame antique cherra de place haute, De mesme secte plusieurs seront occis.

The blood of the just will commit a fault at London, Burnt through lightning of
twenty threes the six: The ancient lady will fall from her high place, Several of
the same sect will be killed.

LII.

Dans plusieurs nuits la terre tremblera: Sur le printemps deux effors suite: Corinthe, Ephese aux deux mers nagera, Guerre s'esmeut par deux vaillans de luite.

For several nights the earth will tremble: In the spring two efforts in succession:
Corinth, Ephesus will swim in the two seas: War stirred up by two valiant in
combat.

LIII.

La grande peste de cité maritime, Ne cessera que mort ne soit vengee
Du iuste sang par pris damné sans crime, De la grand dame par feincte n'outragee.

The great plague of the maritime city Will not cease until there be avenged the

death
Of the just blood, condemned for a price without crime, Of the great lady un-
wronged by pretense.

LIV.

Pour gent estrange, & Romains loingtaine, Leur grand cité apres eaue fort troublee: Fille sans trop different domaine,
Prins chef, ferreure n'auoir esté riblee.

Because of people strange, and distant from the Romans Their great city much
troubled after water: Daughter handless, domain too different,
Chief taken, lock not having been picked.

LV.

Dans le conflict le grand qui peut valloit.
A son dernier fera cas merueilleux. Pendant qu'Hadrie verra ce qu'il falloit, Dans
le banquet pongnale l'orgueilleux.

In the conflict the great one who was worth little At his end will perform a marvelous deed: While "Adria" will see what he was lacking, During the banquet the
proud one stabbed.

LVI.

Que peste & glaiue n'a sceu definer, Mort dans le puys sommet du ciel frappé:
L'abbé mourra quand verra ruiner,
Ceux du naufraige l'escueil voulant grapper.

One whom neither plague nor steel knew how to finish, Death on the summit of
the hills struck from the sky: The abbot will die when he will see ruined
Those of the wreck wishing to seize the rock.

LVII.

Auant conflict le grand tumbera,
Le grand à mort, mort, trop subite & plainte, Nay miparfaict la plus part nagera,
Aupres du fleuue de sang la terre teinte.

Before the conflict the great wall will fall,
The great one to death, death too sudden and lamented, Born imperfect: the greater part will swim:
Near the river the land stained with blood.

LVIII.

Sans pied ne main dend ayguë & forte, Par glob au fort de port & layné nay: Pres du portail desloyal transport, Silene luit, petit, grand emmené.

With neither foot nor hand because of sharp and strong tooth Through the crowd to the fort of the pork and the elder born: Near the portal treacherous proceeds, Moon shining, little great one led off.

LIX.

Classe Gauloyse par apuy de grand garde, Du grand Neptune, & ses tridens souldars.
Rongee Prouence pour soustenir grand bande: Plus Mars Narbon, par iauelotz & dards.

Gallic fleet through support of the great guard Of the great Neptune, and his trident soldiers, Provence reddened to sustain a great band:
More at Narbonne, because of javelins and darts.

LX.

La foy Punicque en Orient rompue.
Grand Iud, & Rosne Loyre & Tag changeront: Quand du mulet la faim sera repue,
Classe espargie, sang & corps nageront.

The Punic faith broken in the East,
Ganges, Jordan, and Rhone, Loire, and Tagus will change: When the hunger of
the mule will be satiated,
Fleet sprinkles, blood and bodies will swim.

LXI.

Enge, Tamins, Gironde & la Rochele, O sang Troyen mort au port de la fleche
Derrier le fleuue au fort mise l'échelle Pointes feu grand meurtre sus la bresche.

Bravo, ye of "Tamins," Gironde and La Rochelle: O Trojan blood! Mars at the
port of the arrow Behind the river the ladder put to the fort,
Points to fire great murder on the breach.

LXII.

Mabus plustost alors mourra, viendra, De gens & bestes vn horrible defaite: Puis
tout à coup la vengeance on verra, Cent, main, faim quand courra la comete.

"Mabus" then will soon die, there will come Of people and beasts a horrible rout:
Then suddenly one will see vengeance,
Hundred, hand, thirst, hunger when the comet will run.

LXIII.

Gaulois, Ausone bien peu subiugera, Pau, Marne & Seine fera Perme l'vrie: Qui
le grand mur contre eux dressera,
Du moindre au mur le grand perdra la vie.

The Gauls Ausonia will subjugate very little, Po, Marne and Seine Parma will
make drunk: He who will prepare the great wall against them, He will lose his
life from the least at the wall.

LXIV.

Secher de faim, de soif, gent Geneuoise, Espoir prochain viendra au defaillir:
Snr point tremblant sera loy Gebenoise, Classe au grand port ne se peut accue-
illir.

The people of Geneva drying up with hunger, with thirst, Hope at hand will
come to fail:
On the point of trembling will be the law of him of the Cevennes, Fleet at the
great port cannot be received.

LXV.

Le pare enclin grande calamité, Par l'Hesperie & Insubre fera: Le feu en nef peste
& captiuité, Mercure en l'Arc Saturne fenera.

The sloping park great calamity
To be done through Hesperia and Insubria: The fire in the ship, plague and cap- ·
tivity, + Mercury in Sagittarius Saturn will fade.

LXVI.

Par grand dangiers le captif eschapé, Peu de temps grand a fortune changee:
Dans le palais le peuple est attrapé, Par bon augure la cité assiegee.

Through great dangers the captive escaped: In a short time great his fortune
changed.
In the palace the people are trapped, Through good omen the city besieged.

LXVII.

Le blonde au nez force viendra commettre, Par la duelle & chassera dehors:
Les exilez dedans fera remettre,
Aux lieux marins commettant les plus fors.

The blond one will come to compromise the fork-nosed one Through the duel

and will chase him out:
The exiles within he will have restored, Committing the strongest to the marine places.

LXVIII.

De l'Aquilon les efforts seront grands: Sus l'Ocean sera la porte ouuerte: Le regne en l'Isle sera reintegrand,
Tremblera Londres par voille descouuerte.

The efforts of "Aquilon" will be great: The gate on the Ocean will be opened, The kingdom on the Isle will be restored: London will tremble discovered by sail.

LXIX.
Le Roy Gaulois par la Celtique dextre, Voyant discorde de la grand Monarchie:
Sur les trois parts fera florir son sceptre, Contre la chappe de la grand Hierarchie.

The Gallic King through his Celtic right arm Seeing the discord of the great Monarchy:
He will cause his sceptre to flourish over the three parts, Against the cope of the great Hierarchy.

LXX.

Le dard du ciel fera son estandue, Morts en parlant grande execution:
La pierre en l'arbre la fiere gent rendue, Bruit humain monstre purge expiation.

The dart from the sky will make its extension, Deaths speaking: great execution.
The stone in the tree, the proud nation restored, Noise, human monster, purge expiation.

LXXI.

Les exilez en Sicile viendront, Pour deliure de faim la gent estrange: Au point du iour les Celtes luy faudront La vie demeure à raison: Roy se range.

The exiles will come into Sicily
To deliver form hunger the strange nation: At daybreak the Celts will fail them: Life remains by reason: the King joins.

LXXII.

Armee Celtique en Italie vexee,
De toutes pars conflict & grande perte: Romains fuis, ô Gaule repoussée, Pres du Thesin Rubicon pugne incerte.

Celtic army vexed in Italy
On all sides conflict and great loss: Romans fled, O Gaul repelled! Near the Ticino, Rubicon uncertain battle.

LXXIII.

Au lac Fucin de Benac le riuage, Prins de Leman au port de l'Orgion: Nay de trois bras predict bellique image, Par trois couronnes au grand Endymi-on.

The shore of Lake Garda to Lake Fucino,
Taken from the Lake of Geneva to the port of "L'Orguion": Born with three arms the predicted warlike image, Through three crowns to the great Endymion.

LXXIV.

De Sens, d'Autun viendront iusques au Rosne, Pour passer outre vers les monts Pyrenees:
La gent sortit de la marque d'Anconne, Par terre & mer suyura à grands trainees.

From Sens, from Autun they will come as far as the Rhone To pass beyond to- '

wards the Pyrenees mountains:
The nation to leave the March of Ancona:
By land and sea it will be followed by great suites.

LXXV.

La voix ouye de l'insolit oyseau, Sur le canon du respiral estage:
Si haut viendra du froment le boisteau Que l'homme d'homme sera Antro-
pophage.

The voice of the rare bird heard, On the pipe of the air-vent floor:
So high will the bushel of wheat rise, That man will be eating his fellow man.

LXXVI.

Foudre en Bourgongne fera cas portenteux. Que par engin oncques ne pourroit
faire, De leur senar sacrist fait boiteux,
Fera s&cced;avoir aux ennemis l'affaire.

Lightning in Burgundy will perform a portentous deed, One which could never
have been done by skill, Sexton made lame by their senate
Will make the affair known to the enemies.

LXXVII.

Par arcs, feux, poix & par feux repoussez, Cris hurlements sur la minuit ouys:
Dedans sont mis par les rampars cassez, Par cunicules les traditeurs fuys.

Hurled back through bows, fires, pitch and by fires: Cries, howls heard at midnight:
Within they are place on the broken ramparts, The traitors fled by the underground passages.

LXXVIII.

Le grand Neptune du profond de la mer, De gent punique & sang Gaulois meslé: ·
Les Isles à sang pour le tardif ramer, Puis luy nuira que l'occult mal celé.

The great Neptune of the deep of the sea With Punic race and Gallic blood
mixed. The Isles bled, because of the tardy rowing:
More harm will it do him than the ill-concealed secret.

LXXIX.

La barbe crespe & noire par engin, Subiuguera la gent cruelle & fiere: Le grand
Chiren ostera du longin. Tous les captifs par Seline banniere.

The beard frizzled and black through skill Will subjugate the cruel and proud
people: The great "Chyren" will remove from far away All those captured by the
banner of "Selin". +

LXXX.

Apres conflict du lesé l'eloquence, Par peu de temps se trame faint repos.
Point l'on n'admet les grands à deliurance, Des ennemis sont remis à propos.

After the conflict by the eloquence of the wounded one For a short time a soft
rest is contrived:
The great ones are not to be allowed deliverance at all: They are restored by the
enemies at the proper time.

LXXXI.

Par feu du ciel la cité presque aduste, L'vne menace encor Deucalion, Vexee Sardaigne par la Punique fuste, Apres que Libra lairra son Phaëton.

Through fire from the sky the city almost burned: The Urn threatens Deucalion
again: Sardinia vexed by the Punic foist,
After Libra will leave her Phaethon.

LXXXII.

Par faim la proye fera loup prisonner, L'assaillant lors en extreme detresse. Le nay
ayant au deuant le dernier,
Le grand n'eschappe au milieu de la presse.

Through hunger the prey will make the wolf prisoner, The aggressor then in
extreme distress.
The heir having the last one before him,
The great one does not escape in the middle of the crowd.

LXXXIII.

Le gros traffic d'vn grand Lyon changé, La plus part tourne en pristine ruine,
Proye aux soldats par pille vendangé: Par Iura mont & Sueue bruine.

The large trade of a great Lyons changed, The greater part turns to pristine ruin
Prey to the soldiers swept away by pillage: Through the Jura mountain and "Sue-
via" drizzle.

LXXXIV.

Entre Campaigne, Sienne, Flora, Tustie, Six mois neuf iours ne pleuura vne
goutte: L'estrange langue en terre Dalmatie, Couurira sus, vastant la terre toute.

Between Campania, Siena, Florence, Tuscany, Six months nine days without a
drop of rain: The strange tongue in the Dalmatian land,
It will overrun, devastating the entire land.

LXXXV.

Le vieux plein barbe soubs le statut seuere, A Lion faict dessus l'Aigle Celtique,
Le petit grand trop outre perseuere, Bruist d'arme au ciel: mer rouge Ligustique.

The old full beard under the severe statute Made at Lyon over the Celtic Eagle:
The little great one perseveres too far:

Noise of arms in the sky: Ligurian sea red.

LXXXVI.

Naufrage à classe pres d'onde Hadriatique, La terre tremble esmeuë sus l'air en terre mis: Egypte tremble augment Mahometique, L'Herault sov rendre à crier est commis.

Wreck for the fleet near the Adriatic Sea:
The land trembles stirred up upon the air placed on land: Egypt trembles Mahometan increase, +
The Herald surrendering himself is appointed to cry out.

LXXXVII.

Apres viendra des extremes contrees, Prince Germain, dessus le throsne doré: La seruitude & eaux rencontrees,
La dame serue, son temps plus n'adoré.

After there will come from the outermost countries A German Prince, upon the golden throne:
The servitude and waters met,
The lady serves, her time no longer adored.

LXXXVIII.

Le circuit du grand faict ruineux, Le nom septiesme du cinquiesme sera:
D'vn tiers plus grand l'estrange belliqueur: Mouton, Lutece, Aix ne garantira.

The circuit of the great ruinous deed, The seventh name of the fifth will be: Of a third greater the stranger warlike: Sheep, Paris, Aix will not guarantee.

LXXXIX.

Vn iour seront demis les deux grands maistres, Leur grand pouuoir se verra augmenté:
La terre neuue sera en ses hauts estres, Au sanguinaire le nombre racompté.

One day the two great masters will be friends, Their great power will be seen
increased:
The new land will be at its high peak, To the bloody one the number recounted.

XC.

Par vie & mort changé regne d'Ongrie, La loy sera plus aspre que seruice:
Leur grand cité d'hurlemens plaincts & crie, Castor & Pollux ennemis dans la
lice.

Though life and death the realm of Hungary changed: The law will be more harsh
than service:
Their great city cries out with howls and laments, Castor and Pollux enemies in
the arena.

XCI.

Soleil leuant vn grand feu l'on verra, Bruit & clarté vers Aquilon tendants: Dedans
le rond mort & cris l'on orra, Par glaiue, feu faim, mort les attendants.

At sunrise one will see a great fire, Noise and light extending towards "Aquilon:"
Within the circle death and one will hear cries,
Through steel, fire, famine, death awaiting them.

XCII.

Feu couleur d'or du ciel en terre veu, Frappé du haut nay, faict cas merueilleux.
Grand meurtre humain: prinse du grand le neueu, Morts d'espactacles eschappé
l'orgueilleux.

Fire colour of gold from the sky seen on earth: Heir struck from on high, marvelous deed done:
Great human murder: the nephew of the great one taken, Deaths spectacular the
proud one escaped.

XCIII.

Biens pres du Tymbre presse la Lybitine, Vn peu deuant grand inondation:
Le chef du nef prins, mis à la sentine, Chasteau, palais en conflagration.

Very near the Tiber presses Death: Shortly before great inundation:
The chief of the ship taken, thrown into the bilge: Castle, palace in conflagration.

XCIV.

Grand Paud, grand mal pour Gaulois receura, Vaine terreur au maritin Lyon:
Peuple infiny par la mer passera, Sans eschapper vn quart d'vn million:

Great Po, great evil will be received through Gauls, Vain terror to the maritime
Lion:
People will pass by the sea in infinite numbers, Without a quarter of a million
escaping.

XCV.

Les lieux peuplez seront inhabitables: Pour champs auoir grande diuision:
Regnes liurez à prudens incapables, Lors les grands freres mort & dissention.

The populous places will be uninhabitable: Great discord to obtain fields:
Realms delivered to prudent incapable ones: Then for the great brothers dissen-
sion and death.

XCVI.

Flambeau ardant au ciel soir sera veu, Pres de la fin & principe du Rosne, Famine, glaiue: tardue secours pourueu, La Perse tourne enuahir Macedoine.

Burning torch will be seen in the sky at night Near the end and beginning of the
Rhone: Famine, steel: the relief provided late,
Persia turns to invade Macedonia.

XCVII.

Romain Pontife garde de t'approcher, De la cité qui deux fleuues arrouse, Ton sang viendra aupres de la cracher Toy & les tiens quand fleurira la rose.

Roman Pontiff beware of approaching The city that two rivers flow through,
Near there your blood will come to spurt, + You and yours when the rose will
flourish.

XCVIII.

Celuy de sang reperse le visage, De la victime proche sacrifiee, Tonant en Leo,
augure par presage,
Mis estre à mort lors pour la fiancee.

The one whose face is splattered with the blood Of the victim nearly sacrificed:
Jupiter in Leon, omen through presage: To be put to death then for the bride.

XCIX.

Terroir Romain qu'interpretoit augure, Par gent Gauloise par trop sera vexee:
Mais nation Celtique craindra l'heure, Boreas, classe trop loing l'auoit poussee.

Roman land as the omen interpreted Will be vexed too much by the Gallic people:
But the Celtic nation will fear the hour,
The fleet has been pushed too far by the north wind.

C.

Dedans les isles si horrible tumulte, Bien on n'orra qu'vne bellique brigue, Tant grand sera de predateurs l'insulte, Qu'on te viendra ranger à la grand ligue.

Within the isles a very horrible uproar, One will hear only a party of war, So great will be the insult of the plunderers That they will come to be joined in the great league.

CENTURY III

APRES combat & bataille nauale,
Le grand Neptune à son plus haut befroy: Rouge aduersaire de peur viêdra pasle,
Mettant le grand Occean en effroy.

After combat and naval battle,
The great Neptune in his highest belfry: Red adversary will become pale with
fear, Putting the great Ocean in dread.

II.

Le diuin Verbe donra à la substance, Côpris ciel, terre, or occult au laict mys-
tique:
Corps, ame esprit ayant toute puissance, Tant soubs ses pieds comme au siege
Celique.

The divine word will give to the substenance, Including heavenm earth, gold
hidden in the mystic milk:
Body, soul, spirit having all power,
As much under its feet as the Heavenly see.

III.

Mars & Mercure, & l'argent ioint ensemble, Vers le midy extreme siccité:
Au fond d'Asie on dira terre tremble, Corinthe, Ephese lors en perplexité.

Mars and Mercury, and the silver joined together, Towards the south extreme
drought:
In the depths of Asia one will say the earth trembles, Corinth, Ephesus then in
perplexity.

IV.

Quand seront proches le defaut des lunaires, De l'vn à l'autre ne distant grandement, Froid, siccité, danger vers les frontieres, Mesme où l'oracle a prins commencement.

When they will be close the lunar ones will fail, From one another not greatly
distant,
Cold, dryness, danger towards the frontiers, Even where the oracle has had its
beginning.

V.

Pres loing defaut de deux grands luminaires.
Qui suruiendra entre l'Auril & Mars:
O quel cherré! mais deux grands debonnaires Par terre & mer secourront toutes
pars.

Near, far the failure of the two great luminaries Which will occur between April
and March.
Oh, what a loss! but two great good-natured ones By land and sea will relieve all
parts.

VI.

Dans temple clos le foudre y entrera, Les citadins dedans leur fort greuez.
Cheuaux, boeufs, hômes, l'onde mur touchera, Par faim, soif, soubs les plus foibles armez.

Within the closed temple the lightning will enter, The citizens within their fort
injured:
Horses, cattle, men, the wave will touch the wall, Through famine, drought, under the weakest armed.

VII.

Les fugitifs, feu du ciel sus les picques, Conflict prochain des corbeaux, s'esbatans
De terre on crie, ayde, secours celiques, Quand pres des murs seront les combat-
ans.

The fugitives, fire from the sky on the pikes: Conflict near the ravens frolicking,
From land they cry for aid and heavenly relief, When the combatants will be near
the walls.

VIII.

Les Cimbres ioints auecques leurs voisins De populer viendront presque l'Espagne: Gens amassez Guienne & Limosins Seront en ligue, & leur feront com-
pagne.

The Cimbri joined with their neighbors Will come to ravage almost Spain:
Peoples gathered in Guienne and Limousin Will be in league, and will bear them
company.

IX.

Bourdeaux Roüan, & la Rochelle ioints, Tiendront autour la grand mer Oc-
ceane, Anglois, Bretons, & les Flamans conioints Les chasseront iusqu'aupres de
Roüane.

Bordeaux, Rouen and La Rochelle joined Will hold around the great Ocean sea,
English, Bretons and the Flemings allied Will chase them as far as Roanne.

X.

De sang & faim plus grand calamité, Sept fois s'appreste à la marine plage:
Monech de faim, lieu pris, captiuité, Le grand, mené croc en ferree cage.

Greater calamity of blood and famine, Seven times it approaches the marine
shore:

Monaco from hunger, place captured, captivity, The great one led crunching in a metaled cage.

XI.

Les armes batre au ciel longue saison L'arbre au milieu de la cité tombé: Verbine rogne, glaiue, en face tison, Lors le monarque d'Hadrie succombé.

The arms to fight in the sky a long time, The tree in the middle of the city fallen: Sacred bough clipped, steel, in the face of the firebrand, Thenm the monarch of "Adria" fallen.

XII.

Par la tumeur de Heb, Po, Timbre, & Rome Et par l'estang Leman & Aretin. Les deux grands chefs & citez de Garonne, Prins, mortz noyez: Partir humain butin.

Because of the swelling of the Ebro, Po, Tagus, Tiber and Rhône And because of the pond of Geneva and Arezzo,
The two great chiefs and cities of the Garonne, Taken, dead, drowned: human booty divided.

XIII.

Par foudre en l'arche or & argent fondu, De deux captifs l'vn l'autre mangera De la cité le plus grand estendu, Quand submergee la classe nagera.

Through lightning in the arch gold and silver melted, Of two captives one will eat the other:
The greatest one of the city stretched out, When submerged the fleet will swim.

XIV.

Par le rameau du vaillant personnage, De France infime, par le pere infelice:
Honneurs, richesses: trauail en son viel aage, Pour auoir creu le conseil d'homme
nice.

Through the branch of the valiant personage Of lowest France: because of the
unhappy father
Honors, riches, travail in his old age,
For having believed the advice of a simple man.

XV.

Coeur, vigueur, gloire le regne changera. De tous points contre ayant son aduersaire: Lors France enfance par mort subiugera, Vn grand Regent sera lors plus
contraire.

The realm, will change in heart, vigor and glory, In all points having its adversary
opposed:
Then through death France an infancy will subjugate, A great Regent will then
be more contrary.

XVI.

Vn prince Anglois Mars à son coeur de ciel, Voudra poursuyure la fortune prospere Des deux duelles l'vn percera le fiel,
Hay de luy bien aymee de sa mere.

An English prince Marc in his heavenly heart Will want to pursue his prosperous
fortune, Of the two duels one will pierce his gall: Hated by him well loved by his
mother.

XVII.

Mont Auentine brusler nuict sera veu, Le ciel obscur tout à vn coup en Flandres
Quand le monarque chassera son neueu,

Leurs gens d'Eglise commettrô les esclandres.

Mount Aventine will be seen to burn at night: The sky very suddenly dark in Flanders: When the monarch will chase his nephew, Then Chirch people will commit scandals.

XVIII.

Apres la pluye laict asses longuette,
En plusieurs lieux de Reims le ciel touché: O quel conflict de sang pres d'eux s'apprester,
Peres & fils Roys n'oseront approcher.

After the rather long rain milk,
In several places in Reims the sky touched: Alas, what a bloody murder is prepared near them,
Fathers and sons Kings will not dare approach.

XIX.

En Luques sang & laict viendra plouuoir, Vn peu deuant changement de preteur:
Grand peste & guerre, faim & soif fera voir Loin où mourra leur prince & recteur.

In Lucca it will come to rain blood and milk, Shortly before a change of praetor:
Great plague and war, famine and drought will be m,ade visible Far away where their prince and rector will die.

XX.

Par les contrees du grand fleuue Bethique, Loin d'Ibere au Royaume de Grenade
Croix repoussees par gens Mahometiques Vn Cordubete ahira le contrade.

Through the regions of the great river Guadalquivir Deep in Iberia to the Kingdom of Grenada
Crosses beaten back by the Mahometan peoples One of Cordova will betray his country

XXI.

Au Crustamin par mer Hadriatique, Apparoistra vn horrible poisson,
De face humaine, & la fin aquatique, Qui se prendra dehors de l'ameçon.

In the Conca by the Adriatic Sea There will appear a horrible fish, With face human and its end aquatic, Which will be taken without the hook.

XXII.

Six iours l'assaut deuant cité donné: Liuree sera forte & aspre bataille: Trois la rendront, & à eux pardonné, Le reste à feu & à sang tranche taille.

Six days the attack made before the city: Battle will be given strong and harsh:
Three will surrender it, and to them pardon:
The rest to fire and to bloody slicing and cutting.

XXIII.

Si France passe outre mert lygustique, Tu te verras en isles & mers enclos.
Mahommet contraire, plus mer Hadriatique Cheuaux & d'Asnes ty rongeras les os.

If, France, you pass beyond the Ligurian Sea, You will see yourself shut up in islands and seas: Mahomet contrary, more so the Adriatic Sea: You will gnaw the bones of horses and asses.

XXIV.

De l'entreprinse grande confusion, Perte de gens thresor innumerable: Tu n'y dois faire encore tension.
France à mon dire fais que sois recordable.

Great confusion in the enterprise, Loss of people, countless treasure: You ought not to extend further there.
France, let what I say be remembered.

XXV.

Qui au royaume Nauarrois paruiendra, Quand le Sicile & Naples seront ioints:
Bigore & Lances par Foyx loron tiendra D'vn qui d'Espagne sera par trop conio-
int.

He who will attain to the kingdom of Navarre When Sicily and Naples will be
joined:
He will hold Bigorre and Landes through Foix and Oloron From one who will be
too closely allied with Spain.

XXVI.

Des Roys & Princes dresseront simulacres, Augures, creuz esleuez aruspices:
Corne, victume d'oree, & d'azur, d'acre, Inrerpretez seront les extipices.

They will prepare idols of Kings and Princes, Soothsayers and empty prophets
elevated: Horn, victime of gold, and azure, dazzling, The soothsayers will be interpreted.

XXVII.

Prince libinique puissant en Occident.
Fran&cced;ois d'Arabe viendra tant enflammer. S&cced;auant aux lettres fera
condescendent La langue Arabe en Fran&cced;ois translater.

Libyan Prince powerful in the West
Will come to inflame very much French with Arabian.
Learned in letters condescending he will Translate the Arabian language into
French.

XXVIII.

De terre foible & pauure parentelle, Par bout & paix paruiendra dans l'empire.
Long temps regner vne ieune femelle, Qu'oncques en regne n'en suruint vn si
pire.

Of land weak and parentage poor,
Through piece and peace he will attain to the empire.
For a long time a young female to reign, Never has one so bad come upon the
kingdom.

XXIX.

Les deux neueux en diuers lieux nourris.
Nauale pugne, terre peres tombez Viendront si haut esleuez enguerris Venger
l'iniure, ennemis succombez.

The two nephews brought up in diverse places: Naval battle, land, fathers fallen:
They will come to be elevated very high in making war To avenge the injury,
enemies succumbed.

XXX.

Celuy qu'en luitte & fer au faict bellique Aura porté plus grand que luy le pris: De
nuict au lict six luy feront la pique Nud sans harnois subit sera surprins.

He who during the struggle with steel in the deed of war Will have carried off
the prize from on greater than he: By night six will carry the grudge to his bed,
Without armor he will surprised suddenly.

XXXI.

Aux champs de Mede, d'Arabe, & d'Armenie Deux grands copies trois fois s'as-
sembleront: Pres du riuage d'Araxes la mesgnie,
Du grand Soliman en terre tomberont.

On the field of Media, of Arabia and of Armenia Two great armies will assemble
thrice:
The host near the bank of the Araxes, They will fall in the land of the great Su-
leiman.

XXXII.

Le grand sepulchre du peuple Aquitanique S'approchera aupres de la Toscane.
Quand Mars sera pres du coing Germanique Et au terroir de la gent Mantuane.

The great tomb of the people of Aquitaine Will approach near to Tuscany,
When Mars will be in the corner of Germany And in the land of the Mantuan
people.

XXXIII.

En la cité où le loup entrera, Bien pres de là les ennemis seront: Copie estrange
grand pays gastera
Aux murs & Alpes les amis passeront.

In the city where the wolf will enter, Very near there will the enemies be: Foreign
army will spoil a great country.
The friends will pass at the wall and Alps.

XXXIV.

Quand le deffaut du Soleil lors sera Sur le plein iour le monstre sera veu: Tout
autrement on l'interpretera, Cherté n'a garde nul n'y aura pouruel.

When the eclipse of the Sun will then be, The monster will be seen in full day:
Quite otherwise will one interpret it,
High price unguarded: none will have foreseen it.

XXXV.

Du plus profond de l'Occident d'Europe, De pauures gens vn ieune enfant naistra, Qui par sa langue seduira grande troupe, Sont bruit au regne d'Orient plus
croistra.

From the very depths of the West of Europe, A young child will be born of poor
people,

He who by his tongue will seduce a great troop: His fame will increase towards the realm of the East.

XXXVI.

Enseuely non mort apopletique, Sera trouué auoir les mains mangees:
Quand la cité damnera l'heretique, Qu'auoit leurs loix, ce leur sembloit changees,

Buried apoplectic not dead,
He will be found to have his hands eaten: When the city will condemn the heretic,
He who it seemed to them had changed their laws.

XXXVII

Auant l'assaut l'oraison prononcee, Milan prins d'Aigle par embusches deceus
Muraille antique par canons enfoncee, Par feu & sang à mercy peu receus.

The speech delivered before the attack,
Milan taken by the Eagle through deceptive ambushes: Ancient wall driven in by cannons,
Through fire and blood few given quarter.

XXXVIII

La gens Gauloise & nation estrange, Outre les motns, morts, prins & profugez:
Au moins contraire & proche de vendange,
Paules Seigneurs en accord redigez.

The Gallic people and a foreign nation Beyond the mountains, dead, captured and killed:
In the contrary month and near vintage time, Through the Lords drawn up in accord.

XXXIX

Les sept en trois moins en concorde, Pour subiuguer des Alpes Apennines: Mais la tempeste & Ligure coüarde, Les profligent en subites ruines.

The seven in three months in agreement To subjugate the Apennine Alps: But the tempest and cowardly Ligurian, Destroys them in sudden ruins.

XL

Le grand theatre se viendra redresser, Les dez iettez & les rets ja tendus: Trop le premier en glaz viendra lasser,
Pars arcs prostrais de long temps ja fendus.

The great theater will come to be set up again: The dice cast and the snares already laid.
Too much the first one will come to tire in the death knell, Prostrated by arches already a long time split.

XLI

Bossu sera esleu par le conseil.
Plus hideux monstre en terre n'apperceu, Le coup voulant creuera l'oeil,
Le traistre au Roy pour fidelle receu.

Hunchback will be elected by the council, A more hideous monster not seen on earth, The willing blow will put out his eye:
The traitor to the King received as faithful.

XLII

L'enfant naistra à deux dents en la gorge, Pierres en Tuscie par pluye tomberont:
Peu d'ans apres ne sera bled ny orge, Pour saouler ceux qui de faim failliront.

The child will be born with two teeth in his mouth, Stones will fall during the rain in Tuscany:

A few years after there will be neither wheat nor barley, To satiate those who will faint from hunger.

XLIII.

Gens d'alentour de Tain Loth, & Garonne Grandez les monts Apenines passer: Vostre tombeau pres de Rome & d'Anconne, Le noir poil crespe fera trophe dresser:

People from around the Tarn, Lot and Garonne Beware of passing the Apennine mountains: Your tomb near Rome and Ancona, The black frizzled beard will have a trophy set up.

XLIV.

Quand l'animal à l'homme domestique, Apres grands peines & sauts viendra parler, Le foudre à vierge sera si malefique, De terre prinse & suspendue en l'air.

When the animal domesticated by man After great pains and leaps will come to speak: The lightning to the virgin will be very harmful, Taken from earth and suspended in the air.

XLV.

Les cinq estranges entrez dedans le temple. Leur sang viendra la terre prophaner. Aux Tholosains sera bien dur exemple, D'vn qui viendra ses lois exterminer.

The five strangers entered in the temple, Their blood will come to pollute the land:
To the Toulousans it will be a very hard example Of one who will come to exterminate their laws.

XLVI.

Le ciel (de Plencus la cité) nous presage, Par clers insignes & par estoilles fixes, Que de son change subit s'approche l'aage, Ne pour son bien, ne pour ses male-fices.

The sky (of Plancus' city) forebodes to us Through clear signs and fixed stars, That the time of its sudden change is approaching, Neither for its good, nor for its evils.

XLVII.

Le vieux monarque dechassé de son regne Aux Oriens son secours ira querre: Pour peut des croix ployera son enseigne, En Mytilene ira par port & par terre.

The old monarch chased out of his realm Will go to the East asking for its help: For fear of the crosses he will fold his banner: To Mitylene he will go through port and by land.

XLVIII.

Sept cens captifs attachez rudement, Pour la moitié meurtrir, donné le sort: Le proche espoir vindra si promptement Mais non si tost qu'vne quinziesme mort.

Seven hundred captives bound roughly. Lots drawn for the half to be murdered: The hope at hand will come very promptly But not as soon as the fifteenth death.

XLIX.

Regne Gaulois tu seras bien changé, En lieu estrange est translaté l'empire: En autres moeurs & loix seras rangé, Rouan, & Chartres te feront bien du pire.

Gallic realm, you will be much changed: To a foreign place is the empire transferred: You will be set up amidst other customs and laws: Rouen and Chartres will do much of the worst to you.

L.

La republique de la grande cité,
A grand rigueur ne voudra consentir: Roy sortir hors par trompette cité, L'eschelle au mur la cité repentir.

The republic of the great city
Will not want to consent to the great severity: King summoned by trumpet to go out,
The ladder at the wall, the city will repent.

LI.

Paris coniure vn grand meurtre commetre Blois le fera sortir en plain effect:
Ceux d'Orleans voudront leur chef remettre Angers, Troye, Langres leur feront vn meffait.

Paris conspires to commit a great murder Blois will cause it to be fully carried out:
Those of Orléans will want to replace their chief, Angers, Troyes, Langres will commit a misdeed against them.

LII.

En la champagne sera si longue pluye, Et en la Poüille si grande siccité
Coq verra l'Aigle, l'aisse mal accomplie, Par Lyon mise sera en extremité.

In Campania there will be a very long rain, In Apulia very great drought.
The Cock will see the Eagle, its wing poorly finished, By the Lion will it be put into extremity.

LIII.

Quand le plus grand emportera le pris
De Nuremberg d'Augbourg, & ceuz de Basle, Par Agippine chef Frankfort repris
Trauerseront par Flamant iusques en Gale.

When the greatest one will carry off the prize Of Nuremberg, of Augsburg, and those of Bâle Through Cologne the chief Frankfort retaken They will cross through Flanders right into Gaul.

LIV.

L'vn des grands fuira aux Espagnes Qu'en longue playe apres viendra saigner:
Passant copies par les hautes montaines,
Deuastant tout, & puis en paix regner.

One of the greatest ones will flee to Spain Which will thereafter come to bleed in a long wound:
Armies passing over the high mountains, Devastating all, and then to reign in peace.

LV.

En l'an qu'vn oeil en France regnera, La court sera en vn bien fascheux trouble:
Le grand de Blois sont amy tuera Le regne mis en mal & doute double.

In the year that one eye will reign in France, The court will be in very unpleasant trouble: The great one of Blois will kill his friend: The realm placed in harm and double doubt.

LVI.

Montaubant, Nismes, Auignon & Besier, Peste, tonnerre, & gresle à fin de Mars:
De Paris Pont, Lyon mur, Montpellier, Depuis six cens & sept vingts trois pars.

Montauban, Nîmes, Avignon and Béziers, Plague, thunder and hail in the wake of Mars: Of Paris bridge, Lyons wall, Montpellier, After six hundreds and seven score three pairs.

LVII.

Sept fois changer verrez gent Britanique, Taints en sang en deux cens nonante an Franche non point par appuy Germanique Aries doubte son pole Bastarnan.

Seven times will you see the British nation change, Steeped in blood in 290 years: Free not at all its support Germanic. Aries doubt his "Bastarnian" pole.

LVIII.

Aupres du Rhin des montaignes Noriques Naistra vn grand de gens trop trard venu, Qui defendra Saurome & Pannoniques, Qu'on ne s&cced;aura qu'il sera deuenu.

Near the Rhine from the Noric mountains Will be born a great one of people come too late, One who will defend Sarmatia and the Pannonians, One will not know what will have become of him.

LIX.

Barbare empire par le tiers vsurpé,
La plus grand part de son sang mettra à mort: Par mort senile par luy le quart frappé,
Pour peur que sang par le sang ne soit mort.

Barbarian empire usurped by the third,
The greater part of his blood he will put to death: Through senile death the fourth struck by him,
For fear that the blood through the blood be not dead.

LX.

Par toute Asie grande proscription, Mesme en Mysie, Lysie, & Pamphilie. Sang versera par absolution, D'vn ieune noir remply de felonnie.

Throughout all Asia (Minor) great proscription, Even in Mysia, Lycia and Pam-

philia.
Blood will be shed because of the absolution Of a young black one filled with felony.

LXI.

La grande bande & secte crucigere, Se dressera en Mesopotamie:
Du proche fleuue compagnie legere, Que telle loy tiendra pour ennemie.

The great band and sect of crusaders Will be arrayed in Mesopotamia: Light company of the nearby river, That such law will hold for an enemy.

LXII.

Proche del duero par mer Cyrrene close, Viendra perser les grands monts Pyrenees La main plus courte & sa perce glose,
A Carcassonne conduira les menees.

Near the Douro by the closed Tyrian sea,
He will come to pierce the great Pyrenees mountains.
One hand shorter his opening glosses, He will lead his traces to Carcassone.

LXIII.

Romain pouuoir sera du tout à bas: Son grand voisin imiter les vestiges: Occultes haines ciuiles & debats, Retarderont au bouffons leurs folies.

The Roman power will be thoroughly abased, Following in the footsteps of its great neighbour: Hidden civil hatreds and debates
Will delay their follies for the buffoons.

LXIV.

Le chef de Perse remplira grande Olchade, Classe Triteme contre gens Mahometiques: De Parthe, & Mede, & piller les Cyclades. Repos long temps au grand port
Ionique.

The chief of Persia will occupy great "Olchades," The trireme fleet against the
Mahometan people From Parthia, and Media: and the Cyclades pillaged: Long
rest at the great Ionian port.

LXV.

Quand le sepulchre du grand Romain trouué Le iour apres sera esleu Pontife:
Du Senat gueres il ne sera prouué Empoisonne, son sang au sacré scyphe.

When the sepulchre of the great Roman is found, The day after a Pontiff will be
elected:
Scarcely will he be approved by the Senate Poisoned, his blood in the sacred
chalice.

LXVI.

Le grand Balif d'Orleans mis à mort Sera par vn de sang vindicatif:
De mort merite ne montra ne par sort Des pieds & mains mal le faisoit captif.

The great Bailiff of Orléans put to death Will be by one of blood revengeful:
Of death deserved he will not die, nor by chance: He made captive poorly by his
feet and hands.

LXVII.

Vne nouuelle secte de Philosophes, Mesprisant mort, or, honneurs & richesses:
Des monts Germanins ne seront limitrophes, A les ensuyure auront appuy &
presses.

A new sect of Philosophers Despising death, gold, honors and riches

Will not be bordering upon the German mountains: To follow them they will
have power and crowds.

LXVIII.

Peuple sans chef d'Espaigne d'Italie, Mors, profliges dedans le Cherronesse Leur
dict trahy par legere folie,
Le sang nager par tout à la traverse.

Leaderless people of Spain and Italy Dead, overcome within the Peninsula:
Their dictator betrayed by irresponsible folly, Swimming in blood everywhere
in the latitude.

LXIX.

Grand exercise conduit par iouuenceau, Se viendra rendre aux mains des
ennemis Mais le vieillard nay au demy pourceau, Fera Chalon & Mascon estre
amis.

The great army led by a young man,
It will come to surrender itself into the hands of the enemies: But the old one
born to the half-pig,
He will cause Châlon and Mâcon to be friends.

LXX.

La grand Bretaigne comprinse d'Angletterre, Viendra par eaux si haut à inonder
La Ligue neuue d'ausonne fera guerre, Que contre eux ils se viendront bander.

The great Britain including England Will come to be flooded very high by waters The new League of Ausonia will make war, So that they will come to strive
against them.

LXXI.

Ceux dans les isles de long temps assiegez, Prendront vigueur force contre ennemis: Ceux par dehors morts de faim profligez, En plus grand faim que ia-mais seront mis.

Those in the isles long besieged
Will take vigor and force against their enemies: Those outside dead overcome
by hunger,
They will be put in greater hunger than ever before.

LXXII.

Le bon vieillard tout vif enseuely,
Pres du grand fleuue par fausse soup&cced;on: Le nouueau vieux de richesse
ennobly,
Prins à chemin tout l'or de la ran&cced;on.

The good old man buried quite alive, Near the great river through false suspicion:
The new old man ennobled by riches, Captured on the road all his gold for ran-
som.

LXXIII.

Quand dans le regne paruiendra le boiteux, Competiteur aura proche bastard:
Luy & le regne viendront si fort roigneux, Qu'ains qu'il guerisse son faict sera
bien tard.

When the cripple will attain to the realm, For his competitor he will have a near
bastard: He and the realm will become so very mangy
That before he recovers, it will be too late.

LXXIV.

Naples, Florence, Fauence, & Imole, Seront en termes de telle facherie,
Que pour complaire aux malheureux de Nolle Plainct d'auoir faict à son chef
moquerie.

Naples, Florence, Faenza and Imola, They will be on terms of such disagreement
As to delight in the wretches of Nola Complaining of having mocked its chief.

LXXV.

Pau, Verone, Vicenne Sarragousse,
De glaiues loings, terroirs de sang humides Peste si grande viendra à la grand
gousse, Proche secours, & bien loing les remedes.

Pau, Verona, Vicenza, Saragossa, From distant swords lands wet with blood:
Very great plague will come with the great shell, Relief near, and the remedies
very far.

LXXVI.

En Germanie naistront diuerses sectes, S'approchant fort de l'heureux pagan-
isme, Le coeur captif & petites receptes,
Feront retour à payer le vray disme.

In Germany will be born diverse sects, Coming very near happy paganism, The
heart captive and returns small,
They will return to paying the true tithe.

LXXVII.

Le tiers climat sous Aries comprins L'an mil sept cens vingt & sept en Octobre,
Le Roy de Perse par d'Egypte prins Conflit mort, perte: à la croix grand oppro-
bre.

The third climate included under Aries The year 1727 in October,

The King of Persia captured by those of Egypt: Conflict, death, loss: to the cross great shame.

LXXVIII.

Le chef d'Escosse, auec six d'Allemagne Par gens de mer Orient aux captif: Trauerseront le Calpre & Espagne, Present en Perse au nouueau Roy craintif.

The chief of Scotland, with six of Germany Captive of the Eastern seamen:
They will pass Gibraltar and Spain, Present in Persia for the fearful new King.

LXXIX.

L'ordre fatal sempiternel par chaisne, Viendra tourner par orpte consequent: Du
port Phocen sera rompue la chaisne, La cité prinse, l'ennemy quant & quant.

The fatal everlasting order through the chain Will come to turn through consis-
tent order: The chain of Marseilles will be broken:
The city taken, the enemy at the same time.

LXXX.

Du regne Anglois le digne dechassé, Le conseiller par ire mis à feu
Ses adherans iront si bas tracer, Que le bastard sera demy receu.

The worthy one chased out of the English realm, The adviser through angur put
to the fire:
His adherents will go so low to efface themselves That the bastard will be half
received.

LXXXI.

Le grand criard sans honte audacieux, Sera esleu gouuerneur de l'armee:
La hardiesse de son contenteur Le pont rompu, cité de pur pasmee.

The great shameless, audacious bawler, He will be elected governor of the army:
The boldness of his contention,
The bridge broken, the city faint from fear.

LXXXII.

Ereins, Antibor, villes autour de Nice, Seront gastees fort par mer & par terre: Les
sauterelles terre & mer vent propice,
Prins morts trousses, pilles sans loy de guerre:

Fréjus, Antibes, towns around Nice,
They will be thoroughly devastated by sea and by land: The locusts by land and
by sea the wind propitious, Captured, dead, bound, pillaged without law of war.

LXXXIII.

Les longs cheueux de la Gaule Celtique, Accompagnes d'estranges nations,
Mettront captif la gent aquitanique, Pour succomber à leurs intentions.

The long hairs of Celtic Gaul Accompanied by foreign nations,
They will make captive the people of Aquitaine, For succumbing to their designs.

LXXXIV.

La grande cité sera bien desolee, Des habitans vn seul n'y demeurera Mur, sexe,
temple & vierge violee,
Par fer, feu, peste canon peuple mourra.

The great city will be thoroughly desolated,
Of the inhabitants not a single one will remain there: Wall, sex, temple and virgin
violated,
Through sword, fire, plague, cannon people will die.

LXXXV.

La cité prinse par tromperie & fraude, Par le moyen d'vn beau ieune attrapé. Assaut donné Raubine pres de LAVDE, Luy & touts morts pour auoir bien trompé.

The city taken through deceit and guile, Taken in by means of a handsome youth:
Assault given by the Robine near the Aude,
He and all dead for having thoroughly deceived.

LXXXVI.

Vn chef d'Ausonne aux Espaignes ira Par mer fera arrest dedans Marseille: Auant sa mort vn long temps languira Apres sa mort on verra grand merueille.

A chief of Ausonia will go to Spain By sea, he will make a stop in Marseilles:
Before his death he will linger a long time: After his death one will see a great marvel.

LXXXVII.

Classe Gauloisse n'approche de Corsegue, Moins de Sardaigne, tu t'en repentiras:
Trestous mourrez frustrez de l'aide grogne.
Sang nagera captif ne me croiras.

Gallic fleet, do not approach Corsica, Less Sardinia, you will rue it:
Every one of you will die frustrated of the help of the cape: You will swim in blood, captive you will not believe me.

LXXXVIII.

De Barselonne par mer si grand' armee, Toute Marseille de frayeur tremblera.
Isles saisies de mer ayde fermee, Ton traditeur en terre nagera.

From Barcelona a very great army by sea, All Marseilles will tremble with terror:
Isles seized help shut off by sea,
Your traitor will swim on land.

LXXXIX.

En ce temps la sera frustree Cypres. De son secours de ceux de mer Egee:
Vieux trucidez, mais par mesles & lyphres Seduict leur Roy, Royne, plus outragee.

At that time Cyprus will be frustrated Of its relief by those of the Aegean Sea:
Old ones slaughtered: but by speeches and supplications Their King seduced,
Queen outraged more.

XC.

Le grand Satyre & Tigre d'Hyrcanie. Dont presenté à ceux de l'Occean: Vn chef
classe istra de Carmanie, Qui prendra texte au Tyrren Phocean.

The great Satyr and Tiger of Hyrcania, Gift presented to those of the Ocean:
A fleet's chief will set out from Carmania, One who will take land at the "Tyrren
Phocaean."

XCI.

L'arbre qu'estoit par long temps mort seché, Dans vne nuict viendra à reuerdir:
Coron Roy malade, Prince pied estaché, Criant d'ennemis fera voile bondir.

The tree which had long been dead and withered, In one night it will come to
grow green again: The Cronian King sick, Prince with club foot,
Feared by his enemies he will make his sail bound.

XCII.

Le monde proche du dernier periode Saturne encor tard sera de retour: Tanslat
empire deuers nation Brodde, L'oeil arraché à Narbon par Autour.

The world near the last period, Saturn will come back again late:
Empire transferred towards the Dusky nation, The eye plucked out by the Gos-
hawk at Narbonne.

XCIII.

Dans Auignon tout le chef de l'empire Fera arrest pour Paris desolé:
Tricast tiendra l'Annibalique ire, Lyon par change sera mal consolé.

In Avignon the chief of the whole empire Will make a stop on the way to desolated Paris:
"Tricast" will hold the anger of Hannibal: Lyons will be poorly consoled for the change.

XCIV.

De cinq cens ans plus compte lon tiendra, Celuy qu'estoit l'ornement de son temps: Puis à vn coup grande clarté donra,
Qui par ce siecle les rendra trescontens.

For five hundred years more one will keep count of him Who was the ornament of his time:
Then suddenly great light will he give,
He who for this century will render them very satisfied.

XCV.

La loy Moricque on verra deffaillir.
Apres vne autre beaucoup plus seductiue: Boristhenes premier viendra faillir.
Par dons & langue vne plus attractiue.

The law of More will be seen to decline: After another much more seductive:
Dnieper first will come to give way:
Through gifts and tongue another more attractive.

XCVI.

Chef de Fossan aura gorge couppee, Par le ducteur du limier & leurier: Le faict par ceux du mont Tarpee, Saturne en Leo 13. de Feurier.

The Chief of Fossano will have his throat cut By the leader of the bloodhound and greyhound: The deed executed by those of the Tarpeian Rock, Saturn in Leo February 13.

XCVII.

Nouuelle loy terre neuue occuper, Vers la Syrie, Iudée & Palestine: Le grand empire barbare corruer, Auant que Phebés son siecle determine.

New law to occupy the new land Towards Syria, Judea and Palestine: The great barbarian empire to decay, Before the Moon completes it cycle.

XCVIII.

Deux royals freres si fort guerroyeront Qu'entre eux sera la guerre si mortelle: Qu'vn chacun places fortes occuperons, De regne & vie sera leur grand querelle.

Two royal brothers will wage war so fierely That between them the war will be so mortal That both will occupy the strong places: Their great quarrel will fill realm and life.

XCIX.

Aux champs herbeux d'Alein & du Varneigne, Du mont Lebron proche de la Durance, Camps de deux parts conflict sera si aigre, Mesopotasie defaillira en la France.

In the grassy fields of Alleins and Vernègues Of the Lubéron range near the Durance, The conflict will be very sharp for both armies, Mesopotamia will fail in France.

C.

Entre Gaulois le dernier honnoré, D'homme ennemy sera victorieux: Force &
terroir en nomment exploré,
D'vn coup de traict quand moura l'enuieux.

The last one honored amongst the Gauls, Over the enemy man will he be victorious: Force and land in a moment explored,
When the envious one will die from an arrow shot.

CENTURY IV

I.

CELA du reste de sang non espandu, Venise quiert secours estre donné. Apres auoir bien loing têps attendu, Cité liuree au premier cornet sonné.

That of the remainder of blood unshed: Venice demands that relief be given:
After having waited a very long time,
City delivered up at the first sound of the horn.

II.

Par mort la France prendra voyage à faire, Classe par mer, marcher monts Pyrenees. Espaigne en trouble, marcher gent militaire: Des plus grands Dames en France emmenees.

Because of death France will take to making a journey, Fleet by sea, marching over the Pyrenees Mountains, Spain in trouble, military people marching:
Some of the greatest Ladies carried off to France.

III.

D'Arras & Bourges, de Brodes grans enseignes, Vn plus grand nombre de Gascons battre à pied, Ceux long du Rosne saigneront les Espaignes: Proche du mont où Sagonte s'assied.

From Arras and Bourges many banners of Dusky Ones, A greater number of Gascons to fight on foot, Those along the Rhône will bleed the Spanish:
Near the mountain where Sagunto sits.

IV.

L'impotent prince faché plaincts & querelles, De rapts & pillé, par coqz & par Libiques: Grands est par terre par mer infinies voilles, Seule Italie sera chassant Celtiques.

The impotent Prince angry, complaints and quarrels, Rape and pillage, by cocks and Africans: Great it is by land, by sea infinite sails, Italy alone will be chasing Celts.

V.

Croix, paix, soubs vn accomply diuin verbe, L'Espaigne & Gaule seront vnis ensemble: Grand clade proche, & combat tres accerbe, Coeur si hardy ne sera qui ne tremble.

Cross, peace, under one the divine word accomplished, Spain and Gaul will be united together:
Great disaster near, and combat very bitter: No heart will be so hardy as not to tremble.

VI.

D'habits nouueaux apres faicte la treuue, Malice tramme & machination: Premier mourra qui en fera la preuue, Couleur venise insidiation.

By the new clothes after the find is made, Malicious plot and machination: First will die he who will prove it, Color Venetian trap.

VII.

Le mineur fils du grand & hay Prince, De lepre aura à vingt ans grande tache, De dueil sa mere mourra bien triste & mince, Et il mourra là où tombe cher lache.

The minor son of the great and hated Prince,

He will have a great touch of leprosy at the age of twenty: Of grief his mother will
die very sad and emaciated,
And he will die where the loose flesh falls.

VIII.

La grand cité d'assaut prompt & repentin, Surprins de nuict, gardes interrompus:
Les excubies & veilles sainct Quintin, Trucidez gardes & les portails rompus.

The great city by prompt and sudden assault Surprised at night, guards interrupted:
The guards and watches of Saint-Quentin Slaughtered, guards and the portals
broken.

IX.

Le chef du camp au milieu de la presse: D'vn coup de fleche sera blessé aux cui-
sses, Lors que Geneue en larmes & detresse, Sera trahie par Lauzan, & Souysses.

The chief of the army in the middle of the crowd Will be wounded by an arrow
shot in the thighs, When Geneva in tears and distress
Will be betrayed by Lausanne and the Swiss.

X.

Le ieune Prince accusé faussement, Mettra en trouble le camp & en querelles:
Meurtry le chef pour le soustenement, Sceptre appaiser: puis guerir escroüelles.

The young Prince falsely accused
Will plunge the army into trouble and quarrels: The chief murdered for his sup-
port,
Sceptre to pacify: then to cure scrofula.

XI.

Celuy qu'aura gouuert de la grand cappe, Sera induict à quelques cas patrer:
Les douze rouges viendront soüiller la nappa, Soubz meurtre, meurtre se viendra
perpetrer.

He who will have the government of the great cope Will be prevailed upon to
perform several deeds: The twelve red one who will come to soil the cloth, Under
murder, murder will come to be perpetrated.

XII.

Le champ plus grand de route mis en fuite, Guaires plus outre ne sera pourchas-
sé:
Ost recampé & legion reduicte, Puis hors des Gaules du tout sera chassé

The greater army put to flight in disorder, Scarcely further will it be pursued:
Army reassembled and the legion reduced, Then it will be chased out completely
from the Gauls.

XIII.

De plus grand perte nouuelles rapportees, Le raport le camp s'estournera.
Ban les vnies encontre reuoltees, Double phalange quand abandonnera.

News of the greater loss reported, The report will astonish the army: Troops
united against the revolted:
The double phalanx will abandon the great one.

XIV.

La mort subite du premier personnage Aura changé & mis vn autre au regne:
Tost, tard venu à si haut & bas aage,
Que terre & mer faudra que on le craigne.

The sudden death of the first personage

Will have caused a change and put another in the sovereignty: Soon, late come
so high and of low age,
Such by land and sea that it will be necessary to fear him.

XV.

D'où pensera faire venir famine, De là viendra se rassasiement: L'oeil de la mer
par auare canine
Pour de l'vn l'autre donra huyle, froment.

From where they will think to make famine come, From there will come the
surfeit:
The eye of the sea through canine greed For the one the other will give oil and
wheat.

XVI.

La cité franche de liberté fait serue. Des profligez & resueurs faict asyle. Le Roy
changé à eux non si proterue: De cent seront deuenus plus de mille.

The city of liberty made servile:
Made the asylum of profligates and dreamers.
The King changed to them not so violent: From one hundred become more than
a thousand.

XVII.

Changer à Banne, Nuy, Chalons, & Dijon, Le duc voulant amander la Barree
Marchât pres fleuue, poisson, bec de plongeon Verra la queüe: porte sera serree.

To change at Beaune, Nuits, Châlon and Dijon, The duke wishing to improve the
Carmelite [nun] Marching near the river, fish, diver's beak
Will see the tail: the gate will be locked.

XVIII.

Des plus lettrez dessus les faits celestes Seront par princes ignorans reprouuez:
Punis d'Edit, chassez, comme scelestes, Et mis à mort là où seront trouuez.

Some of those most lettered in the celestial facts Will be condemned by illiterate
princes: Punished by Edict, hunted, like criminals,
And put to death wherever they will be found.

XIX.

Deuant Roüan d'Insubres mis le siege, Par terre & mer enfermez les passages:
D'haynaut, & Flâdres de Gâd & ceux de Liege, Par dons laenees rauiront les
riuages.

Before Rouen the siege laid by the Insubrians, By land and sea the passages shut
up:
By Hainaut and Flanders, by Ghent and those of Liége Through cloaked gifts
they will ravage the shores.

XX.

Paix vberté long temps lieu loüera: Par tout son regne de sert la fleur de lys:
Corps morts d'eau, terre là l'on aportera, Sperans vain heur d'estre là enseuelis.

Peace and plenty for a long time the place will praise: Throughout his realm the
fleur-de-lys deserted: Bodies dead by water, land one will bring there, Vainly
awaiting the good fortune to be buried there.

XXI.

Le changement sera fort difficile, Cité, prouince au change gain fera:
Coeur haut, prudent mis, chassé luy habile, Mer, terre, peuple son estat changera.

The change will be very difficult: City and province will gain by the change:
Heart high, prudent established, chased out one cunning, Sea, land, people will

change their state.

XXII.

La grand copie qui sera deschassee, Dans vn moment fera besoing au Roy. La foy promise de loing sera faussee, Nud se verra en piteux desarroy.

The great army will be chased out,
In one moment it will be needed by the King: The faith promised from afar will be broken, He will be seen naked in pitiful disorder.

XXIII.

La legion dans la marine classe, Calcine, Magnes soulphre, & poix bruslera: Le long repos de l'asseuree place, Port Selyn, Hercle feu les consumera.

The legion in the marine fleet
Will burn lime, loadstone sulfur and pitch: The long rest in the secure place: "Port Selyn" and Monaco, fire will consume them.

XXIV.

Ouy soubs terre saincte Dame voix fainte, Humaine flamme pour diuine voir luire: Fera des seuls de leur sang terre tainte,
Et les saincts temples pour les impurs destruire.

Beneath the holy earth of a soul the faint voice heard, Human flame seen to shine as divine:
It will cause the earth to be stained with the blood of the monks, And to destroy the holy temples for the impure ones.

XXV.

Corps sublimes sans fin à l'oeil visibles, Ob nubiler viendront par ces raisons:
Corps, front comprins, sens chefs & inuisibles, Diminuant les sacrees oraisons.

Lofty bodies endlessly visible to the eye, Through these reasons they will come to
obscure: Body, forehead included, sense and head invisible,
Diminishing the sacred prayers.

XXVI.

Lou grand eyssame se leuera d'abelhos, Que non salutan don te siegen vengud-
dos.
Denuech l'ẽbousq, lou gach dessous les treilhos Ceiutad trahido per cinq lengos
non nudos.

The great swarm of bees will arise,
Such that one will not know whence they have come; By night the ambush, the
sentinel under the vines City delivered by five babblers not naked.

XXVII.

Salon, Mansol, Tarascon de SEX, l'are, Où est debout encor la piramide: Viendront liurer le Prince Dannemarc, Rachat honny au temple d'Artemide.

Salon, Tarascon, "Mausol", the arch of "SEX.", Where the pyramid is still standing:
They will come to deliver the Prince of "Annemark," Redemption reviled in the
temple of Artemis.

XXVIII.

Lors que Venus du Sol sera couuert, Soubs l'esplendeur sera forme occulte: Mercure au feu les aura descouuert, Par bruit bellique sera mis à l'insulte.

When Venus will be covered by the Sun, Under the splendor will be a hidden
form: Mercury will have exposed them to the fire, Through warlike noise it will

be insulted.

XXIX.

Le Sol caché eclipse par Mercure, Ne sera mis que pour le ciel second: De Vulcan Hermes sera faicte pasture, Sol sera veu peur, rutiland & blond.

The Sun hidden eclipsed by Mercury Will be placed only second in the sky: Of Vulcan Hermes will be made into food, The Sun will be seen pure, glowing red and golden.

XXX.

Plus unze fois Luna Sol ne vouldra, Tous augmenté & baissez de degrez: Et si bas mis que peu or on coudra, Qu'apres faim peste, descouuert le secret.

Eleven more times the Moon the Sun will not want, All raised and lowered by degree: And put so low that one will stitch little gold: Such that after famine plague, the secret uncovered.

XXXI.

La Lune au plain de nuict sur le haut mont, Le nouueau sophe d'vn seul cerueau la veu: Par ses disciples estre immortel semond, Yeux au mydi, en seins mains corps au feu.

The Moon in the full of night over the high mountain, The new sage with a lone brain sees it: By his disciples invited to be immortal, Eyes to the south. Hands in bosoms, bodies in the fire.

XXXII.

Es lieux & temps chair ou poisson donra lieu, La loy commune sera faicte au
contraire: Vieux tiendra fort puis osté du milieu,
Le Panta chiona philon mis fort arriere.

In the places and times of flesh giving way to fish, The communal law will be
made in opposition:
It will hold strongly the old ones, then removed from the midst, Loving of Everything in Common put far behind.

XXXIII.

Iupiter ioinct plus Venus qu'à la Lune, Apparoissant de plenitude blanche: Venus
cachee sous la blancheur Neptune De Mars frappee & par la grauee blanche.

Jupiter joined more to Venus than to the Moon Appearing with white fulness:
Venus hidden under the whiteness of Neptune Struck by Mars through the white
stew.

XXXIV.

Le grand mené captif d'estrange terre, D'or enchainé au Roy Chyren offert:
Qui dans Ausone, Milan perdra la guerre, Et tout son ost mis à feu & à fer.

The great one of the foreign land led captive, Chained in gold offered to King
"Chyren": He who in Ausonia, Milan will lose the war, And all his army put to
fire and sword.

XXXV.

Le feu esteint les vierges trahiront La plus grand part de la bande nouuelle:
Foudre à fer, lance les sels Roy garderont Etrusque & Corse, de nuict gorge al-
lumelle.

The fire put out the virgins will betray The greater part of the new band:

Lightning in sword and lance the lone Kings will guard Etruria and Corsica, by night throat cut.

XXXVI.

Les ieux nouueaux en Gaule redressez, Apres victoire de l'Insubre champaigne: Monts d'Esperie, les grands liez, troussez: De peur trembler la Romaigne & l'Espaigne.

The new sports set up again in Gaul, After victory in the Insubrian campaign: Mountains of Hesperia, the great ones tied and trussed up: "Romania" and Spain to tremble with fear.

XXXVII.

Gaulois par sauts, monts viendra penetrer: Occupera le grand lieu de l'Insubre: Au plus profond son ost fera entrer, Gennes, Monech pousseront classe rubre.

The Gaul will come to penetrate the mountains by leaps: He will occupy the great place of Insubria: His army to enter to the greatest depth, Genoa and Monaco will drive back the red fleet.

XXXVIII.

Pendant que Duc, Roy, Royne occupera, Chef Bizant du captif en Samothrace: Auant l'assauit l'un l'autre mangera, Rebours ferré suyura du sang la trace.

While he will engross the Duke, King and Queen With the captive Byzantine chief in Samothrace: Before the assault one will eath the order: Reverse side metaled will follow the trail of the blood.

XXXIX.

Les Rhodiens demanderont secours, Par le neglet de ses hoirs delaissee. L'empire Arabe reuelera son cours, Par Hesperies la cause redressee.

The Rhodians will demand relief, Through the neglect of its heirs abandoned. The Arab empire will reveal its course, The cause set right again by Hesperia.

XL.

Les forteresses des assiegez serrez, Par poudre à feu profondez en abysmes Les proditeurs seront tous vifs serrez,
Onc aux sacristes n'aduint si piteux scisme.

The fortresses of the besieged shut up, Through gunpowder sunk into the abyss: The traitors will all be stowed away alive,
Never did such a pitiful schism happen to the sextons.

XLI.

Gymnique sexe captiue par hostage, Viendra de nuit custodes deceuoir:
Le chef du camp de&cced;eu par son langage, Lairra à la gente, fera piteux à voir.

Female sex captive as a hostage Will come by night to deceive the guards:
The chief of the army deceived by her language Will abandon her to the people, it will be pitiful to see.

XLII.

Geneue & Lâgres par ceux de Chartres & Dole, Et par Grenoble captif au Mont-limard: Seysset, Lausanne, par fraudulente dole,
Les trahiront par or soixante marc.

Geneva and Langres through those of Chartres and Dôle And through Grenoble captive at Montélimar Seyssel, Lausanne, through fraudulent deceit,
They will betray them for sixty marks of gold.

XLIII.

Seront ouye au ciel armes battre, Celuy au mesme les diuins ennemis:
Voudront loix sainctes iniustement debatre: Par foudre & guerre bien croyans à
mort mis.

Arms will be heard clashing in the sky: That very same year the divine ones
enemies:
They will want unjustly to discuss the holy laws: Through lightning and war the
complacent one put to death.

XLIV.

Deux gros de Mende, de Roudés & Milhau. Cahours, Lymoges, Castres malo
sepmano De nuech l'intrado, de Bourdeaux vn cailhau, Par Perigort au toc de la
campano.

Two large ones of Mende, of Rodez and Milhau Cahors, Limoges, Castres bad
week
By night the entry, from Bordeaux an insult Through Périgord at the peal of the
bell.

XLV.

Par conflict Roy, regne abandonnera, Le plus grand chef faillira au besoing, Mors
profligez peu en reschapera, Tous destranchés, vn en sera tesmoing.

Through conflict a King will abandon his realm: The greatest chief will fail in
time of need: Dead, ruined few will escape it,
All cut up, one will be a witness to it.

XLVI.

Bien deffendu le faict par excellence, Garde toy Tours de ta proche ruine: Londres & Nantes par Reims fera deffense Ne passe outre au temps de la bruine.

The fact well defended by excellence, Guard yourself Tours from your near ruin: London and Nantes will make a defense through Reims Not passing further in the time of the drizzle.

XLVII.

Le noir farouche quand aura essayé Sa main sanguine par teu, fer arcs tendus, Trestous le peuple sera tant effrayé, Voir les plus grans par col & pieds pendus.

The savage black one when he will have tried His bloody hand at fire, sword and drawn bows: All of his people will be terribly frightened, Seeing the greatest ones hung by neck and feet.

XLVIII.

Planure Ausonne fertile, spacieuse, Produira taons si tant de sauterelles: Clarté solaire deuiendra nubileuse, Ronger le tout, grand peste venir d'elles.

The fertile, spacious Ausonian plain Will produce so many gadflies and locusts, The solar brightness will become clouded, All devoured, great plague to come from them.

XLIX.

Deuant le peuple sang sera respandu, Que du haut ciel viendra esloigner. Mais d'vn long temps ne sera entendu, L'esprit d'vn seul le viendra tesmoigner.

Before the people blood will be shed, Only from the high heavens will it come far:
But for a long time of one nothing will be heard,
The spirit of a lone one will come to bear witness against it.

L.

Libra verra regner les Hesperies, De ciel & tenir la monarchie: D'Asie forces nul
ne verra peries,
Que sept ne tiennent par rang la hierarchie.

Libra will see the Hesperias govern, Holding the monarchy of heaven and earth:
No one will see the forces of Asia perished, Only seven hold the hierarchy in
order.

LI.

Vn Duc cupide son ennemy ensuyure, Dans entrera empeschant la phalange,
Hastez à pied si pres viendront poursuyure, Que la iournee conflite pres de
Gange.

A Duke eager to follow his enemy Will enter within impeding the phalanx:
Hurried on foot they will come to pursue so closely That the day will see a conflict near Ganges.

LII.

En cité obsesse aux murs hommes & femmes.
Ennemis hors le chef prest à soy rendre: Vent sera fort encore les gendarmes.
Chassez seront par chaux, poussiere, & cendre.

In the besieged city men and woman to the walls, Enemies outside the chief
ready to surrender: The wind will be strongly against the troops,
They will be driven away through lime, dust and ashes.

LIII.

Les fugitifs & bannis reuoquez, Peres & fils grand garnissant les hauts puis
Le cruel pere & les siens souffoquez, Son fils pire submergé dans le puits.

The fugitives and exiles recalled:

Fathers and sons great garnishing of the deep wells: The cruel father and his people choked:
His far worse son submerged in the well.

LIV.

Du nom qui onque ne fut au Roy Gaulois Iamais ne fut vn foudre si craintif. Tremblant l'Italie, l'Espagne & les Anglois, De femme estrangiers grandement attentif.

Of the name which no Gallic King ever had Never was there so fearful a thunderbolt, Italy, Spain and the English trembling, Very attentive to a woman and foreigners.

LV.

Quand la corneille sur tout de brique ioincte, Durant sept heures ne fera que crier: Mort presagee de sang statue taincte, Tyran meurtri, aux Dieux peuple prier.

When the crow on the tower made of brick For seven hours will continue to scream: Death foretold, the statue stained with blood, Tyrant murdered, people praying to their Gods.

LVI.

Apres victoire de rabieuse langue, L'esprit tempré en tranquil & repos: Victeur sanguin par conflict faict harangue, Roustir la langue & la chair & les os.

After the victory of the raving tongue, The spirit tempered in tranquility and repose:
Throughout the conflict the bloody victor makes orations, Roasting the tongue and the flesh and the bones.

LVII.

Ignare enuie au grand Roy supportee, Tiendras propos deffendre les escripts. Sa femme non femme par vn autre tentee, Plus double deux ne fort ne criz.

Ignorant envy upheld before the great King, He will propose forbidding the writings: His wife not his wife tempted by another, Twice two more neither skill nor cries.

LVIII.

Soloeil ardent dans le grosier coller, De sang humain arrouser terre Etrusque: Chef seille d'eau, mener son fils filer, Captiue dame conduicte terre Turque.

To swallow the burning Sun in the throat, The Etruscan land washed by human blood: The chief pail of water, to lead his son away, Captive lady conducted into Turkish land.

LIX.

Deux assiegez en ardente ferueur:
Ce soif estaincts pour deux plaines tasses Le fort limé, & vn vieillart resueur, Aux Genevois de Nira monstra trasse.

Two beset in burning fervor:
By thirst for two full cups extinguished, The fort filed, and an old dreamer, To the Genevans he will show the track from "Nira."

LX.

Les sept enfans en hostaine laissez, Le tiers viendra son enfant trucider: Deux par son fils seront d'estoc percez. Genues, Florence, les viendra enconder.

The seven children left in hostage, The third will come to slaughter his child: Because of his son two will be pierced by the point, Genoa, Florence, he will come to confuse them.

LXI.

Le vieux mocqué priué de sa place, Par l'estranger qui le subornera:
Mains de son fils mangees deuant sa face, Le frere à Chartres, Orl Roüan trahira.

The old one mocked and deprived of his place, By the foreigner who will suborn
him: Hands of his son eaten before his face,
His brother to Chartres, Orléans Rouen will betray.

LXII.

Vn coronel machine ambition, Se saisira de la grande armee,
Contre son Prince fainte inuention, Et descouuert sera soubs sa ramee.

A colonel with ambition plots, He will seize the greatest army,
Against his Prince false invention, And he will be discovered under his arbor.

LXIII.

L'armee Celtique contre les montaignars, Qui seront s&cced;euz & prins à la
pipee: Paysans frez pouseront rost faugnars, Precipitez tous au fils de l'espee.

The Celtic army against the mountaineers, Those who will be learned and able
in bird-calling:
Peasants will soon work fresh presses, All hurled on the sword's edge.

LXIV.

Le deffaillant en habit de bourgeois, Viendra le Roy tenter de son offense: Quinze
soldats la pluspart Vstagois, Vie derniere & chef de sa cheuance.

The transgressor in bourgeois garb,
He will come to try the King with his offense: Fifteen soldiers for the most part
bandits, Last of life and chief of his fortune.

LXV.

Au deserteur de la grande fortresse, Apres qu'aura son lieu abandonné, Son aduersaire fera grand proüesse, L'empereur tost mort sera condamné.

Towards the deserter of the great fortress, After he will have abandoned his place,
His adversary will exhibit very great prowess, The Emperor soon dead will be
condemned.

LXVI.

Sous couleur fainte de sept testes rasces, Seront semez diuers explorateurs:
Puys & fontaines de poisons arrousees, Au fort de Gennes humains deuorateurs.

Under the feigned color of seven shaven heads Diverse spies will be scattered:
Wells and fountains sprinkled with poisons, At the fort of Genoa devourers of
men.

LXVII.

Lors que Saturne & Mars esgaux combust, L'air fort seiché longue traiection:
Par feux secrets, d'ardeur grand lieu adust, Peu pluye, vent chaut, guerres, incursions.

The year that Saturn and Mars are equal fiery, The air very dry parched long
meteor:
Through secret fires a great place blazing from burning heat, Little rain, warm
wind, wars, incursions.

LXVIII.

En lieu bien proche non esloigné de Venus. Les deux plus grands de l'Asie &
d'Aphrique, Du Ryn & Hister qu'on dira sont venus,
Cris pleurs à Malte & costé Ligustique.

In the place very near not far from Venus, The two greatest ones of Asia and of

Africa,
From the Rhine and Lower Danube they will be said to have come, Cries, tears
at Malta and the Ligurian side.

LXIX.

La cité grande les exilez tiendront, Les citadins morts, meurtris & chassez: Ceux
d'Aquilee à Parme promettront,
Monstrer l'entree par les lieux non trassez.

The exiles will hold the great city,
The citizens dead, murdered and driven out: Those of Aquileia will promise Par-
ma
To show them the entry through the untracked places.

LXX.

Bien contigue des grands monts Pyrenees, Vn contre l'Aigle grand copie address-
er: Ouuertes veines, forces exterminees,
Que iusqu'à Paulle chef viendra chasser.

Quite contiguous to the great Pyrenees mountains, One to direct a great army
against the Eagle: Veins opened, forces exterminated,
As far as Pau will he come to chase the chief.

LXXI.

En lieu d'espouse les filles trucidees, Meurtre à grand faute ne fera superstile:
Dedans se puys vestu les inondees, L'espouse estainte par haute d'Aconile.

In place of the bride the daughters slaughtered, Murder with great error no sur-
vivor to be: Within the well vestals inundated,
The bride extinguished by a drink of Aconite.

LXXII.

Les Attomiques par Agen & l'Estore, A sainct Felix feront leur parlement:
Ceux de Basas viendront à la mal' heure, Saisir Condon & Marsan promptement.

Those of Nîmes through Agen and Lectoure At Saint-Félix will hold their par-
liament: Those of Bazas will come at the unhappy hour To seize Condom and˙
Marsan promptly.

LXXIII.

Le nepueu grand par force prouuera Le pache fait du coeur pusillanime: Ferrare
& Ast le Duc esprouuera, Par lors qu'au soir sera le pantomime

The great nephew by force will test The treaty made by the pusillanimous heart:
The Duke will try Ferrara and Asti,
When the pantomine will take place in the evening.

LXXIV.

Du lac Leman & ceux de Brannonices: Tous assemblez contre ceux d'Aquitaine:
Germains beaucoup encore plus Souisses, Seront desfaicts auec ceux d'Humaine.

Those of lake Geneva and of Mâcon: All assembled against those of Aquitaine:
Many Germans many more Swiss,
They will be routed along with those of "Humane."

LXXV.

Prest à combattre fera defection, Chef aduersaire obtiendra la victoire: L'arriere
garde fera defension.
Les defaillans mort au blanc territoire.

Ready to fight one will desert,
The chief adversary will obtain the victory: The rear guard will make a defense,
The faltering ones dead in the white territory.

LXXVI.

Les Nibobriges par eeux de Perigort, Seront vexez, tenant iusques au Rosne: L'as-
socié de Gascons & Begorne,
Trahir le temple, le prestre estant au prosne:

The people of Agen by those of Périgord Will be vexed, holding as far as the
Rhône: The union of Gascons and Bigorre
To betray the temple, the priest giving his sermon.

LXXVII.

Selin monarque l'Italie pacifique, Regnes vnis par Roy Chrestien du monde:
Mourant voudra coucher en terre blesique,
Apres pyrates auoir chassé de l'onde.

"Selin" monarch Italy peaceful,
Realms united by the Christian King of the World: Dying he will want to lie in
Blois soil,
After having chased the pirates from the sea.

LXXVIII.

La grand' armee de la pugne ciuile, Pour de nuict Parme à l'estrange trouuee,
Septante neuf meurtris dedans la ville,
Les estrangers passez tout à l'espee.

The great army of the civil struggle,
By night Parma to the foreign one discovered, Seventy-nine murdered in the
town,
The foreigners all put to the sword.

LXXIX.

Sang Royal fuis, Monhuit, Mas, Esguillon, Remplis seront de Bourdelois les Landes, Nauuarre, Bygorre poinctes & eguillons, Profonds de faim vorer de Liege

glandes.

Blood Royal flee, Monheurt, Mas, Aiguillon, The Landes will be filled by Bordelais, Navarre, Bigorre points and spurs,
Deep in hunger to devour acorns of the cork oak.

LXXX.

Pres du grand fleuue grand fosse terre egeste, En quinze pars sera l'eau diuisee:
La cité prinse, feu, sang cris conflict mettre.
Et la pluspart concerne au collisee.

Near the great river, great ditch, earth drawn out, In fifteen parts will the water
be divided:
The city taken, fire, blood, cries, sad conflict, And the greatest part involving the
colosseum.

LXXXI.

Pont on fera promptement de nacelles, Passer l'armee du grand Prince Belgique:
Dans profondez & non loing de Brucelles, Outre passez, detranchez sept à picque.

Promptly will one build a bridge of boats, To pass the army of the great Belgian
Prince: Poured forth inside and not far from Brussels,
Passed beyond, seven cut up by pike.

LXXXII.

Amas s'approche venant d'Esclauonie, L'Olestant vieux cité ruynera:
Fort desolee verra sa Romanie,
Puis la grande flamme esteindre ne s&cced;aura.

A throng approaches coming from Slaconia, The old Destroyer the city will ruin:
He will see his "Romania" quite desolated, Then he will not know how to put out
the great flame.

LXXXIII.

Combat nocturne le vaillant capitaine, Vaincu fuyra peu de gens profligé: Son
peuple esmeu, sedition non vaine.
Son propre fils le tiendra assiegé.

Combat by night the valiant captain Conquered will flee few people conquered:
His people stirred up, sedition not in vain, His own son will hold him besieged.

LXXXIV.

Vn grand d'Auxerre mourra bien miserable.
Chassé de ceux qui sous luy ont esté: Serré de chaines, apres d'vn rude cable,
En l'an que Mars, Venus & Sol mis en esté.

A great one of Auxerre will die very miserable, Driven out by those who had
been under him: Put in chains, behind a strong cable,
In the year that Mars, Venus and Sun are in conjunction in summer.

LXXXV.

Le charbon blanc du noir sera chassé, Prisonnier faict mené au tombereau, More
Chameau sur pieds entrelassez, Lors le puisné sillera l'aubereau.

The white coal will be chased by the black one, Made prisoner led to the dung
cart,
Moor Camel on twisted feet,
Then the younger one will blind the hobby falcon.

LXXXVI.

L'an que Saturne en eau sera conioinct, Avecques Sol, le Roy fort puissant, A
Reims & Aix sera receu & oingt,
Apres conquestes meurtrira innocens.

The year that Saturn will be conjoined in Aquarius With the Sun, the very pow-

erful King
Will be received and anointed at Reims and Aix, After conquests he will murder the innocent.

LXXXVII.

Vn fils du Roy tant de langues apprins, A son aisné au regne different:
Son pere beau au plus grand fils comprins, Fera perir principal adherant.

A King's son learned in many languages, Different from his senior in the realm:
His handsome father understood by the greater son, He will cause his principal adherent to perish.

LXXXVIII.

Le grand Antoine de nom de faict sordide De Phthyriaise à son dernier rongé: ꞏ
Vn qui de plomb voudra estre cupide, Passant le port d'esleu sera plongé.

Anthony by name great by the filthy fact Of Lousiness wasted to his end:
One who will want to be desirous of lead, Passing the port he will be immersed by the elected one.

LXXXIX.

Trente de Londres secret coniureront, Contre leur Roy, sur le pont l'entreprise:
Leuy, satalites là mort de gousteront, Vn Roy esleut blonde, natif de Frize.

Thirty of London will conspire secretly Against their King, the enterprise on the
bridge: He and his satellites will have a distaste for death,
A fair King elected, native of Frisia.

XC.

Les deux copies aux mers ne pourrôt ioindre, Dans cest instan trembler Misan,
Ticin:
Faim, soif, doutance si fort les viendra poindre Chair, pain, ne viures n'auront vn
seul boucin.

The two armies will be unable to unite at the walls, In that instant Milan and
Pavia to tremble:
Hunger, thirst, doubt will come to plague them very strongly They will not have
a single morsel of meat, bread or victuals.

XCI.

Au Duc Gaulois contrainct battre au duelle, La nef Mellele monech n'approchera,
Tort accusé, prison perpetuelle, Son fils regner auant mort taschera.

For the Gallic Duke compelled to fight in the duel, The ship of Melilla will not
approach Monaco, Wrongly accused, perpetual prison,
His son will strive to reign before his death.

XCII.

Teste tranchee du vaillant capitaine, Seza iettee deuant son aduersaire:
Son corps pendu de la classe à l'ancienne Confus fuira par rames à vent contraire.

The head of the valiant captain cut off, It will be thrown before his adversary:
His body hung on the sail-yard of the ship, Confused it will flee by oars against
the wind.

XCIII.

Vn serpent veu proche du lict royal, Sera par dame nuict chiens n'abayeront:
Lors naistre en France vn Prince tant royal, Du ciel venu tous les Princes verront.

A serpent seen near the royal bed,

116

It will be by the lady at night the dogs will not bark: Then to be born in France
a Prince so royal,
Come from heaven all the Princes will see him.

XCIV.

Deux grands freres seront chassez d'Espaigne, L'aisne vaincu sous les mons Pyrenees:
Rougir mer, Rosne, sang Lemand d'Alemaigne, Narbon, Blyterre, d'Agth con-
taminees.

Two great brothers will be chased out of Spain, The elder conquered under the
Pyrenees mountains:
The sea to redden, Rhône, bloody Lake Geneva from Germany, Narbonne,
Béziers contaminated by Agde.

XCV.

Le regne à deux l'aissé bien peu tiendront, Trois ans sept mois passez feront la
guere Les deux Vestales contre rebelleront, Victor puisnay en Armenique terre

The realm left to two they will hold it very briefly, Three years and seven months
passed by they will make war:
The two Vestals will rebel in opposition, Victor the younger in the land of Brittany.

XCVI.

La soeur aisnee de l'Isle Britannique Quinze ans deuant le frere aura naissance,
Par son promis moyennant verrifique, Succedera au regne de balance.

The elder sister of the British Isle
Will be born fifteen years before her brother, Because of her promise procuring
verification, She will succeed to the kingdom of the balance.

XCVII.

L'an que Mercure, Mars, Venus retrograde, Du grand Monarque la ligne ne faillir: Esleu du peuple l'vsitant pres de Gaudole.
Qu'en paix & regne viendra fort enuieillir.

The year that Mercury, Mars, Venus in retrogression, The line of the great Monarch will not fail: Elected by the Portuguese people near Cadiz,
One who will come to grow very old in peace and reign.

XCVIII.

Les Albanois passeront dedans Rome, Moyennan Langres demipler affublez.
Marquis & Duc ne pardonnes à homme,
Feu, sang, morbiles point d'eau faillir les bleds.

Those of Alba will pass into Rome,
By means of Langres the multitude muffled up, Marquis and Duke will pardon
no man,
Fire, blood, smallpox no water the crops to fail.
XCIX.

Laisné vaillant de la fille du Roy, Respoussera si profond les Celtiques, Qu'il
mettra foudres, combien en tel arroy Peu & loing, puis profond és Hesperiques.

The valiant elder son of the King's daughter, He will hurl back the Celts very far,
Such that he will cast thunderbolts, so many in such an array Few and distant,
then deep into the Hesperias.

C.

Du feu celeste au Royal edifice.
Quand la lumiere de Mars defaillira,
Sept mois grand guerre, mort gens de malefice Roüan, Eureux au Roy ne faillira.

From the celestial fire on the Royal edifice, When the light of Mars will go out,
Seven months great war, people dead through evil Rouen, Evreux the King will
not fail.

CENTURY V

I.

Avant venuë de ruine Celtique, Dedans le têple deux palementerôs
Poignard coeur, d'vn monté au coursier & picque, Sans faire bruit le grand en-
terreront.

Before the coming of Celtic ruin, In the temple two will parley
Pike and dagger to the heart of one mounted on the steed, They will bury the
great one without making any noise.

II.

Sept coniurez au banquet feront luire, Contre les trois le fer hors de nauire
L'vn les deux classe au grand fera couduire, Quand par le mal. Dernier au front
luy tire.

Seven conspirators at the banquet will cause to flash The iron out of the ship
against the three:
One will have the two fleets brought to the great one, When through the evil the
latter shoots him in the forehead.

III.

Le successeur de la Duché viendra.
Beaucoup plus outre que la mer de Tosquane Gauloise branche la Florence tiendra, Dans son giron d'accord nautique Rane.

The successor to the Duchy will come, Very far beyond the Tuscan Sea:
A Gallic branch will hold Florence, The nautical Frog in its gyron be agreement.

IV.

Le gros mastin de cité dechassé, Sera fasché de l'estrange alliance,
Apres aux champs auoir le cerf chassé Le loups & l'Ours se donront defiance.

The large mastiff expelled from the city Will be vexed by the strange alliance, After having chased the stag to the fields The wolf and the Bear will defy each other.

V.

Soubs ombre feincte d'oster de seruitude, Peuple & cité l'vsurpera luy-mesmes
Pire fera par fraux de ieune pute,
Liuré au champ lisant le faux poësme.

Under the shadowy pretense of removing servitude, He will himself usurp the people and city:
He will do worse because of the deceit of the young prostitute, Delivered in the field reading the false poem.

VI.

Au Roy l'angur sur le chef la main mettre, Viendra prier pour la paix Italique:
A la main gauche viendra changer le sceptre, Du Roy viendra Empereur pacifique.

The Augur putting his hand upon the head of the King Will come to pray for the peace of Italy:
He will come to move the sceptre to his left hand, From King he will become pacific Emperor.

VII.

Du Triumuir seront trouuez les os, Cherchant profond thresor aenigmaique.
Ceux d'alentour ne seroit en repos.
Ce concauuer marbre & plomb metalique.

The bones of the Triumvir will be found, Looking for a deep enigmatic treasure:

Those from thereabouts will not be at rest,
Digging for this thing of marble and metallic lead.

VIII.

Sera laisse' feu vif, mort cache', Dedans les globes horrible espouuantable.
De nuict à classe cité en poudre lasché, La cité à feu, l'ennemy fauorable.

There will be unleashed live fire, hidden death, Horrible and frightful within the globes,
By night the city reduced to dust by the fleet, The city afire, the enemy amenable.

IX.

Iusques au fond la grand arq moluë, Par chef captif l'amy anticipé, N'aistra de dame front, face cheuelue, Lors par astuce Duc à mort atrapé.

The great arch demolished down to its base, By the chief captive his friend fore-stalled,
He will be born of the lady with hairy forehead and face, Then through cunning the Duke overtaken by death.

X.

Vn chef Celtique dans le conflict blessé, Aupres de caue voyant siens mort abba-tre: De sang & playes & d'ennemis pressé,
Et secours par incogneus de quatre.

A Celtic chief wounded in the conflict Seeing death overtaking his men near a cellar: Pressed by blood and wounds and enemies,
And relief by four unknown ones.

XI.

Mer par solaires seure ne passera, Ceux de Venus tiendront toute l'Affrique:
Leur regne plus Saturne n'occupera, Et changera la part Asiatique.

The sea will not be passed over safely by those of the Sun, Those of Venus will
hold all Africa:
Saturn will no longer occupy their realm, And the Asiatic part will change.

XII.

Aupres du lac Leman sera conduite, Par garse estrange cité voulant trahir:
Auant son meurtre à Ausborg la grand suitte, Et ceux du Rhin la viendront in-
uahir.

To near the Lake of Geneva will it be conducted, By the foreign maiden wishing
to betray the city: Before its murder at Augsburg the great suite, And those of the
Rhine will come to invade it.

XIII.

Par grand fureur le Roy Romain Belgique Vexer voudra par phalange barbare:
Fureur grinssent, chassera gent Lybique Depuis Pannons iusques Hercules la
hare.

With great fury the Roman Belgian King Will want to vex the barbarian with his
phalanx: Fury gnashing, he will chase the African people From the Pannonias to
the pillars of Hercules.

XIV.

Saturne & Mars en Leo Espaigne captiue, Par chef Lybique au conflict attrapé,
Proche de Malthe, Herodde prinse viue, Et Romain sceptre sera par Coq frappé.

Saturn and Mars in Leo Spain captive, By the African chief trapped in the conflict,

Near Malta, "Herodde" taken alive,
And the Roman sceptre will be struck down by the Cock.

XV.

En nauigeant captif prins grand Pontife, Grand apres faillir les clercs tumultuez:
Second esleu absent son bien debife, Son fauory bastard à mort rué.

The great Pontiff taken captive while navigating, The great one thereafter to fail
the clergy in tumult: Second one elected absent his estate declines,
His favorite bastard to death broken on the wheel.

XVI.

A son haut pris plus la lerme sabee, D'humaine chair par mort en cendre mettre,
A l'isle Pharos par Croissars pertubee, Alors qu'a Rodes paroistra deux espectre.

The Sabaean tear no longer at its high price, Turning human flesh into ashes
through death, At the isle of Pharos disturbed by the Crusaders, When at Rhodes
will appear a hard phantom.

XVII.

De nuict passant le Roy pres d'vne Androne, Celuy de Cipres & principal guette.
Le Roy failly, la main fuit long du Rosne, Les coniurez l'iron à mort mettre.

By night the King passing near an Alley, He of Cyprus and the principal guard:
The King mistaken, the hand flees the length of the Rhône, The conspirators will
set out to put him to death.

XVIII.

De dueil mourra l'infelix profligé, Celebrera son vitrix l'hecatombe: Pristine loy,
franc edit redigé,

Le mur & Prince au septiesme iour tombe.

The unhappy abandoned one will die of grief, His conqueress will celebrate the hecatomb: Pristine law, free edict drawn up,
The wall and the Prince falls on the seventh day.

XIX.

Le grand Royal d'or, d'airain augmenté, Rompu la pache, par ieune ouuerte guerre: Peuple affligé par vn chef lamenté,
De sang barbare sera couuerte terre.

The great Royal one of gold, augmented by brass, The agreement broken, war opened by a young man: People afflicted because of a lamented chief,
The land will be covered with barbarian blood.

XX.

De là les Alpes grande amour passera, Vn peu deuant naistre monstre vapin: Prodigieux & subit tournera
Le grand Tosquan à son lieu plus propin.

The great army will pass beyond the Alps, Shortly before will be born a monster scoundrel: Prodigious and sudden he will turn
The great Tuscan to his nearest place.

XXI.

Par le trespas du Monarque Latin, Ceux qu'il aura par regne secourus: Le feu luira diuisé le butin.
La mort publique aux hardis incourus.

By the death of the Latin Monarch,
Those whom he will have assisted through his reign: The fire will light up again the booty divided, Public death for the bold ones who incurred it.

XXII.

Auant, qu'a Rome grand aye rendu l'ame Effrayeur grande à l'armee estrangere
Par esquadrons l'embusche pres de Parme, Puis les deux rouges ensemble feront
chere.

Before the great one has given up the ghost at Rome, Great terror for the foreign
army:
The ambush by squadrons near Parma, Then the two red ones will celebrate together.

XXIII.

Les deux contens seront vnis ensemble, Quand la pluspart à Mars seront con-
ionict: Le grand d'Affrique en effrayeur tremble, DVVMVIRAT par la classe de-
sioinct.

The two contented ones will be united together, When for the most part they will
be conjoined with Mars:
The great one of Africa trembles in terror, Duumvirate disjoined by the fleet.

XXIV.

Le regne & loy sous Venus esleué, Saturne aura sus Iupiter empire La loy & regne
par le Soleil leué,
Par Saturnins endurera le pire.

The realm and law raised under Venus, Saturn will have dominion over Jupiter:
The law and realm raised by the Sun,
Through those of Saturn it will suffer the worst.

XXV.

Le prince Arabe Mars Sol, Venus, Lyon Regne d'Eglise par mer succombera:
Deuers la Perse bien pres d'vn million, Bisance, Egypte ver. serp. inuadera.

The Arab Prince Mars, Sun, Venus, Leo, The rule of the Church will succumb by
sea: Towards Persia very nearly a million men,
The true serpent will invade Byzantium and Egypt.

XXVI.

La gent esclaue par vn heur Martial, Viendra en haut degré tant esslevee, Changeront Prince, n'aistra vn prouincial, Passer la mer copie aux monts leuee.

The slavish people through luck in war Will become elevated to a very high degree:
They will change their Prince, one born a provincial, An army raised in the
mountains to pass over the sea.

XXVII.

Par feu & armes non loing de la marnegro, Viendra de Perse occuper Trebisonde:
Trembler Pharos Methelin, Sol alegro, De sang Arabe d'Adrio couuert onde.

Through fire and arms not far from the Black Sea, He will come from Persia to
occupy Trebizond: Pharos, Mytilene to tremble, the Sun joyful,
The Adriatic Sea covered with Arab blood.

XXVIII.

Le bras pendant à la iambe liee, Visage pasle, au sein poignard caché, Trois qui
seront iurez de la meslee
Au grand de Genues sera le fer laschee.

His arm hung and leg bound, Face pale, dagger hidden in his bosom,
Three who will be sworn in the fray
Against the great one of Genoa will the steel be unleashed.

XXIX.

La liberté ne sera recouuree, L'occupera noir, fier, vilain, inique, Quand la mat-
iere du pont sera ouuree, D'Hister, Venise faschee la republique.

Liberty will not be recovered,
A proud, villainous, wicked black one will occupy it, When the matter of the
bridge will be opened, The republic of Venice vexed by the Danube.

XXX.

Tout à l'entour de la grande cité, Seront soldats logez par champs & villes.
Donner l'assaut Paris Rome incité Sur le pont lors sera faicte, grand pille.

All around the great city
Soldiers will be lodged throughout the fields and towns: To give the assault Paris,
Rome incited,
Then upon the bridge great pillage will be carried out.

XXXI.

Par terre Attique chef de la sapience, Qui de present est la rose du monde: Pour
ruiné, & sa grande preeminence Sera subdite & naufrage des ondes.

Through the Attic land fountain of wisdom, At present the rose of the world:
The bridge ruined, and its great pre-eminence Will be subjected, a wreck amidst
the waves.

XXXII.

Où tout bon est, tout bien Soleil & Lune Est abondant, sa ruine s'approche.
Du ciel s'auance vaner ta fortune, En mesme estat que la septiesme roche.

Where all is good, the Sun all beneficial and the Moon Is abundant, its ruin
approaches:
From the sky it advances to change your fortune.

In the same state as the seventh rock.

XXXIII.

Des principaux de cité rebellee Qui tiendront fort pour liberté t'avoir. Detrancher masles, infelice meslee, Crys, heurlemens à Nantes piteux voir.

Of the principal ones of the city in rebellion Who will strive mightily to recover
their liberty: The males cut up, unhappy fray,
Cries, groans at Nantes pitiful to see.

XXXIV.

Du plus profond de l'Occident Anglois Où est le chef de l'isle Britanique Entrera classe dans Gyronne, par Blois Par vin & tel, ceux cachez aux barriques.

From the deepest part of the English West Where the head of the British isle is
A fleet will enter the Gironde through Blois, Through wine and salt, fires hidden
in the casks.

XXXV.

Par cité franche de la grand mer Seline Qui porte encores à l'estomach la pierre,
Angloise classe viendra sous la bruine
Vn rameau prendre, du grand ouuerte guerre.

For the free city of the great Crescent sea, Which still carries the stone in its
stomach, The English fleet will come under the drizzle
To seize a branch, war opened by the great one.

XXXVI.

De soeur le frere par simulte faintise Viendra mesler rosee en myneral: Sur la
placente donne à veille tardiue,
Meurt le goustant sera simple & rural.

The sister's brother through the quarrel and deceit Will come to mix dew in the mineral:
On the cake given to the slow old woman, She dies tasting it she will be simple and rustic.

XXXVII.

Trois cens seront d'vn vouloir & accord, Que pour venir au bout de leur attainte,
Vingt mois apres tous & record
Leur Roy trahy simulant haine fainte.

Three hundred will be in accord with one will To come to the execution of their blow, Twenty months after all memory
Their king betrayed simulating feigned hate.

XXXVIII.

Ce grand monarque qu'au mort succedera, Donnera vie illicite lubrique,
Par nonchalance à tous concedera, Qu'à la parfin faudra la loy Salique,

He who will succeed the great monarch on his death Will lead an illicit and wanton life:
Through nonchalance he will give way to all, So that in the end the Salic law will fail.

XXXIX.

Du vray rameau de fleur de lys issu Mis & logé heritier d'Hetturie:
Son sang antique de longue main tissu, Fera Florence florir en l'harmoirie.

Issued from the true branch of the fleur-de-lys, Placed and lodged as heir of Etruria:
His ancient blood woven by long hand,
He will cause the escutcheon of Florence to bloom.

XL.

Le sang royal sera si tres meslé, Contraints seront Gaulois de l'Hesperie: On attendra que terme soit coulé,
Et que memoire de la voix soit petite.

The blood royal will be so very mixed, Gauls will be constrained by Hesperia:
One will wait until his term has expired,
And until the memory of his voice has perished.

XLI.

Nay sous les ombres & iournee nocturne, Sera en regne & bonté souueraine:
Fera renaistre son sang de l'antique vrne, Renouuellant siecle d'or pour l'airain.

Born in the shadows and during a dark day, He will be sovereign in realm and
goodness:
He will cause his blood to rise again in the ancient urn, Renewing the age of gold
for that of brass.

XLII.

Mars esleué en son plus haut befroy, Fera retraire les Allobrox de France: La gent
Lombarde fera si grand effroy,
A ceux de l'Aigle comprins sous la Balance.

Mars raised to his highest belfry
Will cause the Savoyards to withdraw from France: The Lombard people will
cause very great terror To those of the Eagle included under the Balance.

XLIII.

La grand' ruine des sacrez ne s'eslongue, Prouence, Naples, Scicille, Seez & Ponce,
En Germanie, au Rhin & la Cologne, Vexez à mort par tous ceux de Magonce.

The great ruin of the holy things is not far off, Provence, Naples, Sicily, Sées and

Pons: In Germany, at the Rhine and Cologne,
Vexed to death by all those of Mainz.

XLIV.

Par mer le rouge sera prins de pyrates, La paix sera par son moyen troublee: L'ire
& l'auare commettra par fainct acte, Au grand Pontife sera l'armee doublee.

On sea the red one will be taken by pirates, Because of him peace will be trou-
bled:
Anger and greed will he expse through a false act, The army doubled by the great
Pontiff.

XLV.

Le grand Empire sera tost desolé Et translaté pres d'arduenne silue:
Les deux bastards par l'aisné decollé, Et regnera Aenodarb, nez de milue.

The great Empire will soon be desolated And transferred to near the Ardennes:
The two bastards beheaded by the oldest one, And Bronzebeard the hawk-nose
will reign.

XLVI.

Par chapeaux rouges querelles & nouueaux scismes Quand on aura esleu le Sa-
binois:
On produira contre luy grands sophismes, Et sera Rome lesee par Albanois.

Quarrels and new schism by the red hats When the Sabine will have been elected: They will produce great sophism against him, And Rome will be injured by
those of Alba.

XLVII.

Le grand, Arabe marchera bien auant, Trahy sera par les Bisantinois: L'antique
Rodes luy viendra audeuant, Et plus grand mal par austre Pannonois.

The great Arab will march far forward, He will be betrayed by the Byzantinians:
Ancient Rhodes will come to meet him,
And greater harm through the Austrian Hungarians.

XLVIII.

Apres la grande affliction du sceptre, Deux ennemis par eux seront defaicts:
Classe Affrique aux Pannons viendra naistre, Par mer terre seront horribles faicts.

After the great affliction of the sceptre, Two enemies will be defeated by them:
A fleet from Africa will appear before the Hungarians, By land and sea horrible
deeds will take place.

XLIX.

Nul de l'Espagne, mais de l'antique France Ne sera esleu pour le trembant nacelle
A l'ennemy sera faicte fiance, Qui dans son regne sera peste cruelle.

Not from Spain but from ancient France Will one be elected for the trembling
bark, To the enemy will a promise be made,
He who will cause a cruel plague in his realm.

L.

L'an que les Freres du lys seront en aage, L'vn d'eux tiendra la grande Romanie:
Trembler ses monts, ouuers Latin passage, Fache macher contre fort d'Armenie.

The year that the brothers of the lily come of age, One of them will hold the great
"Romania":
The mountains to tremble, Latin passage opened, Agreement to march against

132

the fort of Armenia.

LI.

La gent de Dace, d'Angleterre, Polonne Et de Boësme feront nouuelle ligue.
Pour passer outre d'Hercules la colonne, Barcins, Tyrrens dresser cruelle brique.

The people of Dacia, England, Poland And of Bohemia will make a new league:
To pass beyond the pillars of Hercules,
The Barcelonans and Tuscans will prepare a cruel plot.

LII.

Vn Roy sera qui donra l'opposite. Les exilz esleuez sur le regne:
De sang nager la gent caste hypolite, Et florira long temps sous telle enseigne.

There will be a King who will give opposition, The exiles raised over the realm:
The pure poor people to swim in blood,
And for a long time will he flourish under such a device.

LIII.

La loy du Sol & Venus contendus Appropriant l'esprit de prophetie: Ne l'vn ne
l'autre ne seront entendus,
Par sol tiendra la loy du grand Messie.

The law of the Sun and of Venus in strife, Appropriating the spirit of prophecy:
Neither the one nor the other will be understood, The law of the great Messiah
will hold through the Sun.

LIV.

Du pont Exine, & la grand Tartarie, Vn Roy sera qui viendra voir la Gaule, Transpercera Alane & l'Armenie,
Et dedans Bisance lairra sanglante gaule

From beyond the Black Sea and great Tartary, There will be a King who will come to see Gaul, He will pierce through "Alania" and Armenia, And within Byzantium will he leave his bloody rod.

LV.

De la Felice Arabie contrade, N'aistra puissant de loy Mahometique: Vexer l'Espagne, conquester la Grenade, Et plus par mer à la gent Lygustique.

In the country of Arabia Felix There will be born one powerful in the law of Mahomet: To vex Spain, to conquer Grenada, And more by sea against the Ligurian people.

LVI.

Par le trespas du tres-vieillard Pontife Sera esleu Romain de bon aage, Qui sera dict que le siege debiffe, Et long tiendra & de picquant ouurage.

Through the death of the very old Pontiff A Roman of good age will be elected, Of him it will be said that he weakens his see, But long will he sit and in biting activity.

LVII.

Istra de mont Gaufier & Auentin, Qui par le trou aduertira l'armee Entre deux rocs sera prins le butin, DE SEXT, mansol faillir la renommee.

There will go from Mont Gaussier and "Aventin," One who through the hole will warn the army: Between two rocks will the booty be taken,   , Of Sectus' mausoleum the renown to fail.

LVIII.

De l'aque duct d'Vticense Gardoing, Par la forest mort inacessible, Ennemy du
pont sera tranché au poing Le chef nemans qui tant sera terrible.

By the aqueduct of Uzès over the Gard, Through the forest and inaccessible
mountain,
In the middle of the bridge there will be cut in the fist The chief of Nîmes who
will be very terrible.

LIX.

Au chef Anglois à Nismes trop seiour, Deuers l'Espagne au secours Aenobarbe
Plusieurs mourront par Mars ouuert ce iour, Quand en Artois faillir estoille en
barbe.

Too long a stay for the English chief at Nîmes, Towards Spain Redbeard to the
rescue: Many will die by war opened that day, When a bearded star will fall in
Artois.

LX.

Par teste rase viendra bien mal eslire, Plus que sa charge ne porter passera. Si
grande fureur & rage fera dire, Qu'à feu & sang tout sexe trenchera.

By the shaven head a very bad choice will come to be made, Overburdened he
will not pass the gate:
He will speak with such great fury and rage, That to fire and blood he will con-
sign the entire sex.

LXI.

L'enfant du grand n'estant à sa naissance, Subiuguera les hauts monts Apennis:
Fera trembler tous ceux de la balance, Et des monts feux iusques à Mont-senis.

The child of the great one not by his birth, He will subjugate the high Apenine

mountains: He will cause all those of the balance to tremble,
And from the Pyrenees to Mont Cenis.

LXII.

Sur les rochers sang on verra pleuuoir, Sol Orient Saturne Occidental:
Pres d'Orgon guerre à Rome grand mal voir, Nefs parfondrees, & prins Tridental.

One will see blood to rain on the rocks, Sun in the East, Saturn in the West:
Near Orgon war, at Rome great evil to be seen, Ships sunk to the bottom, and
the Tridental taken.

LXIII.

De vaine emprinse l'honneur indue plaincte, Galliots errans par latins, froid,
faim, vagues Non loin du Tymbre de sang la terre taincte, Et sur humaine seront
diuerses plagues.

From the vain enterprise honor and undue complaint, Boats tossed about among
the Latins, cold, hunger, waves Not far from the Tiber the land stained with
blood,
And diverse plagues will be upon mankind.

LXIV.

Les assemblez par repos du grand nombre Par terre & mer conseil contremandé:
Pres de l'Antonne Gennes, Nice de l'ombre Par champs & villes le chef contrebandé.

Those assembled by the tranquility of the great number, By land and sea counsel
countermanded:
Near "Antonne" Genoa, Nice in the shadow Through fields and towns in revolt
against the chief.

LXV.

Subit venu l'effrayeur sera grande, Des principaux de l'affaire cachez:
Et dame en brasse plus ne sera en veüe, Ce peu à peu seront les grands fachez.

Come suddenly the terror will be great, Hidden by the principal ones of the
affair:
And the lady on the charcoal will no longer be in sight, Thus little by little will
the great ones be angered.

LXVI.

Sous les antiques edifices vestaux, Non esloignez d'aqueduct ruyne.
De Sol & lune sont les luisans metaux, Ardente lampe, Traian d'or burine.

Under the ancient vestal edifices, Not far from the ruined aqueduct:
The glittering metals are of the Sun and Moon, The lamp of Trajan engraved with
gold burning.

LXVII.

Quand chef Perouse n'osera sa tunique Sans au couuert tout nud s'expolier: Seront prins sept faict Aristocratique,
Le pere & fils mort par poincte au colier.

When the chief of Perugia will not venture his tunic Sense under cover to strip
himself quite naked: Seven will be taken Aristocratic deed,
Father and son dead through a point in the collar.

LXVIII.

Dans le Danube & du Rhin viendra boire Le grand Chameau, ne s'en repentira:
Trembler du Rosne, & plus fort ceux de Loire Et pres des Alpes Coq le ruinera.

In the Danube and of the Rhine will come to drink The great Camel, not repent-
ing it:

Those of the Rhône to tremble, and much more so those of the Loire, and near
the Alps the Cock will ruin him.

LXIX.

Plus ne sera le grand en feux sommeil, L'inquietude viendra prendre repos:
Dresser phalange d'or, azur & vermeil Subiuger Afrique la ronger iusques os.

No longer will the great one be in his false sleep, Uneasiness will come to replace
tranquility:
A phalanx of gold, azure and vermilion arrayed To subjugate Africa and gnaw it
to the bone,

LXX.

Des regions subiectes à la Balance Feront troubler les monts par grande guerre,
Captifs tout sexe deu & tout Bisance, Qu'on criera à l'aube terre à terre.

Of the regions subject to the Balance, They will trouble the mountains with great
war,
Captives the entire sex enthralled and all Byzantium,
So that at dawn they will spread the news from land to land.

LXXI.

Par la fureur d'vn qui attendra l'eau, Par la grand'rage tout l'exercice esmeu:
Chargé des nobles à dix sept barreaux, Au long du Rosne tard messager venu.

By the fury of one who will wait for the water, By his great rage the entire army
moved: Seventeen boats loaded with the noble,
The messenger come late along the Rhône.

LXXII.

Pour le plaisir d'edict voluptueux, On meslera la poison dans la foy: Venus sera
en cours si vertueux, Qu'obfusquera Soleil tout à loy.

For the pleasure of the voluptuous edict, One will mix poison in the faith:
Venus will be in a course so virtuous As to becloud the whole quality of the Sun.

LXXIII.

Persecutee sera de Dieu l'Eglise,
Et les saincts Temples seront expoliez, L'enfant la mere mettra nud en chemise,
Seront Arabes aux Pollons ralliez.

The Church of God will be persecuted, And the holy Temples will be plundered,
The child will put his mother out in her shift, Arabs will be allied with the Poles.

LXXIV.

De sang Troyen naistra coeur, Germanique Qui deuiendra en si haute puissance:
Hors chassera estrange Arabique, Tournant l'Eglise en pristine preeminence.

Of Trojan blood will be born a Germanic heart Who will rise to very high power:
He will drive out the foreign Arabic people, Returning the Church to its pristine
pre-eminence.

LXXV.

Montera haut sur le bien plus à dextre, Demourera assis sur la pierre quarree,
Vers le midy posé à sa senestre, Baston tortu en main bouche serree.

He will rise high over the estate more to the right, He will remain seated on the
square stone, Towards the south facing to his left,
The crooked staff in his hand his mouth sealed.

LXXVI.

En lieu libre tendra son pauillon, Et ne voudra en citez prendre place
Aix, Carpen l'isle volce, mont, Cauaillon, Par tous ses lieux abolira la trasse.

In a free place will he pitch his tent, And he will not want to lodge in the cities:
Aix, Carpentras, L'Isle, Vaucluse "Mont," Cavaillon, Throughout all these places
will he abolish his trace.

LXXVII.

Tous les degrez d'honneur Ecclesiastique Seront changez en dial quirinal:
En Martial quirinal flaminique,
Puis vn Roy de France le rendra vulcanal.

All degrees of Ecclesiastical honor
Will be changed to that of Jupitor and Quirinus: The priest of Quirinus to one
of Mars,
Then a King of France will make him one of Vulcan.

LXXVIII.

Les deux vnis ne tiendront longuement, Et dans treize ans au Barbare Strappe,
Aux deux costez feront tel perdement, Qu'vn benira le Barque & sa cappe.

The two will not be united for very long, And in thirteen years to the Barbarian
Satrap: On both sides they will cause such loss
That one will bless the Bark and its cope.

LXXIX.

Par sacree pompe viendra baisser les aisles, Par la venue du grand legislateur:
Humble haussera, vexera les rebelles, Naistra sur terre aucun aemulateur.

The sacred pomp will come to lower its wings, Through the coming of the great
legislator:

140

He will raise the humble, he will vex the rebels, His like will not appear on this earth.

LXXX.

Logmion grande Bisance approchera. Chassee sera la barbarique Ligue:
Des deux loix l'vne l'estinique laschera, Barbare & franche en perpetuelle brigue.

Ogmios will approach great Byzantium, The Barbaric League will be driven out:
Of the two laws the heathen one will give way, Barbarian and Frank in perpetual strife.

LXXXI.

L'oiseau royal sur la cité solaire, Sept moys deuant fera nocturne augure: Mur d'Orient cherra tonnerre esclaire,
Sept iours aux portes les ennemis à l'heure.

The royal bird over the city of the Sun,
Seven months in advance it will deliver a nocturnal omen: The Eastern wall will fall lightning thunder,
Seven days the enemies directly to the gates.

LXXXII.

Au conclud pache hors la forteresse, Ne sortira celuy en desespoir mis:
Quant ceux d'Arbois, de Langres, contre Bresse, Auront mons Dolle bouscade d'ennemis.

At the conclusion of the treaty outside the fortress Will not go he who is placed in despair:
When those of Arbois, of Langres against Bresse Will have the mountains of Dôle an enemy ambush.

LXXXIII.

Ceux qui auront entreprins subuertir, Nompareil regne, puissant & inuincible:
Feront par fraudes, nuicts trois aduertir, Quand le plus grand à table lira Bible.

Those who will have undertaken to subvert, An unparalleled realm, powerful
and invincible: They will act through deceit, nights three to warn,
When the greatest one will read his Bible at the table.

LXXXIV.

Naistra du gouphre & cité immesuree, Nay de parens obscurs & tenebreux: Qui
la puissance du grand Roy reueree, Voudra destruire par Roüan & Eureux.

He will be born of the gulf and unmeasured city, Born of obscure and dark family:
He who the revered power of the great King Will want to destroy through Rouen
and Evreux.

LXXXV.

Par les Sueues & lieux circonuoisins. Seront en guerre pour cause des nuees.
Camp marins locustes & cousins, Du Leman fautes seront bien desnuees.

Through the Suevi and neighboring places, They will be at war over the clouds:
Swarm of marine locusts and gnats,
The faults of Geneva will be laid quite bare.

LXXXVI.

Par les deux testes, & trois bras separés, La cité grande sera par eaux vexee:
Des grands d'entr'eux par exil esgarés, Par teste perse Bisance fort pressee.

Divided by the two heads and three arms, The great city will be vexed by waters:
Some great ones among them led astray in exile, Byzantium hard pressed by the
head of Persia.

LXXXVII.

L'an que Saturne hors de seruage, Au franc terroir sera d'eau inundé: De sang
Troyen sera son mariage, Et sera seur d'Espaignols circundé.

The year that Saturn is out of bondage,
In the Frank land he will be inundated by water: Of Trojan blood will his mar-
riage be,
And he will be confined safely be the Spaniards.

LXXXVIII.

Sur le sablon par vn hideux deluge, Des autres mers trouué monstre marin:
Proche du lieu sera faicte vn refuge, Venant Sauone esclaue de Turin.

Through a frightful flood upon the sand, A marine monster from other seas
found: Near the place will be made a refuge, Holding Savona the slave of Turin.

LXXXIX.

Dedans Hongrie par Boheme, Nauarre, Et par banniere sainctes seditions:
Par fleurs de lys pays portant la barre, Contre Orleans fera esmotions.

Into Hungary through Bohemia, Navarre, and under that banner holy insurrec-
tions: By the fleur-de-lys legion carrying the bar,
Against Orléans they will cause disturbances.

XC.

Dans le cyclades, en printhe & larisse, Dedans Sparte tout le Peloponnesse:
Si grand famine, peste par faux connisse, Neuf mois tiendra & tout le cheron-
nesse.

In the Cyclades, in Perinthus and Larissa, In Sparta and the entire Pelopennesus:
Very great famine, plague through false dust,
Nine months will it last and throughout the entire peninsula.

XCI.

Au grand marché qu'on dict des mensongiers, Du tout Torrent & champ Athe-
nien:
Seront surprins par les cheuaux legiers, Par Albanois Mars, Leo, Sat. vn versien.

At the market that they call that of liars, Of the entire Torrent and field of Athens:
They will be surprised by the light horses,
By those of Alba when Mars is in Leo and Saturn in Aquarius.

XCII.

Apres le siege tenu dixscept ans, Cinq changeront en tel reuolu terme: Puis sera
l'vn esleu de mesme temps,
Qui des Romains ne sera trop conforme.

After the see has been held seventeen years, Five will change within the same
period of time: Then one will be elected at the same time,
One who will not be too contormable to the Romans.

XCIII.

Soubs le terroir du rond globe lunaire, Lors que sera dominateur Mercure: L'isle
d'Escosse fera vn luminaire, Qui les Anglois mettra à deconfiture.

Under the land of the round lunar globe, When Mercury will be dominating:
The isle of Scotland will produce a luminary, One who will put the English into
confusion.

XCIV.

Translatera en la grand Germanie, Brabant & Flandres, Gand, Bruges, &
Bolongne:
La trefue fainte le grand duc d'Armenie, Assaillira Vienne & la Cologne.

He will transfer into great Germany Brabant and Flanders, Ghent, Bruges and

Boulogne:
The truce feigned, the great Duke of Armenia Will assail Vienna and Cologne.

XCV.

Nautique rame inuitera les vmbres, Du grand Empire lors viendra conciter: La mer Aegee des lignes les en combres Empeschant l'onde Tirrenne defflottez.

The nautical oar will tempt the shadows, Then it will come to stir up the great Empire: In the Aegean Sea the impediments of wood Obstructing the diverted Tyrrhenian Sea.

XCVI.

Sur le milieu du grand monde la rose, Pour nouueaux faicts sang public espandu:
A dire vray on aura bouche close,
Lors au besoing viendra tard l'attendu.

The rose upon the middle of the great world, For new deeds public shedding of blood:
To speak the truth, one will have a closed mouth, Then at the time of need the awaited one will come late.

XCVII.

Le n'ay defforme par horreur suffoqué, Dans la cité du grand Roy habitable: L'edict seuere des captifs reuoqué, Gresle & tonnerre, Condon inestimable.

The one born deformed suffocated in horror, In the habitable city of the great King: The severe edict of the captives revoked, Hail and thunder, Condom inestimable.

XCVIII.

A quarante huict degré climaterique, A fin de Cancer si grande seicheresse:
Poisson en mer, fleuue: lac cuit hectique, Bearn, Bigorre par feu ciel en detresse.

At the forty-eigth climacteric degree, At the end of Cancer very great dryness:
Fish in sea, river, lake boiled hectic,
Béarn, Bigorre in distress through fire from the sky.

XCIX.

Milan, Ferrare, Turin, & Aquilleye, Capue, Brundis vexez per geut Celtique: Par
le Lyon & phalange aquilee
Quant Rome aura le chef vieux Britannique.

Milan, Ferrara, Turin and Aquileia, Capua, Brindisi vexed by the Celtic nation:
By the Lion and his eagles's phalanx, When the old British chief Rome will have.

C.

Le boute feu par son feu attrapé, Du feu du ciel à Calcas & Gominge:
Foix, Aux, Mazere, haut vieillart eschappé, Par ceux de Hasse des Saxons &
Turinge.

The incendiary trapped in his own fire,
Of fire from the sky at Carcassonne and the Comminges: Foix, Auch, Mazères,
the high old man escaped,
Through those of Hesse and Thuringia, and some Saxons.

CENTURY VI

I.

Avtour des monts Pyrenees grans amas De gent estrange secourir Roy nouueau:
Pres de Garonne du grand temple du Mas, Vn Romain chef le craindra dedans
l'eau.

Around the Pyrenees mountains a great throng Of foreign people to aid the new
King:
Near the great temple of Le Mas by the Garonne, A Roman chief will fear him
in the water.

II.

En l'an cinq cens octante plus & moins, On attendra le siecle bien estrange:
En l'an sept cens, & trois cieux en tesmoings, Que plusieurs regnes vn à cinq
feront change.

In the year five hundred eighty more or less, One will await a very strange century:
In the year seven hundred and three the heavens witness thereof, That several
kingdoms one to five will make a change.

III.

Fleuue qu'esprouue le nouueau nay de Celtique Sera en grande de l'Empire dis-
cordes
Le ieune prince par gent ecclesiastique, Ostera le sceptre coronal de concorde.

The river that tries the new Celtic heir Will be in great discord with the Empire:
The young Prince through the ecclesiastical people Will remove the sceptre of
the crown of concord.

IV.

La Celtiq fleuue changera de riuage, Plus ne tiendra la cité d'Agripine: Tout transmué hormis le vieil langage, Saturne, Leo, Mars, Cancer en rapine.

The Celtic river will change its course,
No longer will it include the city of Agrippina: All changed except the old language, Saturn, Leo, Mars, Cancer in plunder.

V.

Si grand famine par vnde pestifere.
Par pluye longue le long du polle arctiques Samatobryn cent lieux de l'hemisphere, Viuront sans loy exempt de pollitique.

Very great famine through pestiferous wave, Through long rain the length of the arctic pole:
"Samarobryn" one hundred leagues from the hemisphere, The will live without law exempt from politics.

VI.

Apparoistra vers le Septentrion Non loing de Cancer l'estoille cheuelue:
Suze, Sienne, Boëce, Eretrion, Mourra de Rome grand, la nuict disperue.

There will appear towards the North Not far from Cancer the bearded star: Susa, Siena, Boeotia, Eretria,
The great one of Rome will die, the night over.

VII.

Norneigre Dace, & l'Isle Britannique, Par les vnis freres seront vexees:
Le chef Romain issu de sang Gallique Et les copies aux forests repoussees.

Norway and Dacia and the British Isle Will be vexed by the united brothers:
The Roman chief sprung from Gallic blood And his forces hurled back into the forests

148

VIII.

Ceux qui estoient en regne pour s&cced;auoir, Au Royal change deuiendront appouuris:
Vns exilez sans appuy or n'auoir, Lettrez & lettres ne seront à grand pris.

Those who were in the realm for knowledge Will become impoverished at the change of King:
Some exiled without support, having no gold, The lettered and letters will not be at a high premium.

IX.

Aux sacrez temples seront faicts escandales, Comptez seront par honneurs & loüanges: D'vn que on graue d'argent d'or les medalles, La fin sera en tourmens bien estranges.

In the sacred temples scandals will be perpetrated, They will be reckoned as honors and commendations:
Of one of whom they engrave medals of silver and of gold, The end will be in very strange torments.

X.

Vn peu de temps les temples des couleurs De blanc & noir des deux entre meslee: Rouges & iaunes leur embleront les leurs, Sang, terre, peste, faim, feu d'eau affollee.

In a short time the temples with colors Of white and black of the two intermixed: Red and yellow ones will carry off theirs from them, Blood, land, plague, famine, fire extinguished by water.

XI.

Des sept rameaux à trois seront reduicts, Les plus aisnez seront surprins par mort, Fratricider les deux seront seduicts,
Les coniurez en dormans seront morts.

The seven branches will be reduced to three, The elder ones will be surprised by death, The two will be seduced to fratricide,
The conspirators will be dead while sleeping.

XII.

Dresser copies pour monter à l'empire, Du Vatican le sang Royal tiendra: Fla-mans, Anglois, Espagne auec Aspire, Contre l'Italie & France contiendra.

To raise forces to ascend to the empire
In the Vatican the Royal blood will hold fast: Flemings, English, Spain with "As-pire" Against Italy and France will he contend.

XIII.

Vn dubieux ne viendra loing du regne, La plus grand part le voudra soustenir.
Vn Capitole ne voudra point qu'il regne, Sa grande charge ne pourra maintenir.

A doubtful one will not come far from the realm, The greater part will want to uphold him:
A Capitol will not want him to reign at all, He will be unable to bear his great burden.

XIV.

Loing de sa terre Roy perdra la bataille, Prompt eschappé poursuiuy suiuant prins, Ignare prins soubs la doree maille,
Soubs feinct habit, & l'ennemy surprins.

Far from his land a King will lose the battle, At once escaped, pursued, then captured, Ignorant one taken under the golden mail, Under false garb, and the enemy surprised.

XV.

Dessoubs la tombe sera trouué le Prince, Qu'aura le pris par dessus Nuremberg: L'espaignol Roy en capricorne mince, Feinct & trahy par le grand Vvitemberg.

Under the tomb will be found a Prince Who will be valued above Nuremberg:
The Spanish King in Capricorn thin,
Deceived and betrayed by the great Wittenberg.

XVI.

Ce que rauy sera de ieune Milue, Par les Normans de France & Picardie: Les noirs du temple du lieu de Negrisilue Feront aulberge & feu de Lombardie.

That which will be carried off by the young Hawk, By the Normans of France and Picardy:
The black ones of the temple of the Black Forest place Will make an inn and fire of Lombardy.

XVII.

Apres les limes bruslez le rasiniers, Contrains seront changer habits divers: Les Saturnins bruslez par les meusniers, Hors la pluspart qui ne sera couuers.

After the files the ass-drivers burned, They will be obliged to change diverse garbs:
Those of Saturn burned by the millers, Except the greater part which will not be covered.

XVIII.

Par les Phisiques le grand Roy delaissé, Par sort non art de l'Ebrieu est en vie, Luy
& son genre au regne haut poussé, Grace donnee à gent qui Christ enuie.

The great King abandoned by the Physicians, By fate not the Jew's art he remains
alive,
He and his kindred pushed high in the realm, Pardon given to the race which
denies Christ.

XIX.

La vraye flamme engloutira la dame, Qui voudra mettre les Innocens à feu: Pres
de l'assaut l'exercite s'enflamme,
Quant dans Seuille monstre en boeuf sera veu.

The true flame will devour the lady
Who will want to put the Innocent Ones to the fire: Before the assault the army
is inflamed,
When in Seville a monster in beef will be seen.

XX.

L'vnion feincte sera peu de duree, Des vn changez reformez la pluspart: Dans les
vaisseaux sera gent endurees, Lors aura Rome vn nouueau Liepart.

The feigned union will be of short duration, Some changed most reformed:
In the vessels people will be in suffering, Then Rome will have a new Leopard.

XXI.

Quant ceux du polle arctic vnis ensemble, Et Orient grand effrayeur & craints:
Esleu nouueau, soustenu le grand tremble, Rodes, Bisence de sang Barbare teinc-
te.

When those of the arctic pole are united together, Great terror and fear in the

East:
Newly elected, the great trembling supported, Rhodes, Byzantium stained with Barbarian blood.

XXII.

Dedans la terre du grand temple celique, Nepueu à Londre par paix feincte meurtry: La barque alors deuiendra scimatique, Liberté feincte sera au corn' & cry.

Within the land of the great heavenly temple, Nephew murdered at London through feigned peace: The bark will then become schismatic, Sham liberty will be proclaimed everywhere.

XXIII.

D'esprit de regne munismes descriés, Et seront peuples esmeuz contre leur Roy, Paix sainct nouueau, sainctes loix empirees, Rapis onc fut en si tredur arroy.

Coins depreciated by the spirit of the realm, And people will be stirred up against their King: New peace made, holy laws become worse, Paris was never in so severe an array.

XXIV.

Mars & le scepte se trouuera conioinct, Dessoubs Cancer calamiteuse guerre: Vn peu apres sera nouueau Roy oingt, Qui par long temps pacifiera la terre.

Mars and the sceptre will be found conjoined Under Cancer calamitous war: Shortly afterwards a new King will be anounted, One who for a long time will pacify the earth.

XXV.

Par Mars contraire sera la monarchie, Du grand pescheur en trouble ruyneux;
Ieune noir rouge prendra la hirarchie, Les proditeurs iront iour bruyneux.

Through adverse Mars will the monarchy Of the great fisherman be in ruinous
trouble:
The young red black one will seize the hierarchy, The traitors will act on a day
of drizzle.

XXVI.

Quatre ans le siege quelque peu bien tiendra, Vn suruiendra libidineux de vie:
Rauenne & Pyse, Veronne soustiendront, Pour esleuer la croix de Pape enuie.

For four years the see will be held with some little good, One libidinous in life
will succeed to it:
Ravenna, Pisa and Verona will give support, Longing to elevate the Papal cross.

XXVII.

Dedans les Isles de cinq fleuues à vn, Par le croissant du grand Chyren Selin: Par
les bruynes de l'air fureur de l'vn, Six eschapez cachez fardeaux de lyn.

Within the Isles of five rivers to one, Through the expansion of the great "Chyren
Selin":
Through the drizzles in the air the fury of one, Six escaped, hidden bundles of
flax.

XXVIII.

Le grand Celtique entrera dedans Rome, Menant amas d'exilez & bannis:
Le grand Pasteur mettra à mort tout homme, Qui pour le coq estoyent aux Alpes
vnis.

The great Celt will enter Rome, Leading a throng of the exiled and banished: The

great Pastor will put to death every man
Who was united at the Alps for the cock.

XXIX.

La vefue saincte entendant les nouuelles, De ses rameaux mis en perplex & trouble: Qui sera duict appaiser les querelles,
Par son pourchas de razes fera comble.

The saintly widow hearing the news,
Of her offspring placed in perplexity and trouble: He who will be instructed to
appease the quarrels,
He will pile them up by his pursuit of the shaven heads.

XXX.

Par l'apparence de faincte saincteté, Sera trahy aux ennemis le siege.
Nuict qu'on cuidoit dormir en seureté, Pres de Brabant marcheront ceux du
Liege.

Through the appearance of the feigned sanctity, The siege will be betrayed to the
enemies:
In the night when they trusted to sleep in safety, Near Brabant will march those
of Liège.

XXXI.

Roy trouuera ce qu'il desiroit tant, Quand le Prelat sera reprins à tort: Responce
au Duc le rendra mal content, Qui dans Milan mettra plusieurs à mort.

The King will find that which he desired so much When the Prelate will be
blamed unjustly:
His reply to the Duke will leave him dissatisfied, He who in Milan will put several to death.

XXXII.

Par trahison de verges à mort battu, Prins surmonté sera par son desordre: Conseil friuole au grand captif sentu,
Nez par fureur quant Berlch viendra mordre.

Beaten to death by rods for treason, Captured he will be overcome through his
disorder:
Frivolous counsel held out to the great captive, When "Berich" will come to bite
his nose in fury.

XXXIII.

Sa main derniere par Alus sanguinaire, Ne se pourra par la mer garentir:
Entre deux fleuues craindre main militaire, Le noir l'ireux le fera repentir.

His last hand through "Alus" sanguinary, He will be unable to protect himself
by sea:
Between two rivers he will fear the military hand, The black and irate one will
make him rue it.

XXXIV.

De feu voulant la machination, Viendra troubler au grand chef assieger:
Dedans sera telle sedition, Qu'en desespoir seront les profligez.

The device of flying fire
Will come to trouble the great besieged chief: Within there will be such sedition
That the profligate ones will be in despair.

XXXV.

Pres de Rion, & proche à blanche laine, Aries, Taurus, Cancer, Leo, la Vierge,
Mars, Iupiter, le Sol ardera grand plaine, Bois & citez lettres cachez au cierge.

Near the Bear and close to the white wool, Aries, Taurus, Cancer, Leo, Virgo,

Mars, Jupiter, the Sun will burn a great plain, Woods and cities letters hidden in the candle.

XXXVI.

Ne bien ne mal par bataille terrestre, Ne paruiendra aux confins de Perouse, Rebeller Pise, Florence voir mal estre, Roy nuict blessé sur mulet à noire house.

Neither good nor evil through terrestrial battle Will reach the confines of Perugia,
Pisa to rebel, Florence to see an evil existence, King by night wounded on a mule with black housing.

XXXVII.

L'oeuure ancienne se paracheuera, Du toict cherra sur le grand mal ruyne: Innocent faict mort on accusera, Nocent cache, taillis à la bruyne.

The ancient work will be finished,
Evil ruin will fall upon the great one from the roof: Dead they will accuse an innocent one of the deed, The guilty one hidden in the copse in the drizzle.

XXXVIII.

Aux profligez de paix les ennemis, Apres auoir l'Italie superee, Noir sanguinaire, rouge. sera commis, Feu, sang verser, eau de sang coloree.

The enemies of peace to the profligates, After having conquered Italy:
The bloodthirsty black one, red, will be exposed, Fire, blood shed, water colored by blood.

XXXIX.

L'enfant du regne, par paternelle prinse Expolier sera pour le deliurer:
Aupres du lac Trasimen l'axur prinse, La troupe hostage par trop fort s'enyurer.

The child of the realm through the capture of his father Will be plundered to deliver him:
Near the Lake of Perugia the azure captive, The hostage troop to become far too drunk.

XL.

Grand de Magonce pour grande soif esteindre, Sera priué de sa grande dignité:
Ceux de Cologne si fort le viendront plaindre, Que la grand groppe au Rhin sera ietté.

To quench the great thirst the great one of Mainz Will be deprived of his great dignity:
Those of Cologne will come to complain so loudly That the great rump will be thrown into the Rhine.

XLI.

Le second chef du regne d'Annemarc, Par ceux de Frize & l'Isle Britannique, Fera despendre plus de cent mille marc, Vain exploicter voyage en Italique.

The second chief of the realm of "Annemark," Through those of Frisia and of the British Isle,
Will spend more than one hundred thousand marks, Exploiting in vain the voyage to Italy.

XLII.

A Logmyon sera laissé le regne, Du grand Selin plus fera de faict: Par les Itales estendra son enseigne, Regi sera par prudent contrefaict.

To Ogmios will be left the realm
Of the great "Selin," who will in fact do more: Throughout Italy will he extend his
banner, He will be ruled by a prudent deformed one.

XLIII.

Long temps sera sans estre habitee, Où Signe & Marne autour vient arrouser:
De la Tamise & martiaux tentee,
De ceux les gardes en cuidant repousser.

For a long time will she remain uninhabited, Around where the Seine and the
Marne she comes to water:
Tried by the Thames and warriors,
The guards deceived in trusting in the repulse.

XLIV.

De nuict par Nantes Lyris apparoistra, Des arts marins susciteront la pluye:
Vrabiq goulfre, grande classe parfondra,
Vn monstre en Saxe naistra d'ours & truye.

By night the Rainbow will appear for Nantes, By marine arts they will stir up
rain:
In the Gulf of Arabia a great fleet will plunge to the bottom, In Saxony a monster
will be born of a bear and a sow.

XLV.

Le gouuerneur du regne bien s&cced;auant, Ne consentir voulant au faict Royal:
Mellile classe par le contraire vent
Le remettra à son plus desloyal.

The very learned governor of the realm, Not wishing to consent to the royal
deed: The fleet at Melilla through contrary wind Will deliver him to his most
disloyal one.

XLVI.

Vn iuste sera en exil renuoyé,
Par pestilence aux confins de Nonseggle, Response au rouge le fera desuoyé, Roy retirant à la Rame & à l'Aigle.

A just one will be sent back again into exile, Through pestilence to the confines of "Nonseggle," His reply to the red one will cause him to be misled, The King withdrawing to the Frog and the Eagle.

XLVII.

Entre deux monts les deux grands assemblez.
Delaisseront leur simulté secrette: Brucelle & Dolle par Langres accablez, Pour à Malignes executeur leur peste.

The two great ones assembled between two mountains Will abandon their secret quarrel:
Brussels and Dôle overcome by Langres, To execute their plague at Malines.

XLVIII.

La saincteté trop feinte & seductiue, Accompagné d'vne langue diserre: La cité vieille, & Parme trop hastiue,
Florence & Sienne, rendront plus desertes.

The too false and seductive sanctity, Accompanied by an eloquent tongue: The old city, and Parma too premature,
Florence and Siena they will render more desert.

XLIX.

De la partie de Mammer grand Pontife, Subiuguera les confins du Danube:
Chasser la croix, par fer raffé ne riffe, Captifs, or, bague plus de cent mille rubes.

The great Pontiff of the party of Mars Will subjugate the confines of the Danube:

The cross to pursue, through sword hook or crook, Captives, gold, jewels more than one hundred thousand rubies.

L.

Dedans le puys seront trouuez les os, Sera l'inceste, commis par la maratre: L'estat changé, on querra bruit & los, Et aura Mars atrendant pour son astre.

Within the pit will be found the bones, Incest will be commited by the stepmoth-
er:
The state changed, they will demand fame and praise, And they will have Mars attending as their star.

LI.

Peuple assemblé, voir nouueau expectacle. Princes & Roys par plusieurs assis-
tans, Pilliers faillir, murs: mais comme miracle Le Roy sauué & trente des instans.

People assembled to see a new spectacle, Princes and Kings amongst many by-
standers, Pillars walls to fall: but as by a miracle
The King saved and thirty of the ones present.

LII.

En lieu du grand qui sera condamné, De prison hors, son amy en sa place:
L'espoir Troyen en six mois ioins, mort né, Le Sol à l'vrne seront peins fleuue en glace.

In place of the great one who will be condemned, Outside the prison, his friend in his place:
The Trojan hope in six months joined, born dead, The Sun in the urn rivers will be frozen.

LIII.

Le grand Prelat Celtique à Roy suspect, De nuict par cours sortira hors de regne:
Par Duc fertile à son grand Roy Bretaine, Bisance à Cypres & Tunes insuspect.

The great Celtic Prelate suspected by the King, By night in flight he will leave the
realm: Through a Duke fruitful for his great British King, Byzantium to Cyprus
and Tunis unsuspected.

LIV.

Au poinct du iour au second chant du coq, Ceux de Tunes, de Fez, & de Bugie,
Par les Arabes, captif le Roy Maroq, L'an mil six cens & sept, de Liturgie.

At daybreak at the second crowing of the cock, Those of Tunis, of Fez and of
Bougie,
By the Arabs the King of Morocco captured, The year sixteen hundred and sev-
en, of the Liturgy.

LV.

Au chalmé Duc en arrachant l'esponce, Voile Arabesque voir, subit descouuerte:
Tripolis, Chio, & ceux de Trapesconce, Duc prins, Marnegro & la cité deserté.

By the appeased Duke in drawing up the contract, Arabesque sail seen, sudden
discovery: Tripolis, Chios, and those of Trebizond,
Duke captured, the Black Sea and the city a desert.

LVI.

La crainte armee de l'ennemy Narbon Effrayera si fort les Hesperidues: Parpignan vuide par l'aueugle d'arbon, Lors Barcelon par mer donra les piques.

The dreaded army of the Narbonne enemy Will frighten very greatly the "Hes-
perians":
Perpignan empty through the blind one of Arbon, Then Barcelona by sea will
take up the quarrel.

LVII.

Celui qu'estoit bien auant dans le regne, Ayant chef rouge proche à hierarchie,
Aspre & cruel, & se fera tant craindre, Succedera à sacré monarchie.

He who was well forward in the realm, Having a red chief close to the hierarchy,
Harsh and cruel, and he will make himself much feared, He will succeed to the sacred monarchy.

LVIII.

Entre les deux monarques esloignez, Lors que le Sol par Selin clair perduë, Simulté grande entre deux indignez, Qu'aux Isles & Sienne la liberte renduë.

Between the two distant monarchs, When the clear Sun is lost through "Selin":
Great enmity between two indignant ones,
So that liberty is restored to the Isles and Siena.

LIX.

Dame en fureur par rage d'adultere, Viendra à son Prince coniurer non de dire:
Mars bref cogneu sera la vitupere,
Que seront mis dixsept à martyre.

The Lady in fury through rage of adultery, She will come to conspire not to tell
her Prince:
But soon will the blame be made known, So that seventeen will be put to martyrdom.

LX.

Le Prince hors de son terroir Celtique Sera trahy, deceu par interprete:
Roüant, Rochelle par ceux de l'Armorique Au port de Blaue deceus par moyne
& prestre.

The Prince outside his Celtic land

Will be betrayed, deceived by the interpreter: Rouen, La Rochelle through those
of Brittany
At the port of Blaye deceived by monk and priest.

LXI.

Le grand tappis plié ne monstrera, Fors qu'à demy la pluspart de l'histoire: Chassé du regne loing aspre apparoistra,
Qu'au faict bellique chacun le viendra croire.

The great carpet folded will not show But by halved the greatest part of history:
Driven far out of the realm he will appear harsh,
So that everyone will come to believe in his warlike deed.

LXII.

Trop tard tous deux les fleurs seront perdues, Contre la loy serpent ne voudra
faire:
Des ligueurs forces par gallots confondues, Sauone, Albingue par monech grand
martyre.

Too late both the flowers will be lost,
The serpent will not want to act against the law: The forces of the Leaguers con-
founded by the French, Savona, Albenga through Monaco great martyrdom.

LXIII.

La dame seule au regne demeuree.
D'vnic esteint premier au lict d'honneur: Sept ans sera de douleur exploree,
Puis longue vie au regne par grand, heur.

The lady left alone in the realm
By the unique one extinmguished first on the bed of honor: Seven years will she
be weeping in grief,
Then with great good fortune for the realm long life.

LXIV.

On ne tiendra pache aucune arresté, Tous receuans iront par tromperie:
De paix & trefue, & terre & mer protesté. Par barcelone classe prins d'industrie.

No peace agreed upon will be kept, All the subscribers will act with deceit:
In peace and truce, land and sea in protest, By Barcelona fleet seized with inge-
nuity.

LXV.

Gris & bureau demie ouuerte guerre, De nuict seront assaillis & pillez: Le bureau
prins passera par la serre,
Son temple ouuert, deux au plastre grillez.

Gray and brown in half-opened war,
By night they will be assaulted and pillaged: The brown captured will pass
through the lock, His temple opened, two slipped in the plaster.

LXVI.

Au fondement de la nouuelle secte, Seront les os du grand Romain trouuez,
Sepulchre en marbre apparoistra couuerte, Terre trembler en Auril, mal enfoüetz.

At the foundation of the new sect,
The bones of the great Roman will be found, A sepulchre covered by marble will
appear, Earth to quake in April poorly buried.

LXVII.

Au grand Empire paruiendra tout vn autre, Bonté distant plus de felicité:
Regi par vn issu non loing du peautre, Corruer regnes grande infelicité.

Quite another one will attain to the great Empire, Kindness distant more so happiness:
Ruled by one sprung not far from the brothel, Realms to decay great bad luck.

LXVIII.

Lors que soldats fureur seditieuse.
Contre leur chef feront de nuict fer luire: Ennemy d'Albe soit par main furieuse,
Lors vexer, Rome, & principaux seduire.

When the soldiers in a seditious fury
Will cause steel to flash by night against their chief: The enemy Alba acts with furious hand,
Then to vex Rome and seduce the principal ones.

LXIX.

La pitié grande sera sans loing tarder, Ceux qui dônoyent seront contraints de prêdre:
Nuds Affamez de froid, soif, soy bander, Les monts passer commettant grand esclandre.

The great pity will occur before long, Those who gave will be obliged to take:
Naked, starving, withstanding cold and thirst,
To pass over the mountains commiting a great scandal.

LXX.

Au chef du monde le grand Chyren sera, Plus outre apres ayme, criant, redouté:
Son bruit & los les cieux surpassera,
Et du seul tiltre victeur fort contenté.

Chief of the world will the great "Chyren" be, Plus Ultra behind, loved, feared, dreaded:
His fame and praise will go beyond the heavens, And with the sole title of Victor will he be quite satisfied.

LXXI.

Quand on viendra le grand Roy parenter Auant qu'il ait du tout l'ame rendue:
Celuy qui moins le viendra lamenrer,
Par Lyons, aigles, croix couronne venduë.

When they will come to give the last rites to the great King Before he has entirely
given up the ghost:
He who will come to grieve over him the least, Through Lions, Eagles, cross
crown sold.

LXXII.

Par fureur feinte d'esmotion diuine, Sera la femme du grand fort violee: Iuges
voulans damner telle doctrine, Victime au peuple ignorant immolee.

Through feigned fury of divine emotion The wife of the great one will be violated:
The judges wishing to condemn such a doctrine, She is sacrificed a victim to the
ignorant people.

LXXIII.

En cité grande vn moyne & artisan, Pres de la porte logez & aux murailles, Contre Moderne secret, caue disant
Trahis pour faire sous couleur d'espousailles.

In a great city a monk and artisan, Lodged near the gate and walls,
Secret speaking emptily against Modena, Betrayed for acting under the guise of
nuptials.

LXXIV.

La dechassee au regne tournera, Ses ennemis trouuez des coniurez:
Plus que iamais son temps triomphera, Trois & septante à mort trop asseurez.

She chased out will return to the realm, Her enemies found to be conspirators:
More than ever her time will triumph, Three and seventy to death very sure.

LXXV.

Le grand pillot par Roy sera mandé, Laisser la classe pour plus haut lieu atteindre:
Sept ans apres sera contrebandé, Barbare armee viendra Venise craindre.

The great Pilot will be commissioned by the King, To leave the fleet to fill a higher post:
Seven years after he will be in rebellion, Venice will come to fear the Barbarian army.

LXXVI.

La cité antique d'antenoree forge, Plus ne pouuant le tyran supporter
Le manche feinct au temple couper gorge, Les siens le peuple à mort viendra bouter.

The ancient city the creation of Antenor, Being no longer ablke to bear the tyrant:
The feigned handle in the temple to cut a throat, The people will come to put his followers to death.

LXXVII.

Par la victoire du deceu fraudulente, Deux classes vne, la reuolte Germanie, Le chef meurtry & son fils dans la tente,
Florence, Imole pourchassez dans Romaine.

Through the fraudulent victory of the deceived, Two fleets one, German revolt:
The chief murdered and his son in the tent, Florence and Imola pursued into "Romania".

LXXVIII.

Crier victoire du grand Selin croissant: Par les Romains sera l'Aigle clamé, Tiecin Millan et Genes y consent,
Puis par eux mesmes Basil grand reclamé.

To proclaim the victory of the great expanding "Selin:" By the Romans will the Eagle be demanded,
Pavia, Milan and Genoa will not consent thereto, Then by themselves the great Lord claimed.

LXXIX.

Pres de Tesin les habitans de Loire, Garonne, Saone, Saine, Tain & Gironde,
Outre les monts dresseront promontoire. Conflict donné Par granci, sumerge onde.

Near the Ticino the inhabitants of the Loire, Garonne and Saône, the Seine, the Tain and Gironde: They will erect a promontory beyond the mountains, Conflict given, Po enlarged, submerged in the wave.

LXXX.

De Fez le regne paruiendra à ceux d'Europe, Feu leur cité & l'anne tranchera.
Le grand d'Asie terre & mer à grand troupe, Que bleux, peres, croix, à mort dechassera.

From Fez the realm will reach those of Europe, Their city ablaze and the blade will cut:
The great one of Asia by land and sea with great troop, So that blues and perses the cross will pursue to death.

LXXXI.

Pleurs cris & plaints heurlemens, effrayeur, Coeur inhumain, cruel, Roy & tran-
sy.
Leman les Isles, de Gennes les maieurs, Sang espacher, fromfaim à nul mercy.

Tears, cries and laments, howls, terror, Heart inhuman, cruel, black and chilly:
Lake of Geneva the Isles, of Genoa the notables, Blood to pour out, wheat famine
to none mercy.

LXXXII.

Par les deserts de lieu libre & farouche, Viendra errer nepueu du grand Pontife:
Assommé à sept auecques lourde souche, Par ceux qu'apres occuperont le Cyphe.

Through the deserts of the free and wild place, The nephew of the great Pontiff
will come to wander:
Felled by seven with a heavy club,
By those who afterwards will occupy the Chalice.

LXXXIII.

Celuy qu'aura tant d'honneur & caresse.
A son entree de la Gaule Belgique. Vn temps apres sera tant de rudesses, Et sera
contre à la fleur tant bellique.

He who will have so much honor and flattery At his entry into Belgian Gaul:
A while after he will act very rudely,
And he will act very warlike against the flower.

LXXXIV.

Celuy qu'en Sparte Claude ne peut regner, Il fera tant par voye seductiue:
Que du court, long, le fera araigner, Que contre Roy fera sa perspectiue.

The Lame One, he who lame could not reign in Sparta, He will do much through

seductive means:
So that by the short and long, he will be accused Of making his perspective against the King.

LXXXV.

La grand'cité de Tharse par Gaulois. Sera destruite, captifs tous à Turban: Secours par mer au grand Portugalois, Premier d'esté le iour du sacre Vrban.

The great city of Tarsus by the Gauls Will be destroyed, all of the Turban captives:
Help by sea from the great one of Portugal,
First day of summer Urban's consecration.

LXXXVI.

Le grand Prelat vn iour apres son songe, Interpreté au rebours de son sens:
De la Gascogne luy suruiendra vn monge, Qui fera eslire le grand prelat de Sens.

The great Prelate one day after his dream, Interpreted opposite to its meaning:
From Gascony a monk will come unexpectedly,
One who will cause the great prelate of Sens to be elected.

LXXXVII.

L'election faicte dans Frankfort, N'aura nul lieu, Milan s'opposera:
Le sien plus proche semblera si grand fort, Qu'outre le Rhin és mareschs cassera.

The election made in Frankfort Will be voided, Milan will be opposed:
The follower closer will seem so very strong
That he will drive him out into the marshes beyond the Rhine.

LXXXVIII.

Vn regne grand demourra desolé, Aupres de l'Hebro se feront assemblees: Monts Pyrenees le rendront consolé,
Lors que dans May seront terres tremblees.

A great realm will be left desolated, Near the Ebro an assembly will be formed:
The Pyrenees mountains will console him,
When in May lands will be trembling.

LXXXIX.

Entre deux cymbes pieds & mains attachez, De miel face oingt, & de laict sub-stanté, Guespes & mouchez, fitine amour fachez Poccilateur faucer, Cyphe tenté.

Feet and hands bound between two boats, Face anointed with honey, and sus-tained with milk:
Wasps and flies, paternal love vexed, Cup-bearer to falsify, Chalice tried.

XC.

L'honnissement puant abominable Apres le faict sera felicité
Grand excuse pour n'estre fauorable, Qu'à paix Neptune ne sera incité.

The stinking abominable disgrace, After the deed he will be congratulated: The great excuse for not being favorable,
That Neptune will not be persuaded to peace.

XCI.

Du conducteur de la guerre nauale, Rouge effrené, suere, horrible grippe, Captif eschappé de l'aisné dans la baste: Quand il naistra du grand vn fils Agrippé.

Of the leader of the naval war,
Red one unbridled, severe, horrible whim, Captive escaped from the elder one in the bale,
When there will be born a sone to the great Agrippa.

XCII.

Prince de beauté tant venuste,
Au chef menee, le second faict trahy. La cité au glaiue de poudre, face aduste, Par
trop grand meurtre le chef du Roy hay.

Prince of beauty so comely,
Around his head a plot, the second deed betrayed: The city to the sword in dust
the face burnt,
Through too great murder the head of the King hated.

XCIII.

Prelat autre d'ambition trompé, Rien ne sera que trop viendra cuider:
Ses messagers & luy bien attrapé, Tout au rebours voit qui les bois fendroit.

The greedy prelate deceived by ambition,
He will come to reckong nothing too much for him: He and his messengers
completely trapped,
He who cut the wood sees all in reverse.

XCIV.

Vn Roy iré sera aux sedifragues, Quand interdicts feront harnois de guerre: La
poison taincte au succre par les fragues Par eaux meurtris, morts, disant serre
serre.

A King will be angry with the see-breakers, When arms of war will be prohibited:
The poison tainted in the sugar for the strawberries, Murdered by waters, dead,
saying land, land.

XCV.

Par detracteur calomnie à puis nay, Quand istront faicts enormes & martiaux: La
moindre part dubieuse à l'aisnay,
Et tost au regne seront faicts partiaux.

Calumny against the cadet by the detractor, When enormous and warlike deeds
will take place:
The least part doubtful for the elder one,
And soon in the realm there will be partisan deeds.

XCVI.

Grande cité à soldats abandonnee, On n'y eu mortel tumult si proche:
O qu'elle hideuse mortalité s'approche, Fors vne offence n'y sera pardonnee.

Great city abandoned to the soldiers, Never was mortal tumult so close to it: Oh,
what a hideous calamity draws near,
Except one offense nothing will be spared it.

XCVII.

Cinq & quarante degrez ciel bruslera Feu approcher de la grand cité neuue Instant grand flamme esparse sautera
Quand on voudra des Normans faire preuue.

At forty-five degrees the sky will burn, Fire to approach the great new city:
In an instant a great scattered flame will leap up, When one will want to demand
proof of the Normans.

XCVIII.

Ruyné aux Volsques de peur si fort terribles Leur grand cité taincte, faict pestilent: Piller Sol, Lune & violer leurs temples:
Et les deux fleuues rougir de sang coulant.

Ruin for the Volcae so very terrible with fear, Their great city stained, pestilential
deed:
To plunder Sun and Moon and to violate their temples: And to redden the two
rivers flowing with blood.

XCIX.

L'ennemy docte se trouuera confus.
Grand camp malade, & defaict par embusches, Môts Pyrenees & Poenus luy serôt faicts refus, Proche du fleuue descouurant antiques roches.

The learned enemy will find himself confused, His great army sick, and defeated by ambushes,
The Pyrenees and Pennine Alps will be denied him, Discovering near the river ancient jugs.

LEGIS CANTIO CONTRA INEPTOS CRITICOS

Quos legent hosce versus maturè censunto, Profanum vulgus & inscium ne attrectato: Omnesq; Astrologi, Blennis, Barbari procul sunto, Qui aliter facit, is rite sacer esto.

INCANTATION OF THE LAW AGAINST INEPT CRITICS

Let those who read this verse consider it profoundly, Let the profane and the ignorant herd keep away: And far away all Astrologers, Idiots and Barbarians, May he who does otherwise be subject to the sacred rite.

CENTURY VII

I.

L'arc du thresor par Achilles deceu, Aux procrées sceu la quadrangulaire: Au faict
Royal le comment sera sceu, Cors veu pendu au veu du populaire.

The arc of the treasure deceived by Achilles, the quadrangule known to the pro-
creators.
The invention will be known by the Royal deed; a corpse seen hanging in the
sight of the populace.

II.

Par Mars ouvert Arles ne donra guerre. De nuict seront les soldartz estonnés:
Noir, blanc à l'inde dissimulés en terre,
Sous la faincte umbre traistres verez & sonnés.

Arles opened up by war will not offer resistance, the soldiers will be astonished
by night.
Black and white concealing indigo on land under the false shadow you will see
traitors sounded.

III.

Apres de France la victoire navale, Les Barchinons, Saillinons, les Phocens,
Lierre d'or, l'enclume serré dedans la basle,
Ceux de Ptolon au fraud seront consens.

After the naval victory of France,
the people of Barcelona the Saillinons and those of Marseilles; the robber of gold,
the anvil enclosed in the the ball,
the people of Ptolon will be party to the fraud.

IV.

Le duc de Langres assiegé dedans Dolle, Accompaigné d'Ostun & Lyonnais:
Geneve, Auspour, joinct ceux de Mirandole, Passer les monts contre les Ancon-
nois.

The Duke of Langres besieged at Dôle accompanied by people from Autun and
Lyons. Geneva, Augsburg allied to those of Mirandola,
to cross the mountains against the people of Ancona.

V.

Vin sur la table en sera respandu Le tiers n'aura celle qu'il pretendoit: Deux fois
du noir de Parme descendu,
Perouse à Pize fera ce qu'il cuidoit.

Some of the wine on the table will be spilt, the third will not have that which he
claimed. Twice descended from the black one of Parma, Perouse will do to Pisa
that which he believed.

VI.

Naples, Palerme, & toute la Secille, Par main barbare sera inhabitee,
Corsique, Salerne & de Sardeigne l'isle, Faim, peste, guerre fin de maux intemp-
tee.

Naples, Palerma and all of Sicily
will be uninhabited through Barbarian hands. Corsica, Salerno and the island of
Sardinia, hunger, plague, war the end of extended evils.

VII.

Sur le combat des grans cheveux, legiers, On criera le grand croissant confond.
De nuict tuer monts, habits de bergiers, Abismes rouges dans le fossé profond.

Upon the struggle of the great light horses,

it will be claimed that the great crescent is destroyed.
To kill by night, in the mountains,
dressed in shephers' clothing, red gulfs in the deep ditch.

VIII.

Flora fuis, fuis le plus proche Romain, Au Fesulan sera conflict donné:
Sang espandu les plus grands prins à main, Tample ne sexe ne sera pardonné.

Florense, flee, flee the nearest Roman, at Fiesole will be conflict given:
blood shed, the greatest one take by the hand, neither tample nor sex will be
pardoned.

IX.

Dame à l'absence de son grand capitaine, Sera priee d'amours du Viceroi,
Faincte promesse & malheureuse estraine, Entre les mains du grand Prince Bar-
rois.

The lady in the absence of her great master will be begged for love by the Viceroy.
Feigned promise and misfortune in love, in the hands of the great Prince of Bar.

X.

Par le grand Prince limitrophe du Mans Preux & vaillant chef de grand excercite:
Par mer & terre de Gallotz & Normans, Caspre passer Barcelone pillé isle.

By the great Prince bordering le Mans, brave and valliant leader of the great
army; by land and sea with Bretons and Normans,
to pass Gibraltar and Barcelona to pillage the island.

XI.

L'enfant Royal contemnera la mere, Oeil, piedz blessés, rude, inobeissant, Nouvelle à dame estrange & bien amere, Seront tués des siens plus de cinq cens.

The royal child will scorn his mother, eye, feet wounded rude disobedient;
strange and very bitter news to the lady;
more than five hundred of here people will be killed.

XII.

Le grand puisné fera fin de la guerre, Aux dieux assemble les excusés: Cahors, Moissac iront long de la serre, Reffus Lestore, les Agenois razés.

The great younger son will make an end of the war, he assembles the pardoned
before the gods;
Ahors and Moissac will go far from the prison, a refusal at Lectoure, the people
of Agen shaved.

XIII.

De la cité marine & tributaire, La teste raze prendra la satrapie: Chasser sordide qui puis sera contraire Par quatorze ans tiendra la tyrannie.

From the marine tributary city,
the shaven head will take up the satrapy;
to chase the sordid man who will the be against him.
For fourteen years he will hold the tyranny.

XIV.

Faux esposer viendra topographie, Seront les cruches des monuments ouvertes: Pulluler secte saincte philosophie, Pour blanches, noirs, & pour antiques verts.

He will come to expose the false topography, the urns of the tombs will be
opened.

Sect and holy philosophy to thrive, black for white and the new for the old.

XV.

Devant cité de l'Insubre contree, Sept and sera le siege devant mis: Le tres grand
Roi y fera son entree, Cité puis libre hors de ses ennemis.

Before the vity of the Insubrain lands, for seven years the siege will be laid; a very
great king enters it,
the city is then free, away from its enemies.

XVI.

Entrée profonde par la grand Roine faicte Rendra le lieu puissant inaccessible:
L'armee des trois lions sera deffaite, Faisant dedans cas hideux & terrible.

The deep entry made by the great Queen will make the place powerful and inaccessible;
the army of the three lions will be defeated causing within a thing hideous and
terrible.

XVII.

Le prince rare de pitié & clemence, Viendra changer par mort grand cognois-
sance:
Par grand repos le regne travaillé, Lors que le grand tost sera estrillé.

The prince who has little pity of mercy
will come through death to change (and become) very knowledgeable.
The kingdom will be attended with great tranquillity, when the great one will
soon be fleeced.

XVIII.

Les assiegés coulouleront leur paches, Sept jours apres feront cruelle issue
Dans repoulsés feu, sang. Sept mis à l'hache Dame captive qu'avoit la paix tissue

The besieged will colour their pacts,
but seven days later they will make a cruel exit: thrown back inside, fire and
blood, seven put to the axe the lady who had woven the peace is a captive.

XIX.

Le fort Nicene ne sera combatu, Vaincu sera par rutilant metal
Son faict sera un long temps debatu, Aux citadins estrange espouvantal.

The fort at Nice will not engage in combat, it will be overcome by shining metal.
This deed will be debated for a long time, strange and fearful for the citizens.

XX.

Ambassadeurs de la Toscane langue, Avril & Mai Alpes & mer passer: Celui de
veay exposera l'harangue, Vie Gauloise ne venant effacer.

Ambassadors of the Tuscan language
will cross the Alps and the sea in April and May.
The man of the calf will deliver an oration, not coming to wipe out the French
way of life.

XXI.

Par pestilente inimitié Volsicque, Dissimulee chassera le tyran:
Au pont de Sorgues se fera la traffique, De mettre à mort lui & son adherent.

By the pestilential enmity of Languedoc, the tyrant dissimulated will be driven
out.
The bargain will be made on the bridge at Sorgues to put to death both him and
his follower

182

Century VII

XXII.

Les citoyens de Mesopotamie, Yrés encontre amis de Tarraconne,
Jeux, ritz, banquetz, toute gent endormie Vicaire au Rosne, prins cité, ceux d'Ausone.

The citizens of Mesopotamia angry with their friends from Tarraconne;
games, rites, banquets, every person asleep,
the vicar at Rhône, the city taken and those of Ausonia.

XXIII.

Le Royal sceptre sera constrainct de prendre, Ce que ses predecesseurs avoient
engaigé: Puis que l'aneau on fera mal entendre,
Lors qu'on viendra le palais saccager.

The Royal sceptre will be forced to take that which his predecessors had pledged.
Because they do not understand about the ring when they come to sack the
palace.

XXIV.

L'enseveli sortira du tombeau, Fera de chaines lier le fort du pont: Empoisonné
avec oeufz de Barbeau,
Grand de Lorraine par le Marquis du Pont.

He who was buried will come out of the tomb,
he will make the strong one out of the bridge to be bound with chains.
Poisoned with the roe of a barbel,
the great one from Lorraine by the Marquis du Pont.

XXV.

Par guerre longue tout l'exercite expuiser, Que pour souldartz ne trouveront pe-
cune: Lieu d'or d'argent, cuir on viendra cuser, Gualois aerain, signe croissant de
Lune.

Through long war all the army exhausted, so that they do not find money for the
soldiers;
instead of gold or silver, they will come to coin leather, Gallic brass, and the
crescent sign of the Moon.

XXVI.

Fustes & galees autour de sept navires, Sera livree une mortelle guerre:
Chef de Madric recevra coup de vivres, Deux eschapeer & cinq menees à terre.

Foists and galleys around seven ships, a mortal war will be let loose.
The leader from Madrid will receive a wound from arrows, two escaped and five
brought to land.

XXVII.

Au cainct de Vast la grand cavalerie, Proche à Ferrage empeschee au bagaige:
Pompt à Turin feront tel volerie,
Que dans le fort raviront leur hostaige.

At the wall of Vasto the great cavalry are impeded by the baggage near Ferrara.
At Turin they will speedily commit such robbery that in the fort they will ravish
their hostage.

XXVIII.

Le capitaine conduira grande proie, Sur la montaigne des ennemis plus proche,
Environné, par feu fera tel voie, Tous eschappez or trente mis en broche.

The captain will lead a great herd on the mountain closest to the enemy.
Surrounded by fire he makes such a way, all escape except for thirty put on the
spit.

XXIX.

Le grand Duc d'Albe se viendra rebeller A ses grans peres fera le tradiment:
Le grand de Guise le viendra debeller, Captif mené & dressé monument.

The great one of Alba will come to rebel, he will betray his great forebears.
The great man of Guise will come to vanquish him, led captive with a monument
erected.

XXX.

Le sac s'approche, feu, grand sang espandu Po, grand fleuves, aux bouviers l'entreprinse, De Gennes, Nice, apres long attendu, Foussan, Turin, à Savillon la
prinse.

The sack approaches, fire and great bloodshed. Po the great rivers, the enterprise
for the clowns; after a long wait from Genoa and Nice,
Fossano, Turin the capture at Savigliano.

XXXI.

De Languedoc, & Guienne plus de dix, Mille voudront les Alpes repasser:
Grans Allobroges marcher contre Brundis Aquin & Bresse les viendront recasser.

From Languedoc and Guienne more than ten thousand will want to cross the
Alps again. The great Savoyards march against Brindisi,
Aquino and Bresse will come to drive them back.

XXXII.

Du mont Royal naistra d'une casane, Qui cave, & compte viendra tyranniser
Dresser copie de la marche MIllane, Favene, Florence d'or & gens espuiser.

From the bank of Montereale will be born one who bores and calculates becom-
ing a tyrant. To raise a force in the marches of Milan,
to drain Faenza and Florence of gold and men

XXXIII.

Par frause regne, forces expolier, La classe obsesse, passages à l'espie: Deux
fainctz amis se viendront rallier, Esveiller haine de long temps assoupie.

The kingdom stripped of its forces by fraud, the fleet blockaded, passages for the
spy; two false friends will come to rally
to awaken hatred for a long time dormant.

XXXIV.

En grand regret sera la gent Gauloise Coeur vain, legier croirera temerité: Pain,
sel, ne vin, eaue : venin ne cervoise Plus grand captif, faim, froit, necessité.

The French nation will be in great grief,
vain and lighthearted, they will believe rash things.
No bread, salt, wine nor water, venom nor ale, the greater one captured, hunger,
cold and want.

XXXV.

La grand pesche viendra plaindre, plorer D'avoir esleu, trompés seront en l'aage:
Guiere avec eux ne voudra demourer, De&cced;ue sera par ceux de son langaige.

The great fish will come to complain and weep for having chosen, deceived concerning his age: he will hardly want to remain with them,
he will be deceived by those (speaking) his own tongue.

XXXVI.

Dieu, le ciel tout le divin verbe à l'unde, Porté par rouger sept razes à Bisance:
Contre les oingz trois cens de Trebisconde,
Deux loix mettront, & l'horreur, puis credence.

God, the heavens, all the divine words in the waves, carried by seven red-shaven
heads to Byzantium: against the anointed three hundred from Trebizond, will
make two laws, first horror then trust.

XXXVII.

Dix emvoyés, ched de nef mettre à mort, D'un adverti, en classe guerre ouverte:
Confusion chef, l'un se picque & mord, Lerin, stecades nefz cap dedans la nerte.

Ten sent to put the captain of the ship to death, are altered by one that there is
open revolt in the fleet.
Confusion, the leader and another stab and bite each other at Lerins and the
Hyerès, ships, prow into the darkness.

XXXVIII.

L'aisné Royal sur coursier voltigeant, Picquer viendra si rudement courir:
Gueulle, lipee, pied dans l'estrein pleignant Trainé, tiré, horriblement mourir.

The elder royal one on a frisky horse will spur so fiercely that it will bolt.
Mouth, mouthfull, foot complaining in the embrace; dragged, pulled, to die hor-
ribly.

XXXIX.

Le conducteur de l'armeé Fran&cced;oise, Cuidant perdre le principal phalange:
Par sus pave de l'avaigne & d'ardoise,
Soi parfondra par Gennes gent estrange.

The leader of the French army will expect to lose the main phalanx.
Upon the pavement of oatrs and slate
the foreign nation will be undermined through Genoa.

XL.

Dedans tonneaux hors oingz d'huile & gresse, Seront vingt un devant le port
fermés,
Au second guet par mont feront prouesse: Gaigner les portes & du guet assom-
més.

Within casks anointed outside with oil and grease twenty-one will be shut before
the harbour,
at second watch; through death they will do great deeds; to win the gates and be
killed by the watch.

XLI.

Les oz des pieds & des main enserrés, Par bruit maison long temps inhabitee:
Seront par songes concavent deterrés, Maison salubre & sans bruit habitee.

The bones of the feet and the hands locked up, because of the noise the house is
uninhabited for a long time.
Digging in dreams they will be unearthed, the house healthy in inhabited without noise.

XLII.

Deux de poison saisiz nouveau venuz, Dans la cuisine du grand Prince verser:
Par le soillard tous deux au faicts cogneuz Prins que cuidoit de mort l'aisné vexer.

Two newly arrived have seized the poison, to pour it in the kitchen of the great
Prince. By the scullion both are caught in the act,
taken he who thought to trouble the elder with death.

CENTURY VIII

I.

PAU, NAY, LORON plus feu qu'à sang sera.
Laude nager, fuir grand au surrez.
Les agassas entree refusera.
Pampon, Durancde les tiendra enferrez.

Pau, Nay, Loron will be more of fire than blood,
to swim in praise, the great one to flee to the confluence (of rivers).
He will refuse entry to the magpies Pampon and the Durance will keep them
confined.

II.

Condon & Aux & autour de Mirande Je voi du ciel feu qui les environne.
Sol Mars conjoint au Lion puis marmande Fouldre, grand gresle, mur tombe
dans Garonne.

Condom and Auch and around Mirande,
I see fire from the sky which encompasses them. Sun and Mars conjoined in Leo,
then at Marmande, lightning, great hail, a wall falls into the Garonne.

III.

Au fort chasteau de Viglanne & Resviers Sera serré le puisnay de Nancy:
Dedans Turin seront ards les premiers, Lors que de dueil Lyon sera transi.

Within the strong castle of Vigilance and Resviers the younger born of Nancy
will be shut up.
In Turin the first ones will be burned, when Lyons will be transported with grief.

IV.

Dedans Monech le coq sera receu, Le Cardinal de France apparoistra Par Loga-
rion Romain sera deceu
Foiblesse à l'aigle, & force au coq naistra.

The cock will be received into Monace, the Cardinal of France will appear;
He will be deceived by the Roman legation; weakness to the eagle, strength will
be born to the cock.

V.

Apparoistra temple luisant orné,
La lampe & cierge à Borne & Bretueil.
Pour la lucerne le canton destorné, Quand on verra le grand coq au cercueil.

There will appear a shining ornate temple, the lamp and the candle at Borne and
Breteuil.
For the canton of Lucerne turned aside, when one will see the great cock in his
shroud.

VI.

Charte fulgure à Lyon apparente Luisant, print Malte subit sera estainte, Sardon,
Mauris traitera decepvante, Geneve à Londes à coq trahison fainte.

Lighting and brightness are seen at Lyons shining, Malta is taken, suddenly it
will be extinguished.
Sardon, Maurice will act deceitfully,
Geneva to London, feigning treason towards the cock.

VII.

Verceil, Milan donra intelligence, Dedans Tycin sera faite la paye.
Courir par Siene eau, sang, feu par Florence. Unique choir d'hault en bas faisant
maie.

Vercelli, Milan will give the news, the wound will be given at Pavia.
To run in the Seine, water, blood and fire through Florence, the unique one falling from high to low calling for help.

VIII.

Pres de Linterne dans de tonnes fermez, Chivaz fera poir l'aigle la menee, L'esleu
cassé lui ses gens enfermez, Dedans Turin rapt espouse emmenee.

Near Focia enclosed in some tuns Chivasso will plot for the eagle.
The elected one driven out, he and his people shut up, rape with Turin, the bride
led away.

IX.

Pendant que l'aigle & le coq à Savone Seront unis Mer Levant & Ongrie,
L'armee à Naples, Palerne, Marque d'Ancone Rome, Venise par BVarb horrible
crie.

While the eagle is united with the cock at Savonna, the Eastern Sea and Hungary.
The army at Naples, Palermo, the marches of Ancona, Rome and Venice a great
outcry by the Barbarian.

X.

Puanteur grande sortira de Lausanne, Qu'on ne seura l'origine du fait,
Lon mettra hors toute le gente loingtaine Feu veu au ciel, peuple estranger deffait.

A great stench will come from Lausanne, but they will not know its origin,
they will put out all people from distant places, fire seen in the sky, a foreign
nation defeated.

XI.

Peuple infini paroistra à Vicence Sans force feu brusler la Basilique
Pres de Lunage deffait grand de Valence, Lors que Venise par more prendra
pique.

A multitude of people will appear at Vicenza without force, fire to burn the Ba-
silica.
Near Lunage the great one of Valenza defeated:
at a time when Venice takes up the quarrel through custom.

XII.

Apparoistra aupres de Buffaloree L'hault & procere entré dedans Milan L'abbé de
Foix avec ceux de saint Morre Feront la forbe abillez en vilan.

He will appear near to Buffalora
the highly born and tall one entered into Milan. The Abbe of Foix with those of
Saint-Meur will cause damage dressed up as serfs.

XIII.

Le croisé frere par amour effrenee Fera par Praytus Bellesophon mourir, Classe à
mil ans la femme forcenee, Beu le breuvage, tous deux apres perir.

The crusader brother through impassioned love will cause Bellerophon to die
through Proetus;
the fleet for a thousand years, the maddened woman, the potion drunk, both of
them then die.

XIV.

Le grand credit d'or, d'argent l'abondance Fera aveugler par libide honneur Sera
cogneu d'adultere l'offense,
Qui parviendra à son grand deshonneur.

The great credit of gold and abundance of silver will cause honour to be blinded by lust;
the offence of the adulterer will become known, which will occur to his great dishonour.

XV.

Vers Aquilon grans efforts par hommasse Presque l'Europe & l'univers vexer,
Les deux eclipse mettra en tel chasse, Et aux Pannons vie & mort renforcer.

Great exertions towards the North by a man-woman to vex Europe and almost all the Universe.
The two eclipses will be put into such a rout
that they will reinforce life or death for the Hungarians.

XVI.

Au lieu que HIERON feit sa nef fabriquer, Si grand deluge sera & si subite,
Qu'on n'aura lieu ne terres s'atacquer L'onde monter Fesulan Olympique.

At the place where HIERON has his ship built, there will be such a great sudden flood,
that one will not have a place nor land to fall upon, the waters mount to the Olympic Fesulan.

XVII.

Les bien aisez subit seront desmis
Par les trois freres le monde mis en trouble, Cité marine saisiront ennemis,
Faim, feu, sang, peste & de tous maux le double.

Those at ease will suddenly be cast down, the world put into trouble by three brothers; their enemies will seize the marine city, hunger, fire, blood, plague, all evils doubled.

XVIII.

De Flora issue de sa mort sera cause, Un temps devant par jeune & vieille bueira,
Par les trois lys luis feront telle pause, Par son fruit sauve comme chair crue
mueire.

The cause of her death will be issued from Florence, one time before drunk by
young and old;
by the three lilies they will give her a great pause. Save through her offspring as
raw meat is dampened.

XIX.

A soubstenir la grand cappe troublee, Pour l'esclaircir les rouges marcheront, De
mort famille sera presque accablee. Les rouges rouges le rouge assomeront.

To support the great troubled Cappe; the reds will march in order to clarify it;
a family will be almost overcome by death, the red, red ones will knock down
the red one.

XX.

Le faux messaige par election fainte Courir par urban rompu pache arreste, Voix
acheptees, de sang chappelle tainte, Et à un autre l'empire contraicte.

The false message about the rigged election to run through the city stopping the
broken pact;
voices bought, chapel stained with blood, the empire contracted to another one.

XXI.

Au port d'Agde trois fustes entreront Portant d'infect non foi & pestilence Passant le pont mil milles embleront, Et le pont rompre à tierce resistance.

Three foists will enter the port of Agde carrying the infection and pestilence, not
the faith.

Passing the bridge they will carry off a million, the bridge is broken by the resistance of a third.

XXII.

Gorsan, Narbonne, par le sel advertir Tucham, la grace Parpignam trahie, La ville rouge n'y vouldra consentir. Par haulte vol drap gris vie faillie.

Coursan, Narbonne through the salt to warn Tuchan, the grace of Perpignan betrayed; the red town will not wish to consent to it, in a high flight, a copy flag and a life ended.

XXIII.

Lettres trouvees de la roine les coffres, Point de subscrit sans aucun nom d'hauteur Par la police seront caché les offres.
Qu'on ne scaura qui sera l'amateur.

Letters are found in the queen's chests, no signature and no name of the author. The ruse will conceal the offers;
so that they do not know who the lover is.

XXIV.

Le lieutenant à l'entree de l'huis, Assommera la grand de Perpignan, En se cuidant saulver à Monpertuis. Sera deceu bastard de Luisgnan.

The lieutenant at the door of the house, will knock down the great man of Perpignag.
Thinking to save himself at Montpertuis, the bastard of Lusignan will be deceived.

XXV.

Coeur de l'amant ouvert d'amour fertive Dans le ruisseau fera ravir la Dame,
Le demi mal contrefera lassive,
Le pere à deux privera corps de l'ame.

The heart of the lover, awakened by furtive love will ravish the lady in the stream.
She will pretend bashfully to be half injured, the father of each will deprive the
body of its soul.

XXVI.

De Caton es trouves en Barcellonne, Mis descouvers lieu retrouvers & ruine,
Le grand qui tient ne tient vouldra Pamplonne.
Par l'abbaye de Montferrat bruine.

The bones of Cato found in Barcelona, placed, discovered, the site found again
and ruined.
The great one who holds, but does not hold, wants Pamplona, drizzle at the abbey of Montserrat.

XXVII.

La voye auxelle l'une sur l'autre forniz Du muy desert hor mis brave & genest
L'escript d'empereur le fenix
Veu en celui ce qu'à nul autre n'est.

The auxiliary way, one arch upon the other,
Le Muy deserted except for the brave one and his genet.
The writing of the Phoenix Emperor, seen by him which is (shown) to no other.

XXVIII.

Les simulacres d'or & argent enflez, Qu'apres le rapt au lac furent gettez
Au desouvert estaincts tous & troublez. Au marbre script prescript intergetez.

The copies of gold and silver inflated, which after the theft were thrown into the lake,
at the discovery that all is exhausted and dissipated by the debt.
All scrips and bonds will be wiped out.

XXIX.

Au quart pillier l'on sacre à Saturne. Par tremblant terre & deluge fendu Soubz l'edifice Saturnin trouvee urne, D'or Capion ravi & puis rendu.

At the fourth pillar which they dedicate to Saturn split by earthquake and by flood;
under Saturn's building an urn is found gold carried off by Caepio and then restored.

XXX.

Dedans Tholoze non loing de Beluzer Faisant un puis long, palais d'espectacle,
Tresor trouvé un chacun ira vexer,
Et en deux locz & pres del vasacle.

In Toulouse, not far from Beluzer making a deep pit a palace of spectacle,
the treasure found will come to vex everyone in two places and near the Basacle.

XXXI.

Premier grand fruit le prince de Perquiere Mais puis viendra bien & cruel malin,
Dedans Venise perdra sa gloire fiere
Et mis à mal par plus joune Celin.

The first great fruit of the prince of Perchiera, then will come a cruel and wicked man.
In Venice he will lose his proud glory, and is led into evil by then younger Selin.

XXXII.

Garde toi roi Gaulois de ton nepveu Qui fera tant que ton unique fils Sera meutri
à Venus faisant voeu,
Accompaigné de nuit que trois & six.

French king, beware of your nephew who will do so much that your only son
will be murdered while making his vows to Venus; accompanied at night by
three and six.

XXXIII.

Le grand naistra de Veronne & Vincence, Qui portera un surnon bien indigne.
Qui à Venise vouldra faire vengeance. Lui mesme prins homme du guet & signe.

The great one who will be born of Verona and Vincenza who carries a very unworthy surname;
he who at Venice will wish to take vengeance, himself taken by a man of the
watch and sign.

XXXIV.

Apres victoire du Lyon au Lyon Sur la montaigne de JURA Secatombe
Delues & brodes septieme million Lyon, Ulme à Mausol mort & tombe.

After the victory of the Lion over the Lion, there will be great slaughter on the
mountain of Jura;
floods and darkcoloured people of the seventh (of a million), Lyons, Ulm at the
mausoleum death and the tomb.

XXXV.

Dedans l'entree de Garonne & Baise Et la forest non loing de Damazan
Du marsaves gelees, puis gresle & bize Dordonnois gelle par erreur de mezan.

At the entrance to Garonne and Baise and the forest not far from Damazan, discoveries of the frozen sea, then hail and north winds. Frost in the Dardonnais through the mistake of the month.

XXXVI.

Sera commis conte oingdre audché De Saulne & sainct Aulbin & Bell'oeuvre Paver de marbre de tours loing espluché Non Bleteram resister & chef d'oeuvre.

It will be committed against the anointed brought from Lons le Saulnier, Saint Aubin and Bell'oeuvre.
To pave with marble taken from distant towers, not to risist Bletteram and his masterpiece.

XXXVII.

La forteresse aupres de la Tamise Cherra par lors le Roi dedans serré, Aupres du pont sera veu en chemise Un devant mort, puis dans le fort barré.

The fortress near the Thames
will fall when the king is locked up inside. He will be seen in his shirt near the bridge,
one facing death then barred inside the fortress.

XXXVIII.

Le Roi de Blois dans Avignon regner Un autre fois le peuple emonopole Dedans le Rhosne par murs fera baigner Jusques à cinq le dernier pres de Nolle.

The King of Blois will reign in Avignon, once again the people covered in blood.
In the Rhône he will make swim
near the wallss up to five, the last one near Nolle.

XXXIX.

Qu'aura esté par prince Bizantin, Sera tollu par prince de Tholoze.
La foi de Foix par le chef Tholentin, Lui faillira ne refusant l'espouse.

He who will have been for the Byzantine prince will be taken away by the prince of Toulouse. The faith of Foix through the leader of Tolentino will fail him, not refusing the bride.

XL.

Le sang du Juste par Taurer la daurade, Pour se venger contre les Saturnins
Au nouveau lac plongeront la marinade.
Puis marcher contre le Albanins.

The blood of the Just for Taur and La Duarade in order to avenge itself against the Saturnines. They will immerse the band in the new lake, then they will march against Alba.

XLI.

Esleu sera Renad ne sonnant mot, Faisant le faint public vivant pain d'orge,
Tyranniser apres tant à un cop,
Mettant à pied des plus grans sus la gorge.

a fox will be elected without speaking one word, appearing saintly in public living on barley bread, afterwards he will suddenly become a tyrant putting his foot on the throats of the greatest men.

XLII.

Par avarice, par force & violence Viendra vexer les siens chiefz d'Orléans, Pres
aint Memire assault & resistance. Mort dans sa tante diront qu'il dort leans.

Through avarice, through force and violence
the chief of Orléans will come to vex his supporters.

Near St. Memire, assault and resistance.
Dead in his tent they will say he is asleep inside.

XLIII.

Par le decide de deux choses bastars Nepveu du sang occupera le regne Dedans
lectoyre seront les coups de dars Nepveu par peur plaire l'enseigne.

Through the fall of two bastard creatures the nephew of the blood will occupy
the throne. Within Lectoure there will be blows of lances,
the nephew through fear will fold up his standard.

XLIV.

Le procreé naturel dogmion,
De sept à neuf du Chemin destorner A roi de longue & ami au mi-hom,
Doit à Navarre fort de PAU prosterner.

The natural offspring off Ogmios will turn off the road from seven to nine. To the
king long friend of the half man,
Navarre must destroy the fort at Pau.

XLV.

La main escharpe & la jambe bandes, Longs puis nay de Calais portera. Au mot
du guet la mort sera tardee
Puis dans le temple à Pasques saignera.

With his hand in a sling and his leg bandaged, the younger brother of Calais will
reach far.
At the word of the watch, the death will be delayed, then he will bleed at Easter
in the Temple.

XLVI.

Pol mensolee mourra trois lieus du Rosne Fuis les deux prochains tarasc detrois:
Cas Mars fera le plus horrible trosne,
De coq & d'aigle de France, freres trois.

Paul the celibate will die three leagues from Rome, the two nearest flee the oppressed monster.
When Mars will take up his horrible throne,
the Cock and the Eagle, France and the three brothers.

XLVII.

Lac Trasmenien portera tesmoignage, Des conjurez serez dedans Perouse, Un despolle contrefera le sage, Truant Tedesque de sterne & minuse.

Lake Trasimene will bear witness
of the conspirators locked up inside Perugia.
A fool will imitate the wise one,
killing the Teutons, destroying and cutting to pieces.

XLVIII.

Saturne en Cancer, Jupiter avec Mars, Dedans Feurier Chaldondon salvaterre.
Sault Castalon affailli de trois pars,
Pres de Verbiesque conflit mortelle guerre.

Saturn in Cancer, Jupiter with Mars in February 'Chaldondon' salva tierra.
Sierra Morena besieged on three sides near Verbiesque, war and mortal conflict.

XLIX.

Saturn: au beuf joue en l'eau, Mars en fleiche, Six de Fevrier mortalité donra,
Ceux de Tardaigne à Briges si grand breche, Qu'à Ponteroso chef Barbarin mourra,

Saturn in Taurus, Jupiter in Aquarius. Mars in Sagittarius, the sixth of February
brings death.
Those of Tardaigne so great a breach at Bruges, that the barbarian chief wilkl die
at Ponteroso.

L.

La pestilence l'entour de Capadille, Un autre faim pres de Sagont s'appreste:
Le chevalier bastard de bon senille, Au grand de Thunes fera trancher la teste.

The plague around Capellades, another famine is near to Sagunto;
the knightly bastard of the good old man will cause the great one of Tunis to lose
his head.

LI.

Le Bizantin faisant oblation, Apres avoir Cordube à soi reprinse: Son chemin
long repos pamplation,
Mer passant proi par la Colongna prinse.

The Byzantine makes an oblation after having taken back Cordoba.
A long rest on his road, the vines cut down, at sea the passing prey captured by
the Pillar.

LII.
Le roi de Blois dans Avignon regner,
D'amboise & seme viendra le long de Lyndre Ongle à Poitiers sainctes aesles
ruiner Devant Boni.

The king of Blois to reign in Avignon, from Amboise and 'Seme' the length of
the Indre:
claws at Poitiers holy wings ruined before Boni. . . .

LIII.

Dedans Bolongne vouldra laves ses fautes, Il ne pourra au temple du soleil,
Il volera faisant choses si haultes En hierarchie n'en fut oncq un pareil.

Within Boulogne he will want to wash away his misdeeds, he cannot at the temple of the Sun.
He will fly away, doing very great things: In the hierarchy he had never an equal.

LIV.

Soubz la colleur du traicte mariage, Fait magnamine par grand Chyren selin.
Quintin, Arras recouvres au voyage D'espaignolz fait second banc macelin.

Under the colour of the mariage treaty, a magnanimous act by the 'Chyren selin':
St. Quintin and Arras recovered on the journey; By the Spanish a second butcher's bench is made.

LV.

Entre deux fleuves se verra enserré, Tonneaux & caques unis à passer outre,
Huict poutz rompus chef à tant enferré, Enfans parfaictz sont jugetez en coultre.

He will find himself shut in between two rivers, casks and barrels joined to cross beyond:
eight bridges broken, their chief run through so many times, perfect children's throats slit by the knife.

LVI.

La bande foible le terra occupera Ceux de hault lieux feront horribles cris, Le
gros troppeau d'estre coin troublera Toute pres D. nebro descouvers les escris.

The weak band will occupy the land, those of high places will make dreadful cries. The large herd of the outer corner troubled,
near Edinburgh it falls discovered by the writings.

LVII.

De soldat simple parviendra en empire, De robe courte parviendra à la longue
Vaillant aux armes en eglise on plus pire
Vexer les prestres comme l'eau fait l'esponge.

From simple soldier he will attain to Empire, from the short robe he will grow
into the long. Brave in arms, much worse towards the Church, he vexes the
priests as water fills a sponge.

LVIII.

Regne en querelle aux freres divisé, Prendre les armes & le nom Britannique Tiltre Anglican sera guard advisé, Surprins de nuict mener à l'air Gallique.

A kingdom divided by two quarrelling brothers to take the arms and the name
of Britain.
The Anglican title will be advised to watch out, surprised by night (the other is
), led to the French air.

LIX.

Par deux fois hault, par deux fois mis à bas L'orient aussie l'occident faiblira
Son adversaire apres plusiers combats, Par mer chassé au besoin faillira.

Twice put up and twice cast down, the East will also weaken the West. Its adversary after several battles chased by sea will fail at time of need.

LX.

Premier en Gaule, premier en Romanie Par mer & terre aux Anglois & Paris
Merveilleux faitz par celle grand mesnie Violent terax perdra le NORLARIS.

First in Gaul, first in Roumania,
over land and sea against the English and Paris.
Marvellous deeds by that great troop, violent, the wild beast will lose Lorraine.

LXI.

Jamais par le descouvrement du jour Ne parviendra au signe sceptrifere
Que tous ses sieges ne soient en sejour, Portant du coq don du TAG amifere.

Never by the revelation of daylight will he attain the mark of the sceptre bearer.
Until all his sieges are at rest,
bringing to the Cock the gift of the armed legion.

LXII.

Lors qu'on verra expiler le saint temple, Plus grand du rosne leurs sacrez profan-
er: Par eux naistra pestilence si ample.
Roi fuit injuste ne fera condamner.

When one sees the holy temple plundered,
the greatest of the Rhône profaning their sacred things; because of them a very
great pestilence will appear, the king, unjust, will not condemn them.

LXIII.

Quand l'adultere blessé sans coup aura Merdri la femme & le filz par despit,
Ferme assoumee l'enfant estranglera: Huit captifz prins, s'estouffer sans respit.

When the adulterer wounded without a blow will have murdered his wife and
son out of spite; his wife knocked down, he will strangle the child;
eight captives taken, choked beyond help.

LXIV.

Dedans les isles les enfans transportez, Les deux de sept seront en desespoir,
Ceux terrouer en seront supportez, Nom pelle prins des ligues fui l'espoir.

The infants transported into the islands, two out of seven will be in despair.
Those of the soil will be supported by it,
the name 'shovel' taken, the hope of the leagues fails.

LXV.

Le vieux frustré du principal espoir, Il parviendra au chef de son empire:
Vingt mois tiendra le regne à grand pouvoir, Tiran, cruel en delaissant un pire.

The old man disappointed in his main hope, will attain to the leadership of his
Empire.
Twenty months he will hold rule with great force, a tyrant, cruel, giving way to
one worse.

LXVI.

Quand l'escritue D.M. trouvee, En cave antique à lampe descouverte, Loi, Roi, &
Prince Ulpian esprouvee
Pavillon rogne & Duc sous la couvert.

When the inscription D.M. is found in the ancient cave, revealed by a lamp. Law,
the King and Prince Ulpian tried,
the Queen and Duke in the pavilion under cover.

LXVII.

PAR. CAR. NERSAF, à ruine grand discord, Ne l'un ne l'autre aura election,
Nersaf du peuple aura amour & concorde.
Ferrare, Callonne grande protection.

Paris, Carcassone, France to ruin in great disharmony, neither one nor the other
will be elected.
France will have the love and good will of the people, Ferara, Colonna great
protection.

LXVIII.

Vieux Cardinal par le jeune deceu, Hors de sa change se verra desarmé, Arles ne
monstres double soit aperceu, Et Liqueduct & le Prince embausmé.

The old Cardinal is deceived by the young one, he will find himself disarmed, out of his position: Do not show, Arles, that the double is perceived, both Liqueduct and the Prince embalmed.

LXIX.

Aupres du jeune le vieux ange baisser Et le viendra surmonter à la fin:
Dix ans esgaux au plus vieux rabaisser, De trois deux l'un huitiesme seraphin.

Beside the young one the old angel falls, and will come to rise above him at the end;
ten years equal to most the old one falls again, of three two and one, the eighth seraphin.

LXX.

Il entrera vilain, mechant, infame Tyrannisant la Mesopotamie, Tous amis fait d'adulterine d'ame,
Terre horrible, noir de phisonomie.

He will enter, wicked, unpleasant, infamous, tyrannizing over Mesopotamia.
All friends made by the adulterous lady, the land dreadful and black of aspect.

LXXI.

Croistra le nombre si grand des astronomes Chassez, bannis & livres consurez,
L'an mil six cents sept par sacre glomes Que nul aux sacres ne seront asseurez.

The number of astrologers will grow so great,
that they will be driven out, banned and their books censored.
In the year 1607 by sacred assemblies
so that none will be safe from the holy ones.

LXXII.

Champ Perusin d'enorme deffaite Et le conflit tout au pres de Ravenne, Passage
sacre lors qu'on fera la feste,
Vainqueur vaincu cheval manger la venne.

Oh what a huge defeat on the Perugian battlefield and the conflict very close to
Ravenna.
A holy passage when they will celebrate the feast, the conquerer banished to eat
horse meat.

LXXIII.

Soldat barbare le grand Roi frappera, Injustement non esloigné de mort, L'avare
mere du fait cause fera Conjurateur & regne en grand remort.

The king is struck by a barbarian soldier, unjustly, not far from death.
The greedy will be the cause of the deed, conspirator and realm in great remorse.

LXXIV.

En terre neufue bien avant Roi entré Pendant subges lui viendront faire acueil,
Sa perfidie aura tel recontré
Qu'aux citadins lieu de feste & receuil.

A king entered very far into the new land while the subjects will come to bid him
welcome;
his treachery will have such a result
that to the citizens it is a reception instead of a festival.

LXXV.

Le pere & fils seront meurdris ensemble Le prefecteur dedans son pavillon
La mere à Tours du filz ventre aura enfle Criche verdure de failles papillon.

The father and son will be murdered together, the leader within his pavilion.
The mother at Tours will have her belly swollen with a son, a verdure chest with little pieces of paper.

LXXVI.

Plus Macelin que roi en Angleterre Lieu obscure nay par force aura l'empire:
Lasche sans foi, sans loi saignera terre, Son temps approche si presque je soupire.

More of a butcher than a king in England,
born of obscure rank will gain empire through force.
Coward without faith, without law he will bleed the land; His time approaches so close that I sigh.

LXXVII.

L'antechrist trois bien tost anniehilez, Vingt & sept ans sang durera sa guerre. Les heretiques mortz, captifs, exilez.
Sang corps humain eau rougi gresler terre.

The antichrist very soon annihilates the three, twenty-seven years his war will last.
The unbelievers are dead, captive, exiled;
with blood, human bodies, water and red hail covering the earth.

LXXVIII.

Un Bragamus avec la langue torte Viendra des dieux le sanctuaire, Aux heretiques il ouvrira la porte En suscitant l'eglise militaire.

A soldier of fortune with twisted tongue will come to the sanctuary of the gods.
He will open the door to heretics and raise up the Church militant.

LXXIX.

Qui par fer pere perdra nay de Nonnaire, De Gorgon sur la sera sang perfetant
En terre estrange fera si tant de taire, Qui bruslera lui mesme & son enfant.

He who loses his father by the sword, born in a Nunnery, upon this Gorgon's
blood will conceive anew;
in a strange land he will do everything to be silent, he who will burn both himself
and his child.

LXXX.

Des innocens le sang de vefue & vierge.
Tant de maulx faitz par moyen se grand Roge Saintz simulacres tremper en ardent cierge De frayeur crainte ne verra nul que boge.

The blood of innocents, widow and virgin,
so many evils committed by means of the Great Red One, holy images placed
over burning candles,
terrified by fear, none will be seen to move.

LXXXI.

Le neuf empire en desolation Sera changé du pole aquilonaire. De la Sicile viendra l'esmotion
Troubler l'emprise à Philip tributaire.

The new empire in desolation
will be changed from the Northern Pole.
From Sicily will come such troub that
it will bother the enterprise tributary to Philip.

LXXXII.

Ronge long, sec faisant du bon valet, A la parfin n'aura que son congie Poignant
poison & lettres au collet Sera saisi eschappé en dangie.

Thin tall and dry, playing the good valet
in the end will have nothing but his dismissal; sharp poison and letters in his
collar,
he will be seized escaping into danger.

LXXXIII.

Le plus grand voile hors de port de Zara, Pres de Bisance fera son entreprinse,
D'ennemi parte & l'ami ne sera,
Le Tiers à deux fera grand pille & prinse.

The largest sail set out of the port of Zara, near Byzantium will carry out its enterprise.
Loss of enemy and friend will not be,
a third will turn on both with great pillage and capture.

LXXXIV.

Paterne orra de la Sicile crie,
Tous les aprests du Goulphre de Trieste, Qui s'entendra jusque à la Trinacrie Tant
de voiles, fui, fuiz, l'horrible peste.

Paterno will hear the cry from Sicily, all the preparations in the Gulf of Trieste;
it will be heard as far as Sicily
flee oh, flee, so may sails, the dreaded pestilence !

LXXXV.

Entre Bayonne & à Saint Jean de Lux Sera posé de Mars la promottoire
Aux Hanix d'Aduilon Nanar hostera lux, Puis suffocqué au lict sans adjutoire.

Between Bayonne and St.Jean de Luz will be placed the promontory of Mars.
To the Hanix of the North, Nanar will remove the light, then suffocate in bed
without assistance.

LXXXVI.

Par Arani Tholoser ville franque, Bande infini par le mont Adrian,
Passe riviere, Hutin par pont la planque Bayonne entrera tous Bihoro criant.

Through Emani, Tolosa and Villefranche,
an infinite band through the mountains of Adrian. Passes the river, Cambat over
the plank for a bridge, Bayonne will be entered all crying Bigoree.

LXXXVII.

Mort conspiree viendra en plein effect, Charge donnee & voiage de mort, Esleu,
crée, receu par siens deffait.
Sang d'innocence devant foi par remort.

A death conspired will come to its full effect, the charge given and the voyage of
death.
Elected, created, received (then) defeated by its followers, in remorse the blood
of innocence in front of him.

LXXXVIII.

Dans la Sardaigne un noble Roi viendra Que ne tiendra que trois ans le royaume,
Plusieurs couleurs avec soi conjoindra,
Lui mesmes apres soin someil marrit scome.

A noble king will come to Sardinia,
who will only rule for three years in the kingdom.
He will join with himself several colours; he himself, after taunts, care spoils
slumber.

LXXXIX.

Pour ne tumber entre mains de son oncle, Qui ses enfans par regner trucidez.
Orant au peuple mettant pied sur Peloncle Mort & traisné entre chevaulx bardez.

In order not to fall into the hands of his uncle who slaughtered his children in order to reign.
Pleasing with the people, puttin his foot on 'Peloncle', dead and dragged between armoured horses.

XC.

Quand des croisez un trouvé de sens trouble En lieu du sacre verra un boeuf cornu
Par vierge porc son lieu lors sera comble Par roi plus ordre ne sera soustenu.

When those of the cross are found their senses troubled, in place of sacred things he will see a horned bull, through the virgin the pig's place will then be filled, order will no longer be maintained by the king.

XCI.

Frymy les champs des Rodans entrees Ou les croisez seront presque unis,
Les deux brassieres en Pisces rencontrees Et un grand nombre par deluge punis.

Entered among the field of the Rhône (dwellers) where those of the cross are almost united,
the two lands meeting in Pisces
and a great number punished by the flood.

XCII.

Loin hors du regne mis en hazard voyage Grand host duira pour soi l'occupera,
Le roi tiendra les siens captif ostrage
A son retour tout pays pillera.

Far distant from his kingdom, sent on a dangerous journey, he will lead a great
army and keep it for himself.
The king will hold his people captive and hostage, he will plunder the whole
country on his return.

XCIII.

Sept mois sans plus obtiendra prelature Par son deces grand scisme fera naistre:
Sept mois tiendra un autre la preture Pres de Venise paix union renaistre.

For seven months, no longer, will he hold the office of prelate, through his death
a great schism will arise;
for seven months another acts as prelate near Venice, peace and union are reborn.

XCIV.

Devant le lac ou plus cher fut getté De sept mois, & son host desconfit Seront
Hispans par Albanois gastez Par delai perte en donnant le conflict.

In front of the lake where the dearest one was destroyed for seven months and
his army routed;
Spaniards will be devastating by means of Alba, through delay in giving battle,
loss.

XCV.

Le seducteur sera mis en la fosse Et estaché jusques à quelque temps, Le clerc uni
le chef avec sa crosse Picante droite attraira les contens.

The seducer will be placed in a ditch and will be tied up for some time.
The scholar joins the chief with his cross. The sharp right will draw the contented
ones.

XCVI.

La synagogue sterile sans nul fruit Sera receu entre les infideles De Babylon la
fille du porsuit
Misere & triste lui trenchera les aisles.

The sterile synagogue without any fruit, will be received by the infidels,
the daughter of the persecuted (man) of Babylon, miserable and sad, they will
clip her wings.

XCVII.

A fin du VAR changer le pompotans, Pres du rivage les trois beaux enfants naistre.
Ruine ay peuple par aage competans. Regne ay pays changer plus voir croistre.

At the end of the Var the great powers change; near the bank three beautiful
children are born.
Ruin to the people when they are of age;
in the country the kingdom is seen to grow and change more.

XCVIII.

Des gens d'eglise sang fera espandu, Comme de l'eau eu si grand abondance; Et
d'un long temps ne sera restranche Ve, ve au clerc ruine & doleance.

Of the church men the blood will bepoured forth as abundant as water in
(amount);
for a long time it will not be restrained, woe, woe, for the clergy ruin and grief.

XCIX.

Par la puissance des trois rois tempoulz, En autre lieu sera mis le saint siege: Où
la substance & de l'esprit corporel,
Sera remis & receu pour vrai siege.

Through the power of three temporal kings, the sacred seat will be put in another place, where the substance of the body and the spirit will be restored and received as the true seat.

C.

Pour l'abondance de larme respandue Du hault en bas par le bas au plus hault.
Trop grande foir par jeu vie perdue De soif mourir par habondant deffault.

By the great number of tears shed,
from top to bottom and from the bottome to the very top, a life is lost through a game with too much faith,
to die of thirst through a great deficiency.

CENTURY IX

I.

Dans la maison du traducteur de Bourc, Seront les lettres trouuees sur la table, Borgne, roux, blanc, chanu tiendra de cours, Qui changera au nouueau Connestable.

In the house of the translator of Bourg, The letters will be found on the table, One-eyed, red-haired, white, hoary-headed will hold the course, Which will change for the new Constable.

II.

Du haut du mont Auentin voix ouye, Vuydez vuydez de tous les deux costez: Du sang des rouges sera l'ire assomye, D'Arimin Prato, Columna debotez.

From the top of the Aventine hill a voice heard, Be gone, be gone all of you on both sides: The anger will be appeased by the blood of the red ones, From Rimini and Prato, the Colonna expelled.

III.

La magna vaqua à Rauenne grand trouble, Conduicts par quinze enserrez à Fornase: A Rome naistra deux monstres à testes double Sang, feu, deluge, les plus grands à l'espase.

The "great cow" at Racenna in great trouble, Led by fifteen shut up at Fornase: At Rome there will be born two double-headed monsters, Blood, fire, flood, the greatest ones in space.

IV.

L'an ensuyuant découuerts par deluge, Deux chefs esleuz, le premier ne tiendra
De fuyr ombre à l'vn d'eux le refuge, Saccagee case qui premier maintiendra.

The following year discoveries through flood, Two chiefs elected, the first one
will not hold: The refuge for the one of them fleeing a shadow,
The house of which will maintain the first une plundered.

V.

Tiers doigt du pied au premier semblera A vn nouveau monarque de bas haut,
Qui Pyse & Luques Tyran occupera
Du precedent corriger le deffaut.

The third toe will seem first To a new monarch from low high,
He who will possess himself as a Tyrant of Pisa and Lucca, To correct the fault
of his predecessor.

VI.

Par la Guyenne infinité d'Anglois Occuperont par nom d'Anglaquitaine, Du
Languedoc Ispalme Bourdeloys, Qu'ils nommeront apres Barboxitaine.

An infinity of Englishmen in Guienne Will settle under the name of Anglaquitaine:
In Languedoc, "Ispalme," Bordelais, Which they will name after "Barboxitaine."

VII.

Qui ouurira le monument trouué, Et ne viendra le serrer promptement, Mal luy
viendra, & ne pourra prouué
Si mieux doit estre Roy Breton ou Normand.

He who will open the tomb found, And will come to close it promptly,
Evil will come to him, and one will be unable to prove, If it would be better to be
a Breton or Norman King.

VIII.

Puisnay Roy fait son pere mettre à mort, Apres conflict de mort tres-inhon-
neste: Escrit trouué, soup&cced;on donna remort, Quand loup chassé pose sur
la couchette.

The younger son made King will put his father to death, After the conflict ver
dishonest death:
Inscription found, suspicion will bring remore, When the wolf driven out lies
down ion the bedstead.

IX.

Quand lampe ardente de feu inextinguible Sera trouué au temple des Vestales.
Enfant trouué feu, eau passant par crible: Perir eau Nymes, Tholose cheoir les
halles.

When the lamp burning with inextinguishable fire Will be found in the temple
of the Vestals:
Child found in fire, water passing through the sieve: To peish in water Nîmes,
Toulouse the markets to fall.

X.

Moyne moynesse d'enfant mort exposé, Mourir par ourse, & rauy par verrier, Par
Fois & Pamyes le camp sera posé Contre Tholose Carcas dresser forrier.

The child of a monk and nun exposed to death, To die through a she-bear, and
carried off by a boar,
The army will be camped by Foix and Pamiers, Against Toulouse Carcassonne
the harbinger to form.

XI.

Le iuste mort à tort à mort l'on viendra mettre Publiquement du lieu esteint:
Si grande peste en ce lieu viendra naistre, Que les iugeans fuyr seront contraints.

Wrongly will they come to put the just one to death, In public and in the middle extinguished:
So great a pestilence will come to arise in this place, That the judges will be forced to flee.

XII.

Le tant d'argent de Diane & Mercure, Les simulachres au lac seront trouuez: Le figurier cherchant argille neuue Lui & les siens d'or seront abbreuuez.

So much silver of Diana and Mercury, The images will be found in the lake: The sculptor looking for new clay,
He and his followers will be steeped in gold.

XIII.

Les exilez autour de la Soulongne Conduits de nuict pour marcher en Lauxois, Deux de Modenne truculent de Bolongne, Mis decouuerts par feu de Buran&cced;ois.

The exiles around Sologne, Led by night to march into Auxois, Two of Modena for Bologna cruel,
Placed discovered by the fire of Buzan&cced;ais.

XIV.

Mis en planure chauderons d'infecteurs, Vin, miel & huyle & bastis sur four-neauxs Seront plongez, sans mal dit malfacteurs Sept fum extaint au canon des bordeaux.

Dyers' caldrons put on the flat surface, Wine, honey and oil, and built over fur-naces:
They will be immersed, innocent, pronounced malefactors, Seven of Borneaux smoke still in the cannon.

XV.

Pres de Parpan les rouges detenus, Ceux du milieu parfondres menez loing: Trois mis en pieces, & cinq mal soustenus, Pour le Seigneur & Prelat de Bourgoing.

Near Perpignan the red ones detained, Those of the middle completely ruined led far off:
Three cut in pieces, and five badly supported, For the Lord and Prelate of Burgundy.

XVI.

De castel Franco sortira l'assemblee, L'ambassadeur non plaisant fera scisme:
Ceux de Ribiere seront en la meslee,
Et au grand goulfre desnie ont l'entree.

Out of Castelfranco will come the assembly, The ambassador not agreeable will cause a schism:
Those of Riviera will be in the squabble, And they will refuse entry to the great gulf.

XVII.

Le tiers premier pis que ne fit Neron, Vuidez vaillant que sang humain respandre: Rédifier fera le forneron,
Siecle d'or mort, nouueau Roy grâd esclandre.

The third one first does worse than Nero, How much human blood to flow, valiant, be gone:
He will cause the furnace to be rebuilt, Golden Age dead, new King great scandal.

XVIII.

Le lys Dauffois portera dans Nansi, Iusques en Flandres electeur de l'Empire Neufue obturee au grand Montmorency, Hors lieux prouuez deliure à clere peine.

The lily of the Dauphin will reach into Nancy, As far as Flanders the Elector of the Empire: New confinement for the great Montmorency, Outside proven places delivered to celebrated punishment.

XIX.

Dans le milieu de la forest Mayenne, Sol au Lyon la fouldre tombera: Le grand bastard yssu du grand du Maine, Ce iour fougeres pointe en sang entrera.

In the middle of the forest of Mayenne, Lightning will fall, the Sun in Leo: The great bastard issued from the great one Maine, On this day a point will enter the blood of Fougères.

XX.

De nuict viendra par la forest de Reines, Deux pars vaultorte Hene la pierre blanche. Le moyne noir en gris dedans Varennes, Esleu cap cause tempeste, feu sang tranche.

By night will come through the forest of "Reines," Two couples roundabout route Queen the white stone, The monk king in gray in Varennes: Elected Capet causes tempest, fire, blood, slice.

XXI.

Au temple haut de Bloys sacre Salonne, Nuict pont de Loyre Prelat, Roy pernicant: Curseur victoire aux marests de la lone, D'où prelature de blancs abormeant.

At the tall temple of Saint-Solenne at Blois, Night Loire bridge, Prelate, King killing outright: Crushing victory in the marshes of the pond, Whence prelacy of whites miscarrying.

Century IX

XXII.

Roy & sa cour au lieu de langue halbe, Dedans le temple vis a vis du palais: Dans le iardin Duc de Mantor & d'Albe, Albe & Mantor poignard langue & palais.

The King and his court in the place of cunning tongue, Within the temple facing the palace:
In the garden the Duke of Mantue and Alba, Alba and Mantua dagger tongue and palace.

XXIII.

Puisnay ioüant au fresch dessoubs la tonne, Le haut du toict du milieu sur la teste, Le pere Roy au temple saint Salonne, Sacrifiant sacrera fum de feste.

The younger son playing outdoors under the arbor, The top of the roof in the middle on his head, The father King in the temple of Saint-Solonne, Sacrificing he will consecrate festival smoke.

XXIV.

Sur le palais au rochier des fenestres, Seront rauis les deux petits royaux: Passer aurelle Luthece, Denis cloistres, Nonnain, Mallods aualler vers noyaux.

Upon the palace at the balcony of the windows, The two little royal ones will be carried off: To pass Orléans, Paris, abbey of Saint-Denis, Nun, wicked ones to swallow green pits.

XXV.

Passant les ponts venir pres de rosiers, Tard arriué plustost qu'il cuidera, Viendront les noues Espagnols à Besiers, Qu'icelle chasse emprinse cassera.

Crossing the bridges to come near the Roisiers, Sooner than he thought, he ar-

rived late.
The new Spaniards will come to Béziers, So that this chase will break the enterprise.

XXVI.

Nice sortie sur nom des lettres aspres, La grande cappe fera present non sien:
Proche de vultry aux murs de vertes capres, Apres plombin le vent à bon essien.

Departed by the bitter letters the surname of Nice, The great Cappe will present something, not his own; Near Voltai at the wall of the green columns, After Piombino the wind in good earnest.

XXVII.

De bois la garde, vent clos ronds pont sera, Haut le receu frappera le Dauphin,
Le vieux teccon bois vnis passera, Passant plus outre du Duc le droit confin.

The forester, the wind will be close around the bridge, Received highly, he will strike the Dauphin.
The old craftsman will pass through the woods in a company, Going far beyond the right borders of the Duke.

XXVIII.

Voile Symacle port Massiliolique, Dans Venise port marcher aux Pannons:
Partir du goufre & sinus Illirique, Vast à Socile, Ligurs coups de canons.

The Allied fleet from the port of Marseilles, In Venice harbour to march against Hungary. To leave from the gulf and the bay of Illyria,
Devastation in Sicily, for the Ligurians, cannon shot.

XXIX.

Lors que celuy qu'à nul ne donne lieu, Abandonner voudra lieu prins non prins:
Feu neuf par saignes, bieument à Charlieu, Seront Quintin Balez reprins.

When the man will give way to none,
Will wish to abandon a place taken, yet not taken; Ship afire through the swamps,
bitumen at Charlieu, St. Quintin and Calais will be recaptured.

XXX.

Au port de Puola & de sainct Nicolas, Perir Normande au goufre Phanatique,
Cap de Bisance rues crier helas,
Secours de Gaddes & du grand Philippique.

At the port of Pola and of San Nicolo,
A Normand will punish in the Gulf of Quarnero: Capet to cry alas in the streets
of Byzantium, Help from Cadiz and the great Philip.

XXXI.

Le tremblement de terre à Morrura, Caffich sainct George à demy perfondrez:
Paix assoupie la guerre esueillera,
Dans temple à Pasques abysmes enfondrez.

The trembling of the earth at Mortara The tin island of St. George half sunk;
Drowsy with peace, war will arise,
At Easter in the temple abysses opened.

XXXII.

De fin porphire profond collon trouuee Dessouz la laze escripts capitolin:
Os poil retors Romain force prouuee, Classe agiter au port de Methelin.

A deep column of fine porphyry is found, Inscriptions of the Capitol under the
base; Bones, twisted hair, the Roman strength tried, The fleet is stirred at the
harbour of Mitylene.

XXXIII.

Hercules Roy de Rome & d'Annemarc, De Gaule trois Guion surnommé, Trembler l'Italie & l'vnde de sainct Marc, Premier sur tous monarque renommé.

Hercules King of Rome and of "Annemark," With the surname of the chief of triple Gaul, Italy and the one of St. Mark to tremble, First monarch renowned above all.

XXXIV.

Le part soluz mary sera mitré, Retour conflict passera sur le thuille: Par cinq cens vn trahyr sera tiltré
Narbon & Saulce par couteaux auons d'huille.

The single part afflicted will be mitred, Return conflict to pass over the tile: For five hundred one to betray will be titled Narbonne and Salces we have oil for knives.

XXXV.

Et Ferdinand blonde sera deserte, Quitter la fleur, suiure le Macedon, Au grand besoin de faillira sa routte, Et marchera contre le Myrmidon.

And fair Ferdinand will be detached,
To abandon the flower, to follow the Macedonian: In the great pinch his course will fail,
And he will march against the Myrmidons.

XXXVI.

Vn grâd Roy prins entre les mains d'vn loyne, Non loin de Pasque confusion coup cultre: Perpet, captifs foudre en la husne,
Lors que trois freres se blesseront & murtre.

A great King taken by the hands of a young man, Not far from Easter confusion knife thrust: Everlasting captive times what lightning on the top, When three brothers will wound each other and murder.

XXXVII.

Pont & moulins en Decembre versez, En si haut lieu montera la Garonne: Meurs, edifices, Tolose renuersez, Qu'on ne s&cced;aura son lieu autant matronne.

Bridge and mills overturned in December, The Garonne will rise to a very high place: Walls, edifices, Toulouse overturned, So that none will know his place like a matron.

XXXVIII.

L'entree de Blaye par Rochelle & l'Anglois, Passera outre le grand Aemathien: Non loin d'Agen attendra le Gaulois, Secours Narbonne deceu par entretien.

The entry at Blaye for La Rochelle and the English, The great Macedonian will pass beyond: Not far from Agen will wait the Gaul, Narbonne help beguiled through conversation.

XXXIX.

En Arbissel à Veront & Carcari, De nuict conduits par Sauonne attraper, Le vifs Gascon Turby, & la Scerry: Derrier mur vieux & neuf palais gripper.

In Albisola to "Veront" and Carcara, Led by night to seize Savona: The guick Gascon La Turbie and L'Escarène: Behind the wall old and new palace to seize.

XL.

Pres de Quintin dons la forest bourlis, Dans l'Abaye seront Flamens ranchés: Les deux puisnais de coups my estourdis, Suitte oppressee & garde tous achés.

Near Saint-Quintin in the forest deceived, In the Abbey the Flemish will be cut up:
The two younger sons half-stunned by blows, The rest crushed and the guard all cut to pieces.

XLI.

Le grand Chyren soy saisir d'Auignon, De Rome lettres en miel plein d'amertu
Lettre ambassade partir de Chanignon, Carpentras pris par duc noir rouge plum

The great "Chyren" will seize Avignon, From Rome letters in honey full of bitterness: Letter and embassy to leave from "Chanignon,"
Carpentras taken by a black duke with a red feather.

XLII.

De Barcellonne, de Gennes & Venise De la Secille peste Monet vnis:
Contre Barbare classe prendront la vise, Barbar poussé bien loing iusqu'à Thunis.

From Barcelona, from Genoa and Venice, From Sicily pestilence Monaco joined:
They will take their aim against the Barbarian fleet, Barbarian driven 'way back as far as Tunis.

XLIII.

Proche à descendre l'armee Crucigere, Sera guettee par les Ismaëlites,
De tous costez batus par nef Rauiere, Prompt assaillis de dix galeres eslites.

On the point of landing the Crusader army Will be ambushed by the Ishmaelites,
Struck from all sides by the ship Impetuosity, Rapidly attacked by ten elite galleys.

Century IX

XLIV.

Migrés, migrés de Geneue trestous. Saturne d'or en fer se changera,
Le contre FAYPOZ exterminera tous, Auant l'aduent le ciel signes fera.

Leave, leave Geneva every last one of you, Saturn will be converted from gold to
iron, "Raypoz" will exterminate all who oppose him, Before the coming the sky
will show signs.

XLV.

Ne sera soul iamais de demander, Grand Mendosus obtiendra son empire: Loing
de la cour fera contremander Pymond, Picard, Paris Tyrron le pire.

None will remain to ask,
Great "Mendosus" will obtian his dominion:
Far from the court he will cause to be countermanded Piedmont, Picardy, Paris,
Tuscany the worst.

XLVI.

Vuydez fuyez de Tolose les ronges, Du sacrifice faire piation.
Le chef du mal dessous l'ombre des courges: Mort estrangler carne omination.

Be gone, flee from Toulouse ye red ones, For the sacrifice to make expiation:
The chief cause of the evil under the shade of pumpkins: Dead to strangle carnal
prognostication.

XLVII.

Les soubz signez d'indigne deliurance, Et de la multe auront contre aduis: Change
monarque mis en perille pence, Serrez en cage le verront vis à vis.

The undersigned to an infamous deliverance, And having contrary advice from
the multitude: Monarch changes put in danger over thought,
Shut up in a cage they will see each other face to face.

XLVIII.

La grand cité d'Occean maritime, Enuironnee de marets en cristal: Dans le solstice hyemal & la prime, Sera tentee de vent espouuantal.

The great city of the maritime Ocean, Surrounded by a crystalline swamp: In the winter solstice and the spring, It will be tried by frightful wind.

XLIX.

Gand & Bruceles marcheront contre Anuers, Senat de Londres mettront à mort leur Roy: Le sel & vin luy seront à l'enuers,
Pour eux auoir le regne en desarroy.

Ghent and Brussels will march against Antwerp, The Senate of London will put to death their King: Salt and wine will overthrow him,
To have them the realm turned upside down.

L.

Mandosus tost viendra à son haut regne, Mettant arriere vn peu les Norlaris: Le rouge blesme, le masle a l'interregne, Le ieune crainte & frayeur Barbaris.

Mendosus will soon come to his high realm, Putting behind a little the Lorrainers:
The pale red one, the male in the interregnum, The fearful youth and Barbaric terror.

LI.

Contre les rouges sectes se banderont, Feu, eau, fer, corde par paix se minera: An point mourir ceux qui machineront, Fors vn que monde sur tout ruinera.

Against the red ones sects will conspire, Fire, water, steel, rope through peace will weaken:
On the point of dying those who will plot, Except one who above all the world will ruin.

LII.

La paix s'approche d'vn costé, & la guerre, Oncques ne fut la poursuitte si grande:
Plaindre hôme, femme sang innocent par terre, Et ce sera de France a toute
bande.

Peace is nigh on one side, and war, Never was the pursuit of it so great:
To bemoan men, women innocent blood on the land, And this will be throughout all France.

LIII.

Le Neron ieune dans le trois cheminees, Fera de paiges vifs pour ardoir ietter:
Heureux qui loing sera de tels menees, Trois de son sang le feront mort guetter.

The young Nero in the three chimneys Will cause live pages to be thrown to
burn:
Happy those who will be far away from such practices, Three of his blood will
have him ambushed to death.

LIV.

Arriuera au port de Corsibonne, Pres de Rauenne, qui pillera la dame: En mer
profonde legat de la Vlisbonne, Sous roc cachez rauiront septante ames.

There will arrive at Porto Corsini,
Near Ravenna, he who will plunder the lady: In the deep sea legate from Lisbon,
Hidden under a rock they will carry off seventy souls.

LV.

L'horrible guerre qu'en l'Occident s'appreste, L'an ensuiuant viendra la pestilence
Si fort l'horrible que ieune, vieux, ne beste, Sang, feu. Mercure, Mars, Iupiter en
France.

The horrible war which is being prepared in the West, The following year will come the pestilence
So very horrible that young, old, nor beast, Blood, fire Mercury, Mars, Jupiter in France.

LVI.

Cam pres de Noudam passera Goussan ville, Et à Maiotes laissera son enseigne:
Conuertira en instant plus de mille,
Cherchât les deux remettre en chaine & legne.

The army near Houdan will pass Goussainville, And at "Maiotes" it will leave its mark:
In an instant more than a thousand will be converted, Looking for the two to put them back in chain and firewood.

LVII.

Au lieu de DRVX vn Roy reposera, Et cherchera loy changeant d'Anatheme:
Pendant le ciel si tresfort tonnera, Portera neufue Roy tuera soy mesme.

In the place of "Drux" a King will rest, And will look for a law changing Anathema: While the sky will thunder so very loudly,
New entry the King will kill himself.

LVIII.

Au costé gauche à l'endroit de Vitry, Seront guettez les trois rouges, de France:
Tous assommez rouge, noir non meurdry, Par les Bretons remis en asseurance.

On the left side at the spot of Vitry,
The three red ones of France will be awaited: All felled red, black one not murdered,
By the Bretons restored to safety.

LIX.

A la Ferté prendra la Vidame, Nicol tenu rouge qu'auoit produit la vie: La grand
Loyse naistra que fera clame,
Donnant Bourgongne à Bretons par enuie.

At La Ferté-Vidame he will seize, Nicholas held red who had produced his life:
The great Louise who will act secretly one will be born, Giving Burgundy to the
Bretons through envy.

LX.

Conflict Barbar en la Cornette noire, Sang espandu, trembler la Dalmatie: Grand
Ismael mettra son promontoire, Ranes trembler secours Lusitanie.

Conflict Barbarian in the black Headdress, Blood shed, Dalmatia to tremble:
Great Ishmael will set up his promontory, Frogs to tremble Lusitania aid.

LXI.

La pille faicte à la coste marine, In cita noua & parens amenez.
Plusieurs de Malte par le fait de Messine, Estroit serrez seront mal guerdonnez.

The plunder made upon the marine coast, In Cittanova and relatives brought
forward: Several of Malta through the deed of Messina
Will be closely confined poorly rewarded.

LXII.

Au grand de Chera mon agora, Seront croisez par ranc tous attachez, Le pertinax
Oppi, & Mandragora,
Raugon d'Octobre le tiers seront laschez.

To the great one of Ceramon-agora, The crusaders will all be attached by rank,
The long-lasting Opium and Mandrake,
The "Raugon" will be released on the third of October.

LXIII.

Plainctes & pleurs cris, & grands hurlemens Pres de Narbon a Bayonne & en Foix,
O quels horribles calamitez changemens, Auant que Mars reuolu quelquefois.

Complaints and tears, cries and great howls, Near Narbonne at Bayonne and in Foix: Oh, what horrible calamities and changes, Before Mars has made several revolutions.

LXIV.

L'Aemathion passer monts Pyrennees, En Mas Narbon ne fera resistance, Par mer & terre fera si grand menee,
Cap. n'ayant terre seure pour demeurance.

The Macedonian to pass the Pyrenees mountains, In March Narbonne will not offer resistance:
By land and sea he will carry on very great intrigue, Capetian having no land safe for residence.

LXV.

Dedans le coing de Luna viendra rendre Où sera prins & mis en terre estrange.
Les fruicts immeurs seront à grand esclandre, Grand vitupere, à l'vn grande loüange.

He will come to go into the corner of "Luna," Where he will be captured and put in a strange land: The unripe fruits will be the subject of great scandal, Great blame, to one great praise.

LXVI.

Paix, vnion sera & changement, Estats, offices bas haut & haut bien bas
Dresser voyage, le fruict premier tourment, Guerre cesser, ciuil proces debats.

There will be peace, union and change, Estates, offices, low high and high very low: To prepare a trip, the first offspring torment, War to cease, civil process, debates.

LXVII.

Du haut des monts à l'entour de Lizere Port à la roche Valent cent assemblez De Chasteauneuf Pierre late en donzere, Contre le Crest Romans foy assemblez.

From the height of the mountains around the Isère, One hundred assembled at the haven in the rock Valence: From Châteauneuf, Pierrelatte, in Donzère, Against Crest, Romans, faith assembled.

LXVIII.

Du mont Aymar sera noble obscurcie, Le mal viendra au ioinct de Saone & Rosne: Dans bois cachez soldats iour de Lucie Qui ne fut onc vn si horrible throsne.

The noble of "Mount Aymar" will be made obscure, The evil will come at the junction of the Saône and Rhône: Soldiers hidden in the woods on Lucy's day, Never was there so horrible a throne.

LXIX.

Sur le mont de Bailly & la Bresle Seront cachez de Grenoble les fiers Outre Lyon, Vien eux si grand gresle. Langoult en terre n'en restera vn tiers.

One the mountain of Sain-Bel and L'Arbresle The proud one of Grenoble will be hidden: Beyond Lyons and Vienne on them a very great hail, Lobster on the land not a third thereof will remain.

LXX.

Harnois trenchans dans les flambeaux cachez, Dedans Lyon, le iour du Sacre-
ment,
Ceux de Vienne seront trestous hachez, Par les cantons Latins Mascon ne ment.

Sharp weapons hidden in the torches. In Lyons, the day of the Sacrament,
Those of Vienne will all be cut to pieces, By the Latin Cantons Mâcon does not
lie.

LXXI.

Aux lieux sacrez animaux veu à trixe, Auec celuy qui n'osera le iour.
A Carcassonne pour disgrace propice, Sera posé pour plus amule seiour.

At the holy places animals seen with hair, With him who will not dare the day:
At Carcassonne propitious for disgrace, He will be set for a more ample stay.

LXXII.

Encor seront les saincts temples pollus, Et expillez par Senat Tholosain, Saturne
deux trois cicles reuollus.
Dans Auril, May, gens de nouueau leuain.

Again will the holy temples be polluted, And plundered by the Senate of Toulouse: Saturn two three cycles completed,
In April, May, people of new leaven.

LXXIII.

Dans Fois entrez Roy ceiulee Turban: Et regnera moins euolu Saturne,
Roy Turban blanc Bizance coeur ban, Sol, Mars, Mercure pres la hurne.

The Blue Turban King entered into Foix, And he will reign less than an evolution
of Saturn:
The White Turban King Byzantium heart banished, Sun, Mars and Mercury near
Aquarius.

LXXIV.

Dans la cité de Fertsod homicide, Fait, & fait multe beuf arant ne macter, Retours
encores aux honneurs d'Artemide
Et à Vulcan corps morts sepulturer.

In the city of "Fertsod" homicide,
Deed, and deed many oxen plowing no sacrifice: Return again to the honors of
Artemis,
And to Vulcan bodies dead ones to bury.

LXXV.

De l'Ambraxie & du pays de Thrace Peuple par mer, mal, & secours Gaulois,
Perpetuelle en prouence la trace,
Auec vestige de leurs coustume & loix.

From Ambracia and the country of Thrace People by sea, evil and help from the
Gauls: In Provence the perpetual trace,
With vertiges of their custom and laws.

LXXVI.

Auec le noir Rapax & sanguinaire, Yssu du peaultre de l'inhumain Neron,
Emmy deux fleuues main gauche militaire, Sera meurtry par Ioyne chaulueron.

With the rapacious and blood-thirsty king, Issued from the pallet of the inhuman Nero: Between two rivers military hand left,
He will be murdered by Yound Baldy.

LXXVII.

Le regne prins le Roy coniurera La dame prinse à mort iurez à sort, La vie à
Royne fils on desniera,
Et la pellix au fort de la consort.

The realm taken the King will conspire, The lady taken to death ones sworn by lot: They will refuse life to the Queen and son, And the mistress at the fort of the wife.

LXXVIII.

La dame Grecque de beauté laydique, Heureuse faicte de procs innumerable, Hors translatee en regne Hispanique, Captiue prinse mourir mort miserable.

The Greek lady of ugly beauty, Made happy by countless suitors: Transferred out to the Spanish realm,
Taken captive to die a miserable death.

LXXIX.

Le chef de classe par fraude stratageme, Fera timides sortir de leurs galees, Sortis meurtris chefs renieux de cresme,
Puis par l'embusche luy rendront le saleres.

The chief of the fleet through deceit and trickery Will make the timid ones come out of their galleys: Come out, murdered, the chief renouncer of chrism, Then through ambush they will pay him his wages.

LXXX.

Le Duc voudra les siens exterminer, Enuoyera les plus forts lieux estranges: Par tyrannie Bize & Luc ruiner,
Puy les Barbares sans vin feront vendanges.

The Duke will want to exterminate his followers, He will send the strongest ones to strange places: Through tyranny to ruin Pisa and Lucca,
Then the Barbarians will gather the grapes without vine.

Century IX

LXXXI.

Le Roy rusé entendra ses embusches, De trois quartiers ennemis assaillir:
Vn nombre estrange larmes de coqueluches, Viendra Lemprin du traducteur
faillir.

The crafty King will understand his snares, Enemies to assail from three sides:
A strange number tears from hoods,
The grandeur of the translator will come to fail.

LXXXII.

Par le deluge & pestilence forte, La cité grande de long temps assiegee: La senti-
nelle & garde de main morte, Subite prinse, mais de nulle outragee.

By the flood and fierce pestilence, The great city for long besieged: The sentry
and guard dead by hand, Sudden capture but none wronged.

LXXXIII.

Sol vingt de Taurus si fort de terre trembler, Le grand theatre remply ruinera:
L'air, ciel & terre obscurcir & troubler, Lors l'infidelle Dieu & saincts voguera.

Sun twentieth of Taurus the earth will tremble very mightily, It will ruin the great
theater filled:
To darken and trouble air, sky and land, Then the infidel will call upon God and
saints.

LXXXIV.

Roy exposé parfera l'hecatombe, Apres auoir trouué son origine:
Torrent ouurir de marbre & plomb la tombe, D'vn grand Romain d'enseigne Medusine.

The King exposed will complete the slaughter, After having discovered his origin:
Torrent to open the tomb of marble and lead, Of a great Roman with "Medusine" device.

LXXXV.

Passer Guienne, Languedoc & le Rosne, D'Agen tenan de Marmande & la Roolle:
D'ouurir par foy parroy, Phocê tiêdra sô trosne Conflict aupres saint Pol de Mauseole.

To pass Guienne, Languedoc and the Rhône, From Agen holding Marmande and La Réole:
To open through faith the wall, Marseilles will hold its throne, Conflict near Saint-Paul-de-Mausole.

LXXXVI.

Du bourg Lareyne paruiêdrôt droit à Chartres, Et feront pres du pont Amhoni pause
Sept pour la paix cauteleux comme Martres, Feront entree d'armee à Paris clause.

From Bourg-la-Reine they will come straight to Chartres, And near Pont d'Antony they will pause:
Seven crafty as Martens for peace, Paris closed by an army they will enter.

LXXXVII.

Par la forest du Touphon essartee, Par hermitage sera posé le temple,
Le Duc d'Estampes par sa ruse inuentee. Du mont Lehori prelat donra exemple.

In the forest cleared of the Tuft,
By the hermitage will be placed the temple: The Duke of Étampes through the ruse he invented
Will teach a lesson to the prelate of Montlhéry.

LXXXVIII.

Calais Arras, secours à Theroanne, Paix & semblant simulera l'escoutte, Soulde
d'Alobrox descendre par Roane.
Destornay peuple qui defera la routte.

Calais, Arras, help to Thérouanne, Peace and semblance the spy will simulate:
The soldiery of Savoy to descend by Roanne,
People who would end the rout deterred.

LXXXIX.

Sept ans sera Philipp. fortune prospere.
Rabaissera des Arabes l'effort, Puis son midy perplex rebors affaire,
Ieune ognion abismera son fort.

For seven years fortune will favor Philip,
He will beat down again the exertions of the Arabs: Then at his noon perplexing
contrary affair, Young Ogmios will destroy his stronghold.

XC.

Vn capitaine de la Grand Germanie Se viendra rendre par simulé secours Au Roy
des Roys aide de Pannoie,
Que sa reuolte fera de sang grand cours.

A captain of Great Germany
Will come to deliver through false help
To the King of Kings the support of Pannonia, So that his revolt will cause a great
flow of blood.

XCI.

L'horrible peste Perynté & Nicopollo, Le Chersonnez tiendra & Marceloyne, La
Thessalie vastera l'Amphipolle, Mal incogneu, & le refus d'Anthoine.

The horrible plague Perinthus and Nicopolis, The Peninsula and Macedonia will it fall upon: It will devastate Thessaly and Amphipolis, An unknown evil, and from Anthony refusal.

XCII.

Le Roy voudra en cité neufue entrer, Par ennemis expugner l'on viendra Captif libere faux dire & perpetrer, Roy dehors estre, loin d'ennemis tiendra.

The King will want to enter the new city, Through its enemies they will come to subdue it: Captive free falsely to speak and act, King to be outside, he will keep far from the enemy.

XCIII.

Les ennemis du fort bien esloignez, Par chariots conduict le bastion. Par sur les murs de Bourges esgrongnez Quand Hercules bastira l'Haemathion.

The enemies very far from the fort, The bastion brought by wagons: Above the walls of Bourges crumbled, When Hercules the Macedonian will strike.

XCIV.

Foibles galeres seront vnies ensemble, Ennemis faux le plus fort en rampart: Foibles assaillies Vratislaue tremble, Lubecq & Mysne tiendront barbare part.

Weak galleys will be joined together, False enemies the strongest on the rampart: Weak ones assailed Bratislava trembles, Lübeck and Meissen will take the barbarian side.

Century IX

XCV.

Le nouueau faict conduira l'exercice, Proche apamé iusqu'aupres du riuage: Tendant secours de Millannoile eslite, Duc yeux priué à Milanfer de cage.

The newly made one will lead the army, Almost cut off up to near the bank: Help
from the Milanais elite straining,
The Duke deprived of his eyes in Milan in an iron cage.

XCVI.

Dans cité entrer exercit desniee, Duc entrera par persuasion,
Aux foibles portes clam armee amenee, Mettront feu, mort, de sang effusion.

The army denied entry to the city, The Duke will enter through persuasion: The
army led secretly to the weak gates,
They will put it to fire and sword, effusion of blood.

XCVII.

De mer copies en trois pars diuisee, A la seconde les viures failleront,
Desesperez cherchant champs Helisees, Premiers en breche entrez victoire auront.

The forces of the sea divided into three parts, The second one will run out of
supplies,
In despair looking for the Elysian Fields,
The first ones to enter the breach will obtain the victory.

XCVIII.

Les affigez par faute d'vn seul taint, Contremenant à partie opposite,
Aux Lygonnois mandera que contraint Seront de rendre le grand chef de Molite.

Those afflicted through the fault of a single one stained, The transgressor in the
opposite party:

He will send word to those of Lyons that compelled They be to deliver the great chief of "Molite."

XCIX.

Vent Aquilon fera partir le siege,
Par meurs ietter cendres, chauls, & poussiere: Par pluye apres, qui leur fera bien pege, Dernier secours encontre leur frontiere.

The "Aquilon" Wind will cause the siege to be raised, Over the walls to throw ashes, lime and dust:
Through rain afterwards, which will do them much worse, Last help against their frontier.

C.

Naualle pugne nuit sera superee. Le feu aux naues à l'Occident ruine: Rubriche neufue, la grand nef coloree,
Ire à vaincu, & victoire en bruine.

Naval battle night will be overcome, Fire in the ships to the West ruin: New trick, the great ship colored,
Anger to the vanquished, and victory in a drizzle.

CENTURY X

I.

A L'ennemy, l'ennemy foy promise Ne se tiendra, les captifs retenus:
Prins preme mort, & le reste en chemise.
Damné le reste pour estre soustenus.

To the ennemy, the enemy faith promised Will not be kept, the captives retained:
One near death captured, and the remainder in their shirts, The remainder
damned for being supported.

II.

Voille gallere voil de nef cachera,
La grande classe viendra sortir la moindre, Dix naues proches tourneront pouss-
er, Grande vaincue vnics à soy ioindre.

The ship's veil will hide the sail galley,
The great fleet will come the lesser one to go out: Ten ships near will turn to drive
it back,
The great one conquered the united ones to join to itself.

III.

En apres cinq troupeau ne mettra hors vn Fuitif pour Penelon laschera,
Faux murmurer, secours vnir pour lors, Le chef le siege pour lors abandonnera.

After that five will not put out the flock, A fugitive for "Penelon" he will turn
loose:
To murmur falsely then help to come, The chief will then abandon the siege.

IV.

Sur la minuict conducteur de l'armee Se sauuera subit esuanouy,
Sept ans apres la fame non blasmee, A son retour ne dira onc ouy.

At midnight the leader of the army Will save himself, suddenly vanished:
Seven years later his reputation unblemished, To his return they will never say
yes.

V.

Albi & Castres feront nouuelle ligue, Neuf Arriens Lis bon & Portugues,
Carcas, Tholouse consumeront leur brigue, Quand chef neuf monstre de Lau-
ragues.

Albi and Castres will form a new league, Nine Arians Lisbon and the Portuguese:
Carcassonne and Toulouse will end their intrigue, When the chief new monster
from the Lauraguais.

VI.

Sardon Nemaus si haut deborderont, Qu'on cuidera Deucalion renaistre. Dans le
collosse la plus part fuyront, Vesta sepulchre feu esteint apparoistre.

The Gardon will flood Nîmes so high That they will believe Deucalion reborn:
Into the colossus the greater part will flee, Vesta tomb fire to appear extinguished.

VII.

Le grand conflit qu'on appreste à Nancy, L'Aemathien dira tout ie soubmets, L'Isle
Britanne par vin sel en solcy:
Hem, mi. deux Phi. long temps ne tiêdra Mets.

The great conflict that they are preparing for Nancy, The Macedonian will say I
subjugate all:
The British Isle in anxiety over wine and salt, "Hem. mi." Philip two Metz will
not hold for long.

VIII.

Index & poulse parfondera le front, De Senegalia le Conte à son fils propre, La
Myrnamee par plusieurs de prin front,
Trois dans sept iours blessés mort.

With forefinger and thumb he will moisten the forehead, The Count of Senigallia
to his own son:
The Venus through several of thin forehead, Three in seven days wounded dead.

IX.

De Castillon figuieres iour de brune, De femme infame naistra souuerain Prince:
Surnom de chausses perhume luy posthume, Onc Roy ne fut si pire en sa prouince.

In the Castle of Figueras on a misty day
A sovereign prince will be born of an infamous woman: Surname of breeches on
the ground will make him posthumous, Never was there a King so very bad in
his province.

X.

Tasche de meurdre, enormes adulteres, Grand ennemy de tout le genre humain:
Que sera pire qu'ayeuls, oncles ne peres, Enfer, feu, eaux, sanguin & inhumain.

Stained with murder and enormous adulteries, Great enemy of the entire human
race:
One who will be worse than his grandfathers, uncles or fathers, In steel, fire,
waters, bloody and inhuman.

XI.

Dessous Ionchere du dangereux passage, Fera passer le posthume sa bande.
Les monts Pyrens passer hors son bagage, De Parpignan courira duc à Tende.

At the dangerous passage below Junquera, The posthumous one will have his band cross:
To pass the Pyrenes mountains without his baggage, From Perpignan the duke will hasten to Tende.

XII.

Esleu en Pape, d'esleu se mocqué, Subit soudain esmeu prompt & timide, Par trop bon doux à mourrir prouoqué,
Crainte esteinte la nuict de sara mort guide.

Elected Pope, as elected he will be mocked, Suddenly unexpectedly moved prompt and timid:
Through too much goodness and kindness provoked to die, Fear extinguished guides the night of his death.

XIII.

Souz la pasture d'animaux ruminant, Par eux conduicts au ventre helbipolique, Soldats cachez, les armes bruit menant,
Non long temptez de cité Antipolique.

Beneath the food of ruminating animals, led by them to the belly of the fodder city: Soldiers hidden, their arms making a noise, Tried not far from the city of Antibes.

XIV.

Vrnel Vaucile sans conseil de soy mesmes, Hardit timide, car crainte prins vaincu, Accompagné de plusieurs putains blesmes.
A Barcellonne au Chartreux conuaincu.

"Urnel Vaucile" without a purpose on his own, Bold, timid, through fear overcome and captured: Accompanied by several pale whores,
Convinced in the Carthusian convent at Barcelona.

XV.

Pere duc vieux d'ans & de soif chargé, Au iour extreme fils desniant l'esguiere.
Dedans le puits vif mort viendra plongé. Senat au fil la mort longue & legere.

Father duke old in years and choked by thirst, On his last day his don denying
him the jug:
Into the well plunged alive he will come up dead, Senate to the thread death long
and light.

XVI.

Heureux au regne de France, heureux de vie, Ignorant sang, mort fureur & rapine:
Par mon flateurs sera mis en enuie, Roy desrobé, trop de foye en cuisine.

Happy in the realm of France, happy in life, Ignorant of blood, death, fury and
plunder: For a flattering name he will be envied,
A concealed King, too much faith in the kitchen.

XVII.

La Royne estrange voyant sa fille blesme, Par vn regret dans l'estomach enclos:
Cris lamentables seront lors d'Angolesme, Et au germains mariage forclos.

The convict Queen seeing her daughter pale, Because of a sorrow locked up in
her breast: Lamentable cries will come then from Angoulême, And the marriage
of the first cousin impeded.

XVIII.

Le ranc Lorrain fera place à Vendosme, Le haut mis bas, & le bas mis en haut,
Le fils de Mamon sera esleu dans Rome, Et les deux grands seront mis en defaut.

The house of Lorraine will make way for Vendôme, The high put low, and the low put high:
The son of Mammon will be elected in Rome, And the two great ones will be put at a loss.

XIX.

Iour que sera par Royne saluee, Le iour apres se salut, la premiere: Le compte fait raison & valbuee,
Par auant humble oncques ne fut si fiere.

The day that she will be hailed as Queen, The day after the benediction the prayer: The reckoning is right and valid,
Once humble never was one so proud.

XX.

Tous les amis qu'auront tenu party, Pour rude en lettres mis mort & saccagé.
Biens publiez par fixe grand neanty, Onc Romain peuple ne fut tant outragé.

All the friend who will have belonged to the party, For the rude in letters put to death and plundered:
Property up for sale at fixed price the great one annihilated.
Never were the Roman people so wronged.

XXI.

Par le despit du Roy soustenant moindre, Sera meurdry luy presentant les ba-
gues: Le pere au fils voulant noblesse poindre,
Fait comme à Perse jadis firent les Magues.

Through the spite of the King supporting the lesser one, He will be murdered presenting the jewels to him: The father wishing to impress nobility on the son
Does as the Magi did of yore in Persia.

XXII.

Pour ne vouloir consentir au diuorce, Qui puis apres sera cogneu indigne: Le
Roy des isles sera chassé par sorte,
Mais à son lieu qui de roy n'aura signe.

For not wishing to consent to the divorce, Which then afterwards will be rec-
ognised as unworthy:
The King of the Isles will be driven out by force, In his place put one who will
have no mark of a king.

XXIII.

Au peuple ingrat faictes les remonstrances.
Par lors l'armee se saisira d'Antibe, Dans l'arc Monech feront les doleances, Et à
Freius l'vn l'autre prendra ribe.

The remonstrances made to the ungrateful people, Thereupon the army will
seize Antibes:
The complaints will place Monace in the arch, And at Fréjus the one will take the
shore from the other

XXIV.

Le captif prince aux Itales vaincu Passera Gennes par mer iusqu'à Marceille,
Par grand effort des forens suruaincu Sauf coup de feu barril liqueur d'abeille.

The captive prince conquered in Italy Will pass Genoa by sea as far as Marseilles:
Through great exertion by the foreigners overcome, Safe from gunshot, barrel of
bee's liquor.

XXV.

Par Nebro ouurir de Bisanne passage, Bien esloignez el tago fara moestra, Dans
Pelligouxe sera commis l'outrage, De la grand dame assise sur l'orchestra

Through the Ebro to open the passage of "Bisanne," Very far away will the Tagus make a demonstration: In "Pelligouxe" will the outrage be commited, By the great lady seated in the orchestra.

XXVI.

Le successeur vengera son beau frere, Occuper regne souz vmbre de vengeance, Occis ostacle son sang mort vitupere, Long temps Bretaigne tiendra auec la France.

The successor will avenge his brother-in-law, To occupy the realm under the shadow of vengeance: Obstacle slain his blood for the death blame, For a long time will Brittany hold with France.

XXVII.

Par le cinquiesme & vn grand Hercules Viendront le temple ouurir de main bellique, Vn Clement, Iule & Ascans recules, L'espee, clef, aigle, n'eurent onc si grand picque.

Through the fifth one and a great Hercules They will come to open the temple by hand of war: One Clement, Julius and Ascanius set back, The sword, key, eagle, never was there such a great animosity.

XXVIII.

Second & tiers qui font prime musique Sera par Roy en honneur sublimee, Par grance & maigre presque demy eticque Raport de Venus faux rendra deprimee.

Second and third which make prime music By the King to be sublimated in honor: Through the fat and the thin almost emaciated, By the false report of Venus to be debased.

Century X

XXIX.

De Pol MANSOL dans cauerne caprine Caché & prins extrait hors par la barbe,
Captif mene comme beste mastine
Par Bergourdans amenee pres de Tarbe.

In a cave of Saint-Paul-de-Mausole a goat Hidden and seized pulled out by the
beard: Led captive like a mastiff beast
By the Bigorre people brought to near Tarbes.

XXX.

Nepveu & sang du sainct nouueau venu, Par le surnom soustient arcs & couuert
Seront chassez mis à mort chassez nu, En rouge & noir conuertiront leur vert.

Nephew and blood of the new saint come, Through the surname he will sustain
arches and roof:
They will be driven out put to death chased nude, Into red and black will they
convert their green.

XXXI.

Le sainct Empire, viendra en Germanie Ismaëlites trouueront lieux ouuerts,
Asnes voudront aussi la Carmanie
Les soustenans de terre tous couuerts.

The Holy Empire will come into Germany, The Ishmaelites will find open places:
The asses will want also Carmania,
The supportes all covered by earth.

XXXII.

Le grand empire chacun an deuoit estre, Vn sur les autres le viendra obtenir:
Mais peu de temps sera son reigne & estre, Deux ans naues se pourra soustenir.

The great empire, everyone would be of it, One will come to obtain it over the

others:
But his realm and state will be of short duration, Two years will he be able to maintain himself on the sea.

XXXIII.

La faction cruelle à robe longue, Viendra cacher souz ses pointus poignards, Saisir Florence le Duc & lieu diphlonque, Sa descouuerte par immurs & flang-nards.

The cruel faction in the long robe Will come to hide under the sharp daggers: The Duke to seize Florence and the diphthong place, Its discovery by immature ones and sycophants.

XXXIV.

Gaulois qu'empire par guerre occupera, Par son beau frere mineur sera trahy: Pour cheual rude voltigeant trainera, Du fait le frere long temps sera hay.

The Gaul who will hold the empire through war, He will be betrayed by his minor brother-in-law: He will be drawn by a fierce, prancing horce, The brother will be hated for the deed for a long time

XXXV.

Puisnay royal flagrant d'ardant libide, Pour se iouyr de cousine germaine: Habit de femme au temple d'Arthemide, Allant meurdry par incognu du Maine.

The younger son of the king flagrant in burning lust To enjoy his first cousin: Female attire in the Temple of Artemis, Going to be murdered by the unknown one of Maine.

XXXVI.

Apres le Roy du soucq guerres parlant, L'Isle Harmotique le tiendra à mespris:
Quelques ans bons rongeant vn & pillant, Par tyrannie à l'isle changeant pris.

Upon the King of the stump speaking of wars, The United Isle will hold him in
contempt:
For several good years one gnawing and pillaging, Through tyranny in the isle
esteem changing.

XXXVII.

L'assemblee grande pres du lac de Borget, Se ralieront pres du Montmelian:
Marchans plus outre pensifs feront proget Chambry, Moraine combat sainct
Iulian.

The great assembly near the Lake of Bourget, They will meet near Montmélian:
Going beyond the thoughful ones will draw up a plan, Chambéry, Saint-Jean-de-
Maurienne, Saint-Julien combat.

XXXVIII.

Amour allegre non loing pose le siege. Au sainct barbar seront les garnisons:
Vrsins Hadrie pour Gaulois feront plaige, Pour peur rendus de l'armee aux
Grisons.

Sprightly love lays the siege not far, The garrisons will be at the barbarian saint:
The Orsini and "Adria" will provide a guarantee for the Gauls, For fear deliverd
by the army to the Grisons.

XXXIX.

Premier fils vefue malheureux mariage, Sans nuls enfans deux Isles en discord:
Auant dixhuict incompetant eage,
De l'autre pres plus bas sera l'accord.

First son, widow, unfortunate marriage, Without any children two Isles in discord: Before eighteen, incompetent age,
For the other one the betrothal will take place while younger.

XL.

Le ieune n'ay au regne Britannique, Qu'aura le pere mourant recommandé, Iceluy mort LONOLE donra topique, Et à son fils le regne demandé.

The young heir to the British realm, Whom his dying father will have recommended: The latter dead "Lonole" will dispute with him,
And from the son the realm demanded.

XLI.

En la frontiere de Caussa & de Charlus, Non guieres loing du fonds de la valee: De ville franche musique à son de luths, Enuironnez combouls & grand mittee.

On the boundary of Caussade and Caylus, Not at all far from the bottom of the valley:
Music from Villefranche to the sound of lutes, Encompassed by cymbals and great stringing.

XLII.

Le regne humain d'Angelique geniture, Fera son regne paix vnion tenir: Captiue guerre demy de sa closture, Long temps la paix leur fera maintenir.

The humane realm of Anglican offspring,
It will cause its realm to hold to peace and union: War half-captive in its enclosure,
For long will it cause them to maintain peace.

XLIII.

Le trop bon temps trop de bonté royale, Fais & deffais prompt subit negligence.
Legier croira faux d'espouse loyalle, Luy mis à mort par beneuolence.

Too much good times, too much of royal goodness, Ones made and unmade,
quick, sudden, neglectful: Lightly will he believe falsely of his loyal wife,
He put to death through his benevolence.

XLIV.

Par lors qu'vn Roy sera contre les siens, Natifs de Bloys subiuguera Ligures,
Mammel, Cordube & les Dalmatiens,
Des sept puis l'ôbre à Roy estrênes & lemeures.

When a King will be against his people,
A native of Blois will subjugate the Ligurians, Memel, Cordoba and the Dalma-
tians,
Of the seven then the shadow to the King handsel and ghosts.

XLV.

L'ombre du regne de Nauarre non vray, Fera la vie de sort illegitime:
La veu promis incertain de Cambray, Roy Orleans donra mur legitime.

The shadow of the realm of Navarre untrue, It will make his life one of fate un-
lawful: The vow made in Cambrai wavering,
King Orléans will give a lawful wall.

XLVI.

Vie soit mort de l'or vilaine indigne, Sera de Saxe non nouueau electeur: De
Brunsuic mandra d'amour signe, Faux le rendant au peuple seducteur.

In life, fate and death a sordid, unworthy man of gold, He will not be a new
Elector of Saxony:

From Brunswick he will send for a sign of love, The false seducer delivering it to the people.

XLVII.

De bourze ville à la dame Guyrlande, L'on mettra sur par la trahison faicte Le grand prelat de Leon par Formande, Faux pelerins & rauisseurs deffaicte.

At the Garland lady of the town of Burgos, They will impose for the treason commited: The great prelate of Leon through "Formande", Undone by false pilgrims and ravishers.

XLVIII.

Du plus profond de l'Espaigne enseigne, Sortant du bout & des fins de l'Europe, Troubles passant aupres du pont de Laigne, Sera deffaicte par bande sa grand troupe.

Banners of the deepest part of Spain, Coming out from the tip and ends of Europe: Troubles passing near the bridge of "Laigne", Its great army will be routed by a band.

XLIX.

Iardin du monde aupres de cité neufue, Dans le chemin des montaignes cauees: Sera saisi & plongé dans la Cuve, Beuuant par force eaux soulphre enuenimees.

Garden of the world near the new city, In the path of the hollow mountains: It will be seized and plunged into the Tub, Forced to drink waters poisoned by sulfur.

L.

La Meuse au iour terre de Luxembourg, Descouurira Saturne & trois en lurne:
Montaigne & pleine, ville cité & bourg, Lorrain deluge, trahison par grand hurne.

The Meuse by day in the land of Luxemburg, It will find Saturn and three in the
urn: Mountain and plain, town, city and borough, Flood in Lorraine, betrayed
by the great urn.

LI.

Des lieux plus bas du pays de Lorraine Seront des basses Allemaignes vnis:
Par ceux du siege Picards, Normâs, du Maisne, Et aux cantons se seront reünis.

Some of the lowest places of the land of Lorraine Will be united with the Low
Germans:
Through those of the see Picards, Normans, those of Main, And they will be
joined to the cantons.

LII.

Au lieu où Laye & Scelde se marient, Seront les nopces de long temps maniees:
Au lieu d'Anuers où la crappe charient, Ieune viellesse consorte intaminee.

At the place where the Lys and the Scheldt unite, The nuptials will be arranged
for a long time:
At the place in Antwerp where they carry the chaff, Young old age wife undefiled.

LIII.

Les trois pelices de loing s'entrebatront, La plus grand moindre demeurera à l'escoute:
Le grand Selin n'en sera plus patron, Le nommera feu pelte blanche routte.

The three concubines will fight each other for a long time, The greatest one the
least will remain to watch:

The great "Selin" will no longer be her patron, She will call him fire shield white route.

LIV.

Nee en ce monde par concupine fertiue, A deux haut mise par les tristes nouuelles, Entre ennemis sera prinse captiue, Et amenee à Malings & Bruxelles.

She born in this world of a furtive concubine, At two raised high by the sad news: She will be taken captive by her enemies, And brought to Malines and Brussels.

LV.

Les malheureuses nopces celebreront En grande ioye mais la fin malheureuse, Mary & mere nore desdaigneront, Le Phybe mort, & nore plus piteuse.

The unfortunate nuptials will be celebrated In great joy but the end unhappy: Husband and mother will slight the daughter-in-law, The Apollo dead and the daughter-in-law more pitiful.

LVI.

Prelat royal son baissant trop tiré, Grand fleux de sang sortira par sa bouche, Le regne Angelicque par regne respiré, Long temps mort vifs en Tunis côme souche.

The royal prelate his bowing too low, A great flow of blood will come out of his mouth: The Anglican realm a realm pulled out of danger, For long dead as a stump alive in Tunis.

LVII.

Le subleué ne cognoistra son sceptre, Les enfans ieunes des plus grands honnira:

Oncques ne fut vn plus ord cruel estre, Pour leurs espouses à mort noir bannira.

The uplifted one will not know his sceptre,
He will disgrace the young children of the greatest ones: Never was there a more
filthy and cruel being,
For their wives the king will banish them to death.

LVIII.

Au temps du dueil que le felin monarque Guerroyera la ieune Aemathien:
Gaule bransler, perecliter la barque, Tenter Phossens au Ponant entretien.

In the time of mourning the feline monarch Will make war upon the young
Macedonian: Gaul to shake, the bark to be in jeopardy, Marseilles to be tried in
the West a talk.

LIX.

Dedans Lyon vingtcinq d'vne haleine, Cinq citoyens Germains, Bressans, Latins:
Par dessous noble conduiront longue traine.
Et descouuers par abbois de mastins.

Within Lyons twenty-five of one mind, Five citizens, Germans, Bressans, Latins:
Under a noble one they will lead a long train, And discovered by barks of mastiffs.

LX.

Ie pleure Nisse, Mannego, Pize, Gennes, Sauonne, Sienne, Capuë Modene, Malte:
Le dessus sang, & glaiue par estrennes, Feu, trembler terre, eau. malheureuse
nolte.

I weep for Nice, Monaco, Pisa, Genoa, Savona, Siena, Capua, Modena, Malta:
For the above blood and sword for a New Year's gift, Fire, the earth to tremble,
water, unfortunate nolition.

LXI.

Betta, Vienne, Emorte, Sacarbance, Voudront liurer aux Barbares Pannone: Par
picque & feu enorme violance,
Les coniurez descouuers par matrone.

"Betta," Vienna, "Emorte," Sopron,
They will want to deliver Pannonia to the Barbarians: Enormous violence
through pike and fire,
The conspirators discovered by a matron.

LXII.

Pres de Sorbin pour assaillir Ongrie, L'heraut de Brudes les viendra aduertir:
Chef Bisantin, Sallon de Sclauonie,
A loy d'Arabes les viendra conuertir.

Near "Sorbia" to assail Hungary,
The herald of "Brudes" will come to warn them: Byzantine chief, Salona of Sla-
vonia,
He will come to convert them to the law of the Arabs.

LXIII.

Cydron, Raguse, la cité au sainct Hieron, Reuerdira le medicant secours:
Mort fils de Roy par mort de deux heron, L'Arabe, Hongrie feront vn mesme
cours.

Cydonia, Ragusa, the city of St. Jerome, With healing help to grow green again:
The King's sone dead because of the death of two heroes, Araby and Hungary
will take the same course.

LXIV.

Pleure Milan, plure Luques, Florence, Que ton grand Duc sur le char montera,
Changer le siege pres de Venise s'aduance, Lors que Colonne à Rome changera.

264

Weep Milan, weep Lucca and Florence, As your great Duke climbs into the char-
iot: The see to change it advances to near Venice,
When at Rome the Colonna will change.

LXV.

O vaste Rome ta ruyne s'approche, Non de tes murs, de ton sang & substance
L'aspre par lettres fera si horrible coche, Fer pointu mis à tous iusques au manche.

O vast Rome, thy ruin approaches,
Not of thy walls, of thy blood and substance:
The one harsh in letters will make a very horrible notch, Pointed steel driven into
all up to the hilt.

LXVI.

Le chef de Londres par regne l'Americh, L'Isle d'Escosse tempiera par gelee: Roy
Reb auront vn si faux Antechrist, Que les mettra trestous dans la meslee.

The chief of London through the realm of America, The Isle of Scotland will be
tried by frost:
King and "Reb" will face an Antichrist so false, That he will place them in the
conflict all together.

LXVII.

Le tremblement si fort au mois de may, Saturne, Caper, Iupiter, Mercure au
boeuf: Venus aussi, Cancer, Mars, en Nonnay, Tombera gresle lors plus grosse
qu'vn oeuf.

A very mighty trembling in the month of May, Saturn in Capricorn, Jupiter and
Mercury in Taurus: Venus also, Cancer, Mars in Virgo,
Hail will fall larger than an egg.

LXVIII.

L'armee de mer deuant cité tiendra, Puis partira sans faire longue allee: Citoyens
grande proye en terre prendra,
Retourner classe prendre grande emblee.

The army of the sea will stand before the city, Then it will leave without making
a long passage: A great flock of citizens will be seized on land, Fleet to return to
seize it great robbery.

LXIX.

Le fair luysant de neuf vieux esleué, Se ront si grands par Midy, Aquilon: De sa
soeur propre grandes alles leué, Fuyant meurdry au buisson d'Ambellon.

The shining deed of the old one exalted anew, Through the South and "Aquilon"
they will be very great:
Raised by his own sister great crowds, Fleeing, murdered in the thicket of "Ambellon."

LXX.

L'oeil par obiect fera telle excroissance, Tant & ardante que tombera la neige:
Champ arrousé viendra en decroissance, Que le primat succombera à Rege.

Through an object the eye will swell very much, Burning so much that the snow
will fall: The fields watered will come to shrink,
As the primate succumbs at Reggio.

LXXI.

La terre & lair geleront si grand eau, Lors qu'on viendra pour Ieudy venerer: Ce
qui sera iamais ne fut si beau,
Des quatre parts le viendront honorer.

The earth and air will freeze a very great sea, When they will come to venerate Thursday: That which will be never was it so fair, From the four parts they will come to honor it.

LXXII. (*)

L'an mil neuf cens nonante neuf sept mois, Du ciel viendra vn grand Roy d'effrayeur: Resusciter le grand Roy d'Angolmois, Auant apres Mars regner par bonheur.

The year 1999, seventh month, From the sky will come a great King of Terror: To bring back to life the great King of the Mongols, Before and after Mars to reign by good luck.

LXXIII.

Le temps present auecques le passé, Sera iugé par grand Iouialiste: Le monde tard luy sera lassé, Et desloyal par le clergé iuriste.

The present time together with the past Will be judged by the great Jovialist: The world too late will be tired of him, And through the clergy outh-taker disloyal.

LXXIV.

Au reuolu du grand nombre septiesme, Apparoistra au temps ieux d'Hecatombe: Non esloigné du grand aage milliesme, Que les entrez sortiront de leur tombe.

The year of the great seventh number accomplished, It will appear at the time of the games of slaughter: Not far from the great millennial age, When the buried will go out from their tombs.

LXXV.

Tant attendu ne reuiendra iamais, Dedans l'Europe en Asie apparoistra: Vn de la ligue yssu du grand Hermes, Et sur tous Roys des Orients croistra.

Long awaited he will never return In Europe, he will appear in Asia:
One of the league issued from the great Hermes, And he will grow over all the Kings of the East.

LXXVI.

Le grand Senat discernera la pompe, A l'vn qu'apres sera vaincu chassé: Ses adherans seront à son de trompe Biens publiez, ennemis dechassez.

The great Senate will ordain the triumph
For one who afterwards will be vanquished, driven out: At the sound of the trumpet of his adherents there will be Put up for sale their possessions, enemies expelled.

LXXVII.

Trente adherans de l'ordre des quirettes Bannis, leurs biens donnez ses aduersaires: Tous leurs bienfaits seront pour demerites, Classe espargie deliurez aux Corsaires.

Thirty adherents of the order of "Quirites" Banished, their possessions given their adversaries: All their benefits will be taken as misdeeds,
Fleet dispersed, delivered to the Corsairs.

LXXVIII.

Subite ioye en subite tristesse, Sera à Rome aux graces embrassees:
Dueil, cris, pleurs, larm. sang, excellent liesse Contraires bandes surprinses & troussees.

Sudden joy to sudden sadness,
It will occur at Rome for the graces embraced: Grief, cries, tears, weeping, blood,
excellent mirth, Contrary bands surprised and trussed up.

LXXIX.

Les vieux chemins seront tous embellys, Lon passera à Memphis somentree:
Le grand Mercure d'Hercules fleur de lys, Faisant trembler terre, mer & contree.

The old roads will all be improved,
One will procedd on them to the modern Memphis: The great Mercury of Hercules fleur-de-lys, Causing to tremble lands, sea and country.

LXXX.

Au regne grand du grand regne regnant, Par force d'armes les grands portes
d'airain: Fera ouurir, le Roy & Duc ioignant,
Fort demoly, nef à fons, iour serain.

In the realm the great one of the great realm reigning, Through force of arms the
great gates of brass
He will cause to open, the King and Duke joining, Fort demolished, ship to the
bottom, day serene.

LXXXI.

Mis tresors temple citadins Hesperiques, Dans iceluy retiré en secret lieu:
Le temple ouurir les liens fameliques, Reprens, rauis, proye horrible au milieu.

A treasure placed in a temple by "Hesperian" citizens, Therein withdrawn to a
secret place:
The hungry bonds to open the temple, Retaken, ravished, a horrible prey in the
midst.

LXXXII.

Cris, pleurs, larmes viendront auec couteaux, Semblant fuyr, donront dernier assaut, L'entour parques planter profonds plateaux, Vifs repoussez & meurdris de plinsaut.

Cries, weeping, tears will come with knives, Seeming to flee, they will deleiver a final attack, Parks around to set up high platforms, The living pushed back and murdered instantly.

LXXXIII.

De batailler ne sera donné signe, Du parc seront contraints de sortir hors: De Gand l'entour sera cogneu l'ensigne, Qui fera mettre de tous les siens à morts.

The signal to give battle will not be given, They will be obliged to go out of the park: The banner around Ghent will be recognized, Of him who will cause all his followers to be put to death.

LXXXIV.

La naturelle à si haut non bas, Le tard retour fera marris contens: Le Recloing ne sera sans debats, En employant & perdant tout son temps.

The illegitimate girl so high, high, not low, The late return will make the grieved ones contended: The Reconciled One will not be without debates, In employing and losing all his time.

LXXXV.

Le vieil tribun au point de la trehemide Sera pressee, captif ne deliurer, Le vueil, non vueil, le mal parlant timide, Par legitime à ses amis liurer.

The old tribune on the point of trembling, He will be pressed not to deliver the captive: The will, non-will, speaking the timid evil, To deliver to his friends lawfully.

LXXXVI.

Comme vn gryphon viendra le Roy d'Europe, Accompagné de ceux d'Aquilon, De rouges & blancs conduira grand troupe, Et iront contre le Roy de Babylon.

Like a griffin will come the King of Europe, Accompanied by those of "Aquilon": He will lead a great troop of red ones and white ones, And they will go against the King of Babylon.

LXXXVII.

Grâd Roy viendra prendre port pres de Nisse, Le grand empire de la mort si en fera Aux Antipolles, posera son genisse, Par mer la Pille tout esuanouyra.

A Great King will come to take port near Nice, Thus the death of the great empire will be completed: In Antibes will he place his heifer, The plunder by sea all will vanish.

LXXXVIII.

Pieds & Cheual à la seconde veille, Feront entree vastient tout par la mer: Dedans le poil entrera de Marseille, Pleurs, crys, & sang, onc nul temps si amer.

Foot and Horse at the second watch, They will make an entry devastating all by sea: Within the port of Marseilles he will enter, Tears, cries, and blood, never times so bitter.

LXXXIX.

De brique en mabre seront les murs reduits, Sept & cinquante annees pacifiques:
Ioye aux humains, renoué l'aqueduict,
Santé, temps grands fruicts, ioye & mellifiques.

The walls will be converted from brick to marble, Seven and fifty pacific years:
Joy to mortals, the aquaduct renewed,
Health, abundance of fruits, joy and mellifluous times.

XC.

Cent fois mourra le tyran inhumain, Mis à son lieu s&cced;auant & debonnaire,
Tout le Senat sera dessous sa main, Fasché sera par malin temeraire.

A hundred times will the inhuman tyrant die, In his place put one learned and mild,
The entire Senate will be under his hand, He will be vexed by a rash scoundrel.

XCI.

Clergé Romain l'an mil six cens & neuf, Au chef de l'an feras election:
D'vn gris & noir de la Compagnie yssu, Qui onc ne fut si maling.

In the year 1609, Roman clergy,
At the beginning of the year you will hold an election: Of one gray and black issued from Campania,
Never was there one so wicked as he.

XCII.

Deuant le pere l'enfant sera tué, Le pere apres entre cordes de ionc, Geneuois peuple sera esuertue,
Gisant le chef au milieu comme vn tronc.

Before his father the child will be killed, The father afterwards between ropes of rushes:
The people of Geneva will have exerted themselves, The chief lying in the middle like a log.

XCIII.

La barque neufue receura les voyages, Là & aupres transfereront l'Empire:
Beaucaire, Arles retiendrons les hostages, Pres deux colomnes trouuees de Porphire.

The new bark will take trips,
There and near by they will transfer the Empire: Beaucaire, Arles will retain the hostages, Near by, two columns of Porphyry found.

XCIV.

De Nismes d'Arles, & Vienne contemner, N'obeyr à ledict d'Hespericque:
Aux labouriez pour le grand condamner, Six eschappez en habit seraphicque.

Scorn from Nîmes, from Arles and Vienne, Not to obey the "Hesperian" edict:
To the tormented to condemn the great one, Six escaped in seraphic garb.

XCV.

Dans les Espaignes viendra Roy trespuissant, Par mer & terre subiugant or Midy:
Ce ma fera, rabaissant le croissant, Baisser les aisles à ceux du Vendredy.

To the Spains will come a very powerful King, By land and sea subjugating the South:
This evil will cause, lowering again the crescent, Clipping the wings of those of Friday.

XCVI.

Religion du nom de mers vanicra, Contre la secte fils Adaluncatif, Secte obstinee
deploree craindra
Des deux blessez par Aleph & Aleph.

The Religion of the name of the seas will win out Against the sect of the son of
"Adaluncatif": The stubborn, lamented sect will be afraid
Of the two wounded by A and A.

XCVII.

Triremes pleines tout aage captif, Temps bon à mal, le doux pour amertume:
Proye à Barbares trop tost seront hatifs, Cupid de voir plaindre au vent la plume.

Triremes full of captives of every age, Good time for bad, the sweet for the bitter:
Prey to the Barbarians hasty they will be too soon, Anxious to see the feather
wail in the wind.

XCVIII.

La splendeur claire à pucelle ioyeuse, Ne luyra plus, long temps sera sans sel:
Auec marchans, ruffiens, loups odieuse, Tous pesle mesle monstre vniuersel.

For the merry maid the bright splendor
Will shine no longer, for long will she be without salt: With merchants, bullies,
wolves odious,
All confusion universal monster.

XCIX.

La fin le loup, le lyon, beuf, & l'asne, Timide dama seront auec mastins: Plus ne
cherra à eux la douce manne, Plus vigilance & custode aux mastins.

The end of wolf, lion, ox and ass, Timid deer they will be with mastiffs:
No longer will the sweet manna fall upon them, More vigilance and watch for
the mastiffs.

C.

Le grand empire sera par Angleterre, Le pempotam des ans de trois cens: Grandes
copies passer par mer & terre, Les Lusitains n'en seront par contens.

The great empire will be for England,
The all-powerful one for more than three hundred years: Great forces to pass by
sea and land,
The Lusitanians will not be satisfied thereby.

OTHER PROPHECIES
FOR THE EVENTS IN THIS CENTURY

I.

Siecle nouueau, alliance nouuelle, Vn Marquisat mis dans la nacelle,
A qui plus fort des deux l'emportera, D'vn Duc d'vn Roy, gallere de Florance, Port
à Marseil, Pucelle dans la France, De Catherine fort chef on rasera.

New century, new alliance, A Marquisate put in the bark,
To him who the stronger of the two will carry it off, Of a Duke and of a King,
falley of Florence,
Port at Marseilles, the Damsel in France, The chief fort of Catherine will be razed.

II.

Que d'or d'argent fera despendre, Quand Comte voudra Ville prendre, Tant de
mille & mille soldats, Tuez, noyez, sans y rien faire,
Dans plus forte mettra pied terre, Pigmée ayde des Censuarts.

How much gold and silver will have to be spent When the Count will desire
to take the town, Many thousands and thousands of soldiers, Drowned, killed,
without doing anything there, In stronger land will he set foot,
Pygmy aid by the Copy-holders.

III.

La Ville sans dessus dessous, Renuersée de mille coups
De canons: & forts dessous terre: Cinq ans tiendra: le tout remis, Et lasche à ses
ennemis,

L'eau leur fera apres la guerre.

The Town without above below, Overturned by a thousand shots
From cannons: and fortifications underground: Five years will it hold: everything delivered up, And left for its enemies,

The water will make war upon them afterwards.

IV.

D'vn rond, d'vn lis, naistra vn si grand Prince, Bien tost, & tard venu dans sa
Prouince, Saturne en Libra en exaltation:

Maison de Venus en descroissante force, Dame en apres masculin soubs l'es-
corse, Pour maintenir l'heureux sang de Bourbon.

Of a circle, of a lily, there will be born a very great Prince, Very soon, and late
come into his Province,

Saturn in Libra in exaltation:

The House of Venus in decreasing force, The Lady thereafter masculine under
the bark, In order to maintain the happy Bourbon blood.

V.

Celuy qui la Principauté, Tiendra par grande cruauté,
A la fin verra grand phalange: Par coup de feu tres dangereux, Par accord pourroit faire mieux, Autrement boira suc d'Orange.

He who the Principality Will hold through great cruelty,
He will see his great phalanx at its end: By very dangerous gunshot,
By agreement he could do better, Otherwise he will drink Orange juice.

VI.

Quand de Robin la traistreuse entreprise, Mettra Seigneurs & en peine vn grand
Prince, Sceu par la Fin, chef on luy tranchera:

La plume au vent, amye dans Espagne, Poste attrappé estant dans la campagne,
Et l'escriuain dans l'eauë se jettera.

When the treacherous enterprise of Robin Will cause Lords and a great Prince
trouble, Known by Lafin, his head will be cut off:
The feather in the wind, female friend to Spain, The messenger trapped while in
the country, And the scribe will throw himself into the water.

VII.

La sangsuë au loup se ioindra, Lorsqu'en mer le bled defaudra, Mais le grand
Prince sans enuie, Par ambassade luy donra
De son bled pour luy donner vie, Pour vn besoin s'en pouruoira.

The leech will attach itself to the wolf, When the grain will sink into the sea, But
the great Prince without envy, Through his embassy he will give him Of his own
grain to give him life,
He will provide himself with it for time of need.

VIII.

Vn peu deuant l'ouuert commerce, Ambassadeur viendra de Perse, Nouuelle au
franc pays porter: Mais non receu, vaine esperance A son grand Dieu sera l'of-
fance, Feignant de le vouloir quitter.

Shortly before the opening of commerce, An ambassador will come from Persia,
To bring news to the Frank land:
But unreceived, vain hope,
It will be an offense to his great God, Pretending to desire to abandom him.

IX.

Deux estendars du costé de l'Auuergne, Senestre pris, pour un temps prison
regne, Et vne Dame enfans voudra mener,
Au Censuart mais descouuert l'affaire, Danger de mort murmure sur la terre,
Germain, Bastille frere & soeur prisonnier.

Two standards from the direction of Auvergne, The left one taken, for a time
prison rule, And a Lady will want to lead her child
To the Copy-holder but the affair is discovered, Danger of death and murmur

throughout the land, German, brother and sister prisoner in the Bastille.

X.

Ambassadeur pour vne Dame, A son vaisseau mettra la rame, Pour prier le grand medecin: Que de l'oster de telle peine, Mais en ce s'opposera Royne, Grand peine auant qu'en veoir la fin.

The Ambassador for a Lady To his vessel will put the oar, To beseech the great physician That he relieve her of such pain, But to this a Queen will be opposed, Great pain before seeing the end of it.

XI.

Durant le siecle on verra deux ruisseaux, Tout vn terroir inonder de leurs eaux, Et submerger par ruisseaux & fontaines: Coups & Monfrin Beccoyran, & ales, Par le gardon bien souuant trauaillez, Six cens & quatre alez, & trente moines.

During the century one will see two streams Flood an entire land with their waters, And to be submerged by streams and fountains: Shots at Montfrin Bou&c-ced;oiron and Alais, Very often troubled by the Gardon, Six hundred and four, and thirty monks.

XII.

Six cens & cinq tres grand nouuelle, De deux Seigneurs la grand querelle, Proche de Genaudan sera, A vne Eglise apres l'offrande Meurtre commis, prestre demande Tremblant de peur se sauuera.

Six hundred and five very great news, The great quarrel of the two Lords, It will take place near Gevaudan, At a church after the offering Murder committed, the priest begs Trembling with fear he will flee.

XIII.

L'auanturier six cens & six ou neuf, Sera surpris par fiel mis dans vn oeuf, Et peu apres sera hors de puissance Par le puissant Empereur general Qu'au monde n'est vn pareil ny esgal, Dont vn chascun luy rend obeïssance.

Six hundred and six or nine, the adventurer Will be surprised by gall put in an egg,
And shortly afterwards he will be out of power Through the powerful Emperor-General
To whom the world has not an equal, Of which each iwll render him obedience.

XIV.

Au grand siege encor grands forfaits, Recomman&cced;ans plus que iamais Six cens & cinq sur la verdure,
La prise & reprise sera, Soldats és champs iusqu'en froidure
Puis apres recommencera.

At the great siege great crimes again, Starting again worse than ever
Six hundred and five in the spring, There will take place the capture and recapture,
Soldiers in the fields until winter Then afterwards it will begin again.

XV.

Nouueau esleu patron du grand vaisseau, Verra long temps briller le cler flambeau Qui sert de lampe à ce grand territoire, Et auquel temps armez sous son nom, Ioinctes à celles de l'heureux de Bourbon Leuant, Ponant, & Couchant sa memoire.

The newly elected master of the great vessel, He will see shining for a long time the clear flame
Which serves this great territory as a lamp, And at which time armed under his name, Joined with the happy ones of Bourbon East, West and West his memory.

XVI.

En Octobre six cens & cinq. Pouruoyeur du monstre marin, Prendra du souuerain le cresme, Ou en six cens & six, en Iuin,
Grand' ioye aux grands & au commun, Grands faits apres ce grand baptesme.

In October six hundred and five, The purveyor of the marine monster
Will take the unction from the sovereign, Or in six hundred and six, in June,
Great joy for the common and the great ones alike, Great deeds after this great
baptism.

XVII.

Au mesme temps vn grand endurera, Ioyeux mal sain, l'an complet ne verra, Et
quelques vns qui seront de la feste, Feste pour vn seulement, à ce iour, Mais peu
apres sans faire long seiour,
Deux se donront l'vn à l'autre de la teste. At the same time a great one will suffer,
Merry, poor health, he will not see the completion of the year, And several who
will be at the feast,
Feast for one only, on this day,
But shortly afterwards without delaying long, Two will knock their heads together.

XVIII.

Considerant la triste Philomelle Qu'en pleurs & cris sa peine renouuelle, Racour-
sissant par tel moyen ses iours,
Six cens & cinq, elle en verra l'issuë, De son tourment, ia la toille tissuë, Par son
moyen senestre aura secours.

Considering the sad Nightingale
Who with tears and laments renews her anguish, By such means making her
days shorter,
Six hundred and five, she will see the end of it, Of her torment, the cloth already
woven, By means of it sinister aid will she have.

XIX.

Six cens & cinq, six cens & six & sept, Nous monstrera iusques à l'an dix sept, Du
boutefeu l'ire, hayne & enuie,
Soubz l'oliuier d'assez long temps caché, Le Crocodril sur la terre acaché,
Ce qui estoit mort, sera pour lors en vie.

Six hundred and five, six hundred and six and seven, It will show us up to the
year seventeen,
The anger, hatred and jealousy of the incendiary, For a long enough time hidden
under the olive tree, The Crocodile has hidden on the land,
That which was dead will then be alive.

XX.

Celuy qui a par plusieurs fois Tenu la cage & puis les bois, R'entre à son premier
estre Vie sauue peu apres sortir,
Ne se sc,achant encor congnoistre, Cherchera sujet pour mourir.

He who several times has Held the cage and then the woods,
He will return to the first state
His life safe shortly afterwards to depart, Still not knowing how to know,
He will look for a subject in order to die.

XXI.

L'autheur des maux commencera regner En l'an six cens & sept sans espargner
Tous les subiets qui sont à la sangsuë, Et puis apres s'en viendra peu à peu,
Au franc pays r'allumer son feu, S'en retournant d'où elle est issuë.

The author of the evils will begin to reign
In the year six hundred and seven without sparing All her subjects who belong
to the leach,
And then afterwards she will come little by little To the Frank country to relight
her fire, Returning whence whe has come.

XXII.

Cil qui dira, descouurissant l'affaire, Comme du mort, la mort pourra bien faire
Coups de poignards par vn qu'auront induit, Sa fin sera pis qu'il n'aura fait faire
La fin conduit les hommes sur la terre, Guete' par tout, tant le iour que la nuit.

He who will tell, revealing the affair, As with death, death will be able to do well
Blows of daggers which will have been incited by one, His end will be worse than
he will have devised to make The end leads the men on land,
Watched for everywhere, as much by day as by night.

XXIII.

Quand la grand nef, la prouë & gouuernal, Du franc pays & son esprit vital, D'es-
cueils & flots par la mer secoüée,
Six cens & sept, & dix coeur assiegé Et des reflus de son corps affligé, Sa vie estant
sur ce mal renoüée.

When the great ship, the prow and rudder Of the Frank land and its vital spirit,
By the sea shaken over reef and billow, Six hundred and seven and ten, heart
besieged
And afflicted by the ebbings of its body, Upon this evil its life being renewed.

XXIV.

Le Mercurial non de trop longue vie, Six cens & huict & vingt, grand maladie,
Et encor pis danger de feu & d'eau, Son grand amy lors luy sera contraire,
De tels hazards se pourroit bien distraire, Mais bref, le fer luy fera son tombeau.

The Mercurial not of too long a life,
Six hundred and eight and twenty, great sickness, And yet worse danger from
fire and water,
His great friend will the be against him,
With such hazards he could divert himself well enough, But in brief, the sword
will cause his death.

XXV.

Six cens & six, six cens & neuf, Vn Chancelier gros comme vn boeuf, Vieux com-
me le Phoenix du monde,
En ce terroir plus ne luyra, De la nef d'oubly passera,
Aux champs Elisiens faire ronde.

Six hundred and six, six hundred and nine, A Chancellor large as an ox,
Old as the Phoenix of the world, In this world will shine no more,
He will pass with the ship of oblivion, To the Elysian Fields to make his round.

XXVI.

Deux freres sont de l'ordre Ecclesiastique, Dont l'vn prendra pour la France la
picque, Encor vn coup si l'an six cens & six
N'est affligé d'vne grande maladie, Les armes en main iusques six cens & dix,
Gueres plus loing ne s'estendant sa vie.

Two brothers are of the Ecclesiastical order, One of them will take up the pike for
France, Another blow if in the year six hundred and six He is not afflicted with
a great malady,
Arms in his hand up to six hundred and ten, Scarcely much further does his life
extend.

XXVII.

Celeste feu du costé d'Occident,
Et du Midy, courir iusques au Leuant, Vers demy morts sans point trouuer racine, Troisiesme aage, à Mars le Belliqueux, Des Escarboucles on verra briller
feux, Aage Escarboucle, & à la fin famine.

Celestial fire from the Western side, And from the South, running up to the East,
Worms half dead without finding even a root.
Third age, for Mars the Warlike,
One will see fires shing from the Carbuncles.
Age a Carbuncle, and in the end famine.

XXVIII.

L'an mil six cens & neuf ou quatorziesme, Le vieux Charon fera Pasques en
Caresme, Six cens & six, par escript le mettra
Le Medecin, de tout cecy s'estonne, A mesme temps assigné en personne
Mais pour certain l'vn d'eux comparoistra.

The year one thousand six hundred and nine or fourteen, The old Charon will
celebrate Easter in Lent,
Six hundred and six, in writing he will place it The Physician, by all this is astonished,
At the same time summoned in person But for certain one of them will appear.

XXIX.

Le Griffon se peut aprester Pour à l'ennemy resister,
Et renforcer bien son armée, Autrement l'Elephant viendra Qui d'vn abord le
surprendra,
Six cens & huict, mer enflammée.

The Griffon is able to prepare himself For resisting the enemy,
And to reinforce will his army, Otherwise the Elephant will come He who will
suddenly surprise him,
Six hundred and eight, the sea aflame.

XXX.

Dans peu de temps Medecin du grand mal, Et la sangsuë d'ordre & rang inegal,
Mettront le feu à la branche d'Oliue, Poste courir, d'vn & d'autre costé,
Et par tel feu leur Empire accosté, Se r'alumant du franc finy saliue.

In a short while the Physician of the great disease, And the leech of the unequal
rank and order, They will set fire to the Olive branch,
Post running, from one side and another,
And by means of such fire their Empire approached, Being rekindled by the
Frank saliva finished.

XXXI.

Celuy qui a, les hazards surmonté, Qui fer, feu, eauë, n'a iamais redouté, Et du
pays bien proche du Basacle, D'vn coup de fer tout le monde estouné,
Par Crocodil estrangement donne', Peuple raui de veoir vn tel spectacle.

He who has overcome the hazards, Who has ne'er dreaded sword, fire, water,
And of the country very close to Toulouse,
By a blow of steel the entire world astonished, Strangely given by the Crocodile,
People delighted to see such a spectacle.

XXXII.

Vin a` foison, tres bon pour les gendarmes, Pleurs & souspirs, plainctes cris &
alarme Le Ciel fera ses tonnerres pleuuoir
Feu, eau & sang, le tout mesle' ensemble, Le Ciel de sol, en fremit & en tremble,
Viuant n'a veu ce qu'il pourra bien veoir.

Wine in abundance, cery good for the troops, Tears and sighs, complaints, groans
and alarm The Sky will cause its thunderbolts to rain Fire, water and blood, all
mixed together, Sun's heaven, shaking and trembling from it,
That which can be seen clearly no living person has e'er seen.

XXXIII.

Bien peu apres sera tres grande misere, Du peu de bled, qui sera sur la terre, Du
Dauphine', Prouence & Viuarois, Au Viuarois est vn pauure presage, Pere du fils,
sera entropophage,
Et mangeront racine & gland du bois.

Very soon after there will be very great misery, From the scarcity of grain, which
will be on the land Of Dauphiny, Provence and Vivarais,
To Vivarais it is a poor prediction, Father will eat his own son,
And from the woods they will eat root and acorn.

XXXIV.

Princes & Seigneurs tous se feront la guerre, Cousin germain le frere auec le
frere, Finy l'Arby de l'heureux de Bourbon,
De Hierusalem les Princes tant aymables, Du fait commis enorme & execrable,
Se ressentiront sur la bourse sans fond.

Princes and Lords will all make war against one another, First cousin brother
against brother,
Araby by the happy ones of Bourbon finished, The Princes of Jerusalem very
agreeable,
Of the heinous and execrable deed committed, They will feel the effects on the
bottomless purse.

(Editor's Note: The original translation of the verses ended here)

XXXV.

Dame par mort grandement attristée, Mere & tutrice au sang qui la quittée,
Dame & Seigneurs, faits enfans orphelins, Par les aspics & par les Crocodilles,
Seront surpris forts Bourgs, Chasteaux Villes Dieu tout puissant les garde des
malins.

XXXVI.

L grand rumeur qui sera par la France, Les impuissans voudront auoir puissance,
Langue emmiellée & vrays Cameleons, De boutefeux, allumeurs de Chandelles,
Pyes & geyes, rapporteurs de nouuelles Dont la morsure semblera Scorpions.

XXXVII.

Foible & puissant seront en grand discord, Plusieurs mourront auant faire l'accord Foible au puissant vainqueur se fera dire, Le plus puissant au ieune cedera,
Et le plus vieux des deux decedera, Lors que l'vn d'eux enuahira l'Empire.

XXXVIII.

Par eauë, & par fer, & par grande maladie, Le pouuoyeur à l'hazer de sa vie S&c-
ced;aura combien vaut le quintal du bois, Six cens & quinze, ou le dixneufiesme,
On grauera d'vn grand Prince cinquiesme L'immortel nom, sur le pied de la
Croix.

XXXIX.

Le pouruoyeur du monstre sans pareil, Se fera veoir ainsi que le Soleil, Montant
le long la ligne Meridienne, En poursuiuant l'Elephant & le loup, Nul Empereur
ne fit iamais tel coup, Et rien plus pis à ce Prince n'aduienne.

XL.

Ce qu'en viuant le pere n'auoit sceu, Il acquerra ou par guerre ou par feu Et com-
batre la sangsuë irritée,
Ou iouyra de son bien paternel Et fauory du grand Dieu Eternel Aura bien tost
sa Prouince heritée.

XLI.

Vaisseaux, galleres auec leur estendar, S'entrebattront prés du mont Gilbattar Et
lors sera fors faits à Pampelonne, Qui pour son bien souffrira mille maux,
Par plusieurs fois soustiendra les assaux, Mais à la fin vnie à la Couronne.

XLII.

La grand'Cité où est le premier homme, Bien amplement la ville ie vous nomme,
Tout en alarme, & le soldat és champs Par fer & eaue", grandement affligée,
Et a` la fin des Franc,ois soulagée, Mais ce sera de's six cens & dix ans.

XLIII.

Le petit coing, Prouinces mutinées Par forts Chasteaux se verront dominées,
Encor vn coup par la gent militaire, Dans bref seront fortement assiegez, Mais ils
seront d'vn tres grand soulagez, Qui aura fait entree dans Beaucaire.

XLIV.

La belle rose en la France admiree, D'vn tres grand Prince à la fin desirée, Six
cens & dix, lors naistront ses amours Cinq ans apres, sera d'vn grand blessée,
Du trait d'Amour, elle sera enlassée, Si a` quinze ans du Ciel rec,oit secours.

XLV.

De coup de fer tout le monde estonné, Pa Crocodil estrangement donné,
A vn bien grand, parent de la sangsuë, Et peu apres sera vn autre coup
De guet à pens, commis contre le loup, Et de tels faits on ne verra l'issuë.

XLVI.

Le pouruoyeur mettra tout en desroute, Sansuë & loup, en mon dire n'escoute
Quand Mars sera au signe du Mouton Ioint à Saturne, & Saturne à la Lune, Alors
sera ta plus grande infortune,
Le Soleil lors en exaltation.

XLVII.

Le grand d'Hongrie, ira dans la nacelle, Le nouueau né fera guerre nouuelle A
son voisin qu'il tiendra assiegé,
Et le noireau auec son altesse,
Ne souffrira, que par trop on le presse, Durant trois ans ses gens tiendra rangé.

XLVIII.

Du vieux Charron on verra le Phoenix, Estre premier & dernier des fils,
Reluyre en France, & d'vn chascun aymable, Regner long temps auec tous les
honneurs Qu'auront iamais eu ses precesseurs
Dont il rendra sa gloire memorable.

XLIX.

Venus & Sol, Iupiter & Mercure Augmenteront le genre de nature Grande alliance en France se fera, Et du Midy la sangsuë de mesme,
Le feu esteint par ce remede extreme, En terre ferme Oliuer plantera.

L.

Vn peut deuant ou apres l'Angleterre Par mort de loup, mise aussi bas que terre,
Verra le feu resister contre l'eau, Le r'alumant auecques telles force
Du sang humain, dessus l'humaine escorce Faite de pain, bondance de cousteau.

LI.

La Ville qu'auoit en ses ans Combatu l'iniure du temps,
Qui de son vainqueur tient la vie, Celuy qui premier l'a surprist, Que peu apre
Franc,ois reprist Par combats encor affoiblie.

LII.

La grand Cité qui n'a pain à demy, Encor vn coup la sainct Barthelemy, Engrau-
era au profond de son ame,
Nismes, Rochelle, Geneue & Montpellier, Castres, Lyon, Mars entrant au Belier,
S'entrebattront le tout pour vne Dame.

LIII.

Plusieurs mourront auant que Phoenix meure, Iusques six cens septante est sa
demeure, Passé quinze ans, vingt & vn trente neuf.
Le premier est subiet à maladie, Et le second au fer, danger de vie,
Au feu à l'eau, est subiect à trente-neuf.

LIV.

Six cens & quinze, vingt, grand Dame mourra, Et peu apres vn fort long temps
plouura, Plusieurs pays, Flandres & l'Angleterre, Seront par feu & par fer affligez,
De leurs voisins longuement assiegez, Contraints seront de leurs faire la guerre.

LV.

Vn peu deuant ou apres tres grand' Dame, Son ame au Ciel, & son corps soubs la
lame, De plusieurs gens regrettée sera,
Tous ses parens seront en grand' tristesse, Pleurs & souspirs d'vne Dame en ieu-
nesse, Et à deux grands, le dueil delaissera.

LVI.

Tost l'Elephant de toutes parts verra Quand pouruoyeur au Griffon se ioindra,
Sa ruine proche, & Mars qui tousiours gronde: Fera grands faits aupres de terre
saincte, Grands estendars sur la terre & sur l'onde,
Si la nef a este' de deux freres enceinte

LVII.

Peu apres l'aliance faicte, Auant solemniser la feste, L'Empereur le tout troublera,
Et la nouuelle mariée,
Au franc pays par sort liée, Dans peu de temps apres mourra.

LVIII.

Sangsuë en peu de temps mourra, Sa mort bon signe nous donra, Pour l'accroissement de la France, Alliance se trouueront,
Deux grands Royaumes se ioindront, aura sur eux puissance.

Erebus Society

Made in the USA
Las Vegas, NV
22 October 2022